WORDS TO PRAY BY

Your people will rebuild the ancient ruins and will raise up the age-old foundations; you will be called repairer of broken walls, restorer of streets with dwellings. (Isaiah 58:12)

WANDA ALGER

Alger Publications
Winchester, VA

Words to Pray By
by Wanda Alger

Copyright © 2022 Wanda Alger

Published by
Alger Publications
Winchester, VA
wandaalger.me

ISBN 978-0-9996752-3-6

Cover design by Jenn David
Cover artwork by Danny Hahlbohm

**Additional Resources
from Wanda Alger:**

Oracles of Grace: Building a Legacy of Wisdom and Revelation

Prayer That Sparks National Revival

Moving From Sword to Scepter: Ruling Through Prayer as the Ecclesia of God

Making Room for His Presence: A 21-Day Community Devotional

Prophetic Mentoring Training Course Video Series

Getting Free of Religious, Jezebel, and Leviathan Spirits Video Series

Dream Interpretation Audio Series

THE COVER DESIGN

When I began to pray about the artwork for the book's cover, the Lord gave me two people to contact. One was Danny Hahlbohm (Inspired Art by Danny Hahlbohm). His prophetic artwork has been seen and celebrated all over the world for many years, inspiring countless people in their walk with the Lord. I felt he was to have a part in illustrating the purpose of this book – and he delivered! Little did I know he had a vision years prior that was to be the inspiration for this commissioned artwork.

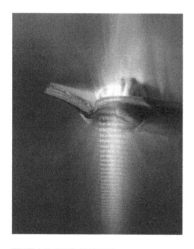

THE LIVING WORD
copyright 2022 Danny Hahlbohm
www.dannyhahlbohm.net

"In the vision, the Lord showed me a Bible, then opened the Bible to where I could see the text written inside. Then a certain passage seemed to illuminate before me. As it did, the Bible turned slightly so I was seeing it from a side view. From that perspective I saw thousands of words shoot down into infinity. I asked the Lord what this was, and He told me that the Word of God contains far more than what we hold in our hands. It is not a book, but truly, a living extension of God Himself. It is, indeed, a living entity in itself which has no limits to that which it is." (Danny H.)

Thank you, Danny, for creating this piece that beautifully reminds us of our ongoing relationship with the Living Word. He continually reveals Himself in new ways and loves to speak to those who search for Him.

The other person I contacted was Jenn David of Creative2. She is a young graphic designer and part of the creative team that helped me create my new website (launched in the fall of 2022). In creating the "mood board" for my website, she seemed to capture my heart through colors, graphics, and seemingly small details that, when put together, reflected the essence of the message I carry. I knew that she, too, was to have a part to play.

Only the Holy Spirit could merge these two artists together so beautifully for a cover that illustrates a powerful prophetic message of generational heritage. Danny's artwork is the foundation and Jenn's added design elements complete this amazing picture that reveals the power of the Living Word. Indeed, God is doing a work to bring out the best in all of us to establish something extremely powerful – and lasting.

TABLE OF CONTENTS

How to Use This Prayer Concordance

This is the confidence we have in approaching God: that if we ask anything according to His will, He hears us. And if we know that He hears us-whatever we ask-we know that we have what we asked of Him. (1 John 5:14-15)

When the Lord gave me the vision for this book, I knew it was to be a timeless resource for years to come. As the Body of Christ, we are in a season of rebuilding our spiritual foundations and discipling the next generation. Ungodly belief systems and doctrines of men have infiltrated the Church. We need to reestablish God's timeless truths that will strengthen our faith and secure our spiritual inheritance for the long haul. A major part of a healthy foundation is knowing God's will and building a strong relationship with Him through prayer.

My inspiration for this book came from my own prayer journal that I started as a teenager. Knowing that God would answer my prayers if I prayed according to His will, I wanted to know what His will was. I wanted to target my prayers the right way and have the faith and confidence that He would answer.

I began to search the various topics that were important to me and wrote down all the verses I could find on those particular topics. Using various concordances that were available at the time, I collected enough scriptures from both Old and New Testaments to feel confident of God's intentions and purposes concerning those specific topics. And then I began to pray.

Not only did my understanding of the Word deepen, I began to see answers to prayer. I saw a direct correlation to my targeted prayers and the breakthroughs that came in my life. My faith grew every time I saw a direct result of praying and applying God's Word.

My prayer journal became my personalized concordance – my "go to" - when I needed to know how to pray about something. Whether it was a family disagreement, a financial decision, or a stronghold to overcome,

I prayed according to the various scriptures I had already recorded in my journal.

Little did I know how significant this was going to be in establishing a solid biblical foundation for the rest of my life. Not only did it strengthen my own faith in many spiritual matters, but the scriptures began to spill out of me when I started praying for others. Various scriptures would come to mind from my prayer concordance, and I found myself praying with greater assurance and authority in my intercession. Truly, they became my *words to pray by.*

I kept adding to my prayer journal/concordance for the next ten to fifteen years, and even made one for my mother who asked for her own copy. As an intercessor, she saw how rich the resource was and saw many of the results to my answered prayers. Even in my young adult years I somehow knew the journal was a priceless treasure that would be used in the years to come.

Thus, what you hold in your hands is the fruit of those humble beginnings and a start to establishing your own prayer concordance for the days ahead. It is certainly not an exhaustive one, but I have included enough topics to cover some of the most common issues we all face in our journey as believers. I've also included a few blank pages at the end of each topic for you to add additional scriptures the Lord might give you.

After each scripture verse is a short prayer that is based on that verse. These are written as "jump starters," not set-in-stone liturgical readings! Feel free to paraphrase them as the Spirit directs you to pray. This is YOUR prayer journal, not mine. I'm just giving you a head start in building your own style of communication with the Lord.

Though I personally use the English Standard Version as my choice for study, I chose the New International Version as the primary source for the scripture references, simply because it is the most common. I also wrote this prayer concordance with some specific priorities in mind:

It is FOUNDATIONAL

The topics I have chosen and the scriptures I present are meant to establish a solid biblical foundation. Whether you are a new believer or a mature saint, a strong scriptural foundation is critical at a time when so many voices seek to compromise our faith and water down the gospel. By reading many different scriptures on the same topic, it is easier to see a bigger picture and understand God's heart and ways which are eternal. Though some of the specifics we look for may not be in Scripture, we can find enough of His heart and character throughout the Word so as to determine how He might think and act in a given situation.

It is PERSONAL

Part of praying effectively for others is experiencing the power of prayer in our own lives. Faith always starts on a personal level. Thus, I have written all the prayers in first person. They can certainly be changed to third person when needed but allowing the Lord to demonstrate His will in our own lives first will build our faith to pray more effectively for others.

It is CONVERSATIONAL

Though there is a place to decree and declare – and I've included several of those in the prayers – the majority of the prayers are written to encourage conversation. After all, prayer is first and foremost, about our relationship with the Lord. We must establish a heart connection before anything else. We don't have to command or demand His will to be done. He longs to answer our prayers simply because we are His sons and daughters.

It is PRACTICAL

Part of the challenge in prayer is to be specific and targeted. If we want to know He has heard us and will answer, we have to give Him something to work with. We have to pray in a way that will bring measurable results. The more specific we are with our requests, the more specific He will be in showing us if we've hit the target. Be practical with your prayers and look for ways to apply the Word in tangible ways.

My prayer is that this book will launch you into an amazing journey of discovery with the Word of God. He is the Living Word and loves to speak to His sons and daughters. He delights in showing you His will and revealing the secrets of His heart. I pray you meet Him in the pages to follow.

SPIRITUAL GROWTH

Words for Knowing God's Will

Psalms 16:5-6
Lord, You alone are my portion and my cup; You make my lot secure. The boundary lines have fallen for me in pleasant places; surely I have a delightful inheritance.

Father, You have already determined my call and my purpose and given me the grace to fulfill Your will. You are my greatest desire and the source from which all my life flows. It is You that makes me secure. Thank You for preparing my inheritance which will give me great delight. Thank You for keeping me within the boundaries of Your grace.

Proverbs 16:3
Commit to the Lord whatever you do, and He will establish your plans.

I commit my ways to You, Lord! Establish my steps and show me which way to turn. I want You to direct me in everything I do. I trust You with my life. Show me the way to go and I will gladly follow!

Proverbs 16:33
The lot is cast into the lap, but its every decision is from the Lord.

Lord, as I put You first in my life, thank You for directing me in Your paths and not letting me follow my own. Direct my decisions so that they will honor You and align with Your will and purpose. When I make bad decisions or unwise choices, show me how to redeem them and bring good out of every situation.

Proverbs 19:21
Many are the plans in a person's heart, but it is the Lord's purpose that prevails.

I desire to do Your will, God. May Your purposes prevail, even when my plans fall short of Yours. Thank You for redeeming my mistakes and giving me grace to learn the lessons I need to learn. My life is in Your hands!

Psalms 32:8

I will instruct you and teach you in the way you should go; I will counsel you with My loving eye on you.

Thank you, Lord, for teaching me and helping to know which way to go. Thank You for keeping Your eyes on me and giving me the counsel I need in order to succeed. Consecrate my eyes and ears so that I can discern Your leading more carefully and hear Your voice more clearly.

Jeremiah 29:11

For I know the plans I have for you, declares the Lord, plans to prosper you and not to harm you, plans to give you hope and a future.

You have plans for me, God! You want to prosper me and protect me and have planned a great future filled with hope. I praise You for preparing the way for me and giving me so much to look forward to! I declare over my life that I will fulfill my destiny and be all that You have created me to be!

Jeremiah 33:3

Call to Me and I will answer you and tell you great and unsearchable things you do not know.

Thank you, Lord, for sharing with me the secrets of Your heart. Thank You for helping me understand Your words and Your ways. Thank you for answering my questions and filling in the necessary blanks. I call upon You now to show me what I need to know to take the next step in my journey.

Mark 4:22-23

For whatever is hidden is meant to be disclosed, and whatever is concealed is meant to be brought out into the open. If anyone has ears to hear, let them hear.

I desire to hear Your words, Lord! Thank You for showing me those things that have been hidden or concealed that will reveal Your working in the earth. Give me ears to hear You and not miss the truths You want to show me – even those which may be hard to understand.

Romans 8:28

And we know that in all things God works for the good of those who love Him, who have been called according to His purpose.

Father, I love You and desire to fulfill the call on my life. Thank You for using everything in my life, both the good and even the bad, to accomplish Your will. Even when things get rough, help me to see how You are using the situation for my good and for Your glory.

Romans 12:2

Do not conform to the pattern of this world, but be transformed by the renewing of your mind. Then you will be able to test and approve what God's will is - His good, pleasing, and perfect will.

Lord, I do not want to be molded to this world's way of thinking. I want to think like You! I want to know Your Word more than the words of others. I want to test and discern what Your good, pleasing, and perfect will is for my life. Keep me from giving in to my flesh and help me to grow in discernment and wisdom for each day.

1 Corinthians 2:12

What we have received is not the spirit of the world, but the Spirit who is from God, so that we may understand what God has freely given us.

Thank You, Lord, for giving me access to Your Spirit. Thank You for giving me a way out of the world's ways of doing things. I choose to walk in the Spirit of God so that I can understand all that You have freely given me. May I be set apart in how I live my life to give honor to You and draw others to see how good You really are.

1 Corinthians 2:16

"For who has known the mind of the Lord so as to instruct him?" But we have the mind of Christ.

Thank you for giving me the mind of Christ so that I can understand Your ways! Thank You for giving me access to Your truth and the ability to apply it in my life! Show me how to access Your thoughts so that I will walk in Your wisdom and not my own ideas.

Ephesians 5:17
Therefore do not be foolish but understand what the Lord's will is.

You say that we can know Your will. Thank You, Lord, that I don't have to guess! Help me to understand Your will and to not be foolish or presumptuous. I desire wisdom in the inmost places so that my choices will be a blessing and my life a reflection of Your truth.

Philippians 1:6
Being confident of this, that He who began a good work in you will carry it on to completion until the day of Christ Jesus.

Thank You, Lord, that I can rest in Your sovereign grace to finish the work that You've started in me. Thank You for giving me everything I need to finish the course and fulfill Your will. Alert me if I begin to take the reins away from You! You started this work in me and I know You can finish it.

Philippians 2:13
For it is God who works in you to will and to act in order to fulfill His good purpose.

Lord, thank You for working in me to choose what You want. Thank You for turning my heart and even giving me the desire to do Your will! I submit my thoughts and ideas to You. Mold them and shape them so that I do Your will out of a sincere desire to please You, and not out of any obligation.

Colossians 1:9-10
For this reason, since the day we heard about you, we have not stopped praying for you. We continually ask God to fill you with the knowledge of His will through all the wisdom and understanding that the Spirit gives, so that you may live a life worthy of the Lord and please Him in every way: bearing fruit in every good work, growing in the knowledge of God

Thank you, Lord, for filling me with the knowledge of Your will and giving me all spiritual wisdom and understanding so that I can walk in Your ways. I want to please You fully and bear fruit in the things I put my hands to. Expand my heart and mind so that I can grow in the knowledge of God.

1 Thessalonians 5:16-18

Rejoice always, pray continually, give thanks in all circumstances; for this is God's will for you in Christ Jesus.

Remind me, Lord, to always rejoice in You as I bring my requests before You. I know a thankful heart is a powerful deterrent against discouragement and defeat. Remind me when I complain too much and don't see the amazing things You're already doing in my life! Help me to focus on the good more than on the bad.

2 Timothy 1:9

He has saved us and called us to a holy life - not because of anything we have done but because of His own purpose and grace. This grace was given us in Christ Jesus before the beginning of time.

It is Your purpose and grace, Lord, that saved me and gave me the ability to live a holy life. Thank you for thinking ahead and preparing the way from the very foundation of the world! I desire to be set apart for Your purposes. I desire to live in a way that is honorable and pure. Thank You for giving me the grace to be just like You!

James 1:5

If any of you lacks wisdom, you should ask God, who gives generously to all without finding fault, and it will be given to you.

Father, I ask you to fill me with Your wisdom so that I might know Your heart and Your ways more clearly. I know that You want me to ask! Thank You for answering my questions and not turning away from my doubts. Thank You for always being there and listening to my heart.

James 3:17

But the wisdom that comes from heaven is first of all pure; then peace-loving, considerate, submissive, full of mercy and good fruit, impartial and sincere.

Lord, fill me with the wisdom of Your Spirit. Help me to recognize and walk in that which is pure, peace-loving, considerate, submissive, full of mercy and good fruit, impartial and sincere. May these qualities mark my decisions and guide my discernment so as to reflect the ways and wisdom of heaven.

2 Peter 1:3

His divine power has given us everything we need for a godly life through our knowledge of Him who called us by His own glory and goodness.

Lord, thank You for giving me everything I need to succeed in this life. Help me to be a good steward of Your Word and to understand the principles in practical ways. I trust You to teach me and show me what I need to know. May I apply this knowledge in a way that honors You and reflects Your goodness to those around me.

1 John 2:17

The world and its desires pass away, but whoever does the will of God lives forever.

God, I want to stay faithful to Your Word and Your will so that all that I do in this life will count for eternity. I don't want to waste my time here by doing things that are worthless and meaningless. May my life be remembered where it counts the most.

1 John 5:3-4

In fact, this is love for God: to keep His commands. And His commands are not burdensome, for everyone born of God overcomes the world. This is the victory that has overcome the world, even our faith.

Thank You, Lord, for giving me directives that are not going to be hard for me to obey. Where my flesh may struggle to submit, my spirit will breathe easy when I yield to Your ways. Because I belong to You, I have the victory to overcome all the traps of the flesh and the world. I believe in You and place my faith in Your perfect plans, rejoicing in the battles already won!

NOTES

NOTES

WORDS FOR HEARING GOD'S VOICE

Exodus 19:9

The Lord said to Moses, "I am going to come to you in a dense cloud, so that the people will hear Me speaking with you and will always put their trust in you." Then Moses told the Lord what the people had said.

Lord, help me to hear Your voice, even when my thoughts seem cloudy. Help me to recognize Your voice and to put my trust in You. Thank You for cutting through the fog and speaking so clearly! Give me ears to hear and obey.

Exodus 20:18-20

When the people saw the thunder and lightning and heard the trumpet and saw the mountain in smoke, they trembled with fear. They stayed at a distance and said to Moses, "Speak to us yourself and we will listen. But do not have God speak to us or we will die." Moses said to the people, "Do not be afraid. God has come to test you, so that the fear of God will be with you to keep you from sinning."

Lord, I ask that the fear of the Lord be present in my life so that I will always recognize Your holiness and Your presence. I will not let the weight of Your glory keep me from listening to You. May I hear it in reverential awe with an increased desire to do Your will. Thank You for wanting to speak to me!

1 Samuel 3:10

The Lord came and stood there, calling as at the other times, "Samuel! Samuel!" Then Samuel said, "Speak, for Your servant is listening."

Give me an ear for Your voice, Lord. Remind me to set aside time to sit in Your presence and incline my heart toward You. Give me even greater sensitivity to recognize when You speak and are calling my name. May I always respond with a readiness to obey.

1 Kings 19:11-12

The Lord said, "Go out and stand on the mountain in the presence of the Lord, for the Lord is about to pass by." Then a great and powerful wind tore the mountains apart and shattered the rocks before the Lord, but the Lord was not in the wind. After the wind there was an earthquake, but the Lord was not in the earthquake. After the earthquake came a fire, but the Lord was not in the fire. And after the fire came a gentle whisper.

Help me to recognize the ways You speak to me, Lord. I give you my expectations and invite You to teach me how to listen so that I will not miss Your voice. I give you permission to speak in new and unexpected ways. May my heart be ready and my mind be prepared to recognize You and respond rightly.

Psalms 5:3

In the morning, Lord, You hear my voice; in the morning I lay my requests before You and wait expectantly.

I commit to listen for Your voice each day as I consistently set aside time to commune with You. I will tell You what is on my heart, knowing You will answer and give me what I need because You are a faithful God.

Psalms 32:8-9

I will instruct you and teach you in the way you should go; I will counsel you with My loving eye on you. Do not be like the horse or the mule, which have no understanding but must be controlled by bit and bridle or they will not come to you.

Thank you, Lord, for instructing me and teaching me the way I should go. I yield my control and submit to Your ways for my life. Forgive me for being stubborn and unwilling to follow. Turn my heart so that I will listen more carefully and respond more quickly. You alone know what is best for my ultimate good and for Your greatest glory.

Psalms 66:18-19

If I had cherished sin in my heart, the Lord would not have listened; but God has surely listened and has heard my prayer.

Cleanse my heart and show me anything that is blocking my ability to hear Your voice, Lord. Show me how to hear You more clearly and to keep my heart and mind free of any distractions or roadblocks in perceiving Your presence and Your direction.

Proverbs 3:5-6

Trust in the Lord with all your heart and lean not on your own understanding; in all your ways submit to Him, and He will make your paths straight.

Lord, show me whenever my own ideas and expectations get in the way of hearing Your voice. You are intricately involved in every aspect of my life and You know the best way through! Alert me when my own ideas are getting in the ways of Yours. Thank You for straightening out the crooked paths in my life and clearing the way for my future.

Isaiah 30:20-21

Although the Lord gives you the bread of adversity and the water of affliction, your teachers will be hidden no more; with your own eyes you will see them. Whether you turn to the right or to the left, your ears will hear a voice behind you, saying, "This is the way; walk in it."

Thank you, Lord, for guiding my every step! I incline my ear to what You are saying and determine to carefully consider every decision I make. I only want to go where You tell me to go. Keep me from presumption and steer me to the right path.

Jeremiah 6:10

To whom can I speak and give warning? Who will listen to me? Their ears are closed so they cannot hear. The word of the Lord is offensive to them; they find no pleasure in it.

Do not hold back Your words from me, God! I delight in hearing Your voice and listening to what You say – even the corrections and warnings – for I know they are right and good. Remove any rebellion in my heart or fear concerning Your ways so that I can receive the fullness of what You have to say.

Habakkuk 2:1

I will stand at my watch and station myself on the ramparts; I will look to see what He will say to me, and what answer I am to give to this complaint.

Lord, I commit myself to daily watch and listen for Your voice. Prepare my heart and mind to receive Your instructions so that they might bring life and hope to all who hear them. Remind me when I forget to listen and help me stay on the alert for Your directives.

Luke 8:18

Therefore, consider carefully how you listen. Whoever has will be given more; whoever does not have, even what they think they have will be taken from them.

Thank You, Lord, for speaking to Me and giving me understanding. I want to be a good steward of what You say so that I can receive even more. May I be a storehouse of Your truth so that I can share with others what You have shown to me.

Luke 11:28

He replied, "Blessed rather are those who hear the word of God and obey it."

I desire Your blessing on my life, Lord! I will obey Your Word when I hear it and follow through with Your direction. Help me to stay accountable and to not postpone obedience when You speak. Stop me when I don't listen or turn away from Your voice. Keep my heart centered with a desire to do Your will.

John 6:63

The Spirit gives life; the flesh counts for nothing. The words I have spoken to you - they are full of the Spirit and life.

Your words bring life, Lord! I will celebrate what You speak to me as Your words are always full of truth and filled with power from Your Spirit! Continue to show the difference between the voice of my flesh, the voice of the enemy, and the voice of Your Spirit. Thank You for making it clear so I can follow You.

John 8:47

Whoever belongs to God hears what God says. The reason you do not hear is that you do not belong to God."

I belong to You, Lord, and I will follow no other voice! Thank you for giving me access to Your heart. I want to know what You have to say and desire to do Your will. Show me if there's anything in my life that is blocking Your voice coming through.

John 10:27

My sheep listen to My voice; I know them, and they follow Me.

I am listening for Your voice, Lord, and will follow where You lead me. I know that delayed obedience will hinder my ability to hear You. I choose to follow where You lead. I trust You as my Shepherd and lean on You as my Guardian in everything I do and everywhere I go.

John 14:26

But the Advocate, the Holy Spirit, whom the Father will send in My name, will teach you all things and will remind you of everything I have said to you.

Thank you for Holy Spirit, my Counselor and Friend! I gladly receive the Spirit's instruction for my life. May He remind me of what You have said in the past so that I might be strengthened in my faith and more certain of my future. May the Spirit establish Your word in my heart for all eternity.

John 16:13-14

But when He, the Spirit of truth, comes, He will guide you into all the truth. He will not speak on His own; He will speak only what He hears, and He will tell you what is yet to come. He will glorify Me because it is from Me that He will receive what He will make known to you.

Guide me to the Spirit of Truth so that I may know You better, Lord. Help me to recognize the voice that gives all honor and attention to You as my Father and that reveals the fullness of Your glory. Show me what I need to know for the days ahead so I can be faithful and diligent in fulfilling Your call.

Romans 10:17

Consequently, faith comes from hearing the message, and the message is heard through the word about Christ.

Teach me Your word, God, so that I will recognize Your voice and Your will. I desire to build a strong foundation of Your Word in my life so that I can rightly discern the voices that speak to me. Help me to feed my spirit with truth and not with worthless things. I want my faith to be strong as I apply Your words to my life in practical ways.

Hebrews 4:2

For we also have had the good news proclaimed to us, just as they did; but the message they heard was of no value to them, because they did not share the faith of those who obeyed.

As I listen for Your voice, Lord, I position my heart and mind in absolute faith concerning Your purposes. I will not waver in what You say or doubt Your intentions towards me. I believe that what You speak is good and right and true, and I want to obey without hesitation.

James 1:19

My dear brothers and sisters, take note of this: Everyone should be quick to listen, slow to speak, and slow to become angry.

Help me to listen more than speak, Lord. May any negative emotions take a back seat to waiting on You and listening carefully to Your perspective in every matter. Thank you for giving me sensitive hearing!

1 John 5:14-15

This is the confidence we have in approaching God: that if we ask anything according to His will, He hears us. And if we know that He hears us - whatever we ask - we know that we have what we asked of Him.

Your Word says that when I ask according to Your will, You hear me and will answer. Teach me to know Your will so that I can ask the right things. Help me to fill my heart and mind with Your Word so that my conversations with You will flow from Your truth. Give me even greater understanding in Your ways so that my prayers will be effective and hit the mark.

NOTES

NOTES

Words for Living by the Spirit

Ezekiel 36:26-27

I will give you a new heart and put a new spirit in you; I will remove from you your heart of stone and give you a heart of flesh. And I will put My Spirit in you and move you to follow My decrees and be careful to keep My laws.

Take my heart of stone, Lord, and give me a soft heart that is sensitive to You. Remove any hardness of heart or apathy towards Your will for my life. Draw me and move me to follow where You lead me. Sanctify and cleanse my heart so that Your desire will be my desire, and Your will my will.

Isaiah 11:2-3a

The Spirit of the Lord will rest on him - the Spirit of wisdom and of understanding, the Spirit of counsel and of might, the Spirit of the knowledge and fear of the Lord - and he will delight in the fear of the Lord.

Father, I pray that the fullness of Your Spirit will rest upon me. May I walk in the Spirit of wisdom and understanding, the Spirit of counsel and might, and the Spirit of knowledge and the fear of the Lord. I cannot do this on my own, so I ask You to come upon me now and fill me to the brim. Thank You for providing this seven-fold blessing from Your throne.

Zechariah 4:6

So he said to me, "This is the word of the Lord to Zerubbabel: 'Not by might nor by power, but by My Spirit,' says the Lord Almighty.

Thank You, Lord, that victory does not depend on my own might or my own power, but on Your Holy Spirit. Remind me when I strive to defeat the enemy with my own resources. I trust in the power of Your Spirit to defeat whatever comes against me, and I will give You all the credit for the victory.

Matthew 10:19-20

But when they arrest you, do not worry about what to say or how to say it. At that time you will be given what to say, for it will not be you speaking, but the Spirit of your Father speaking through you.

Lord, I will not be anxious when feeling under pressure or am being challenged in my faith, for You will teach me what to say! Holy Spirit, I give You permission to speak to me and through me when I don't know what to say to those who question me. Thank You for Your perfect wisdom and prevailing truth that overrides the knowledge of men. May I be a good steward of the words You reveal to me.

Luke 4:1

Jesus, full of the Holy Spirit, left the Jordan and was led by the Spirit into the wilderness

Lord, I know there will be times when You will lead me into wilderness seasons. But, thank You for filling me with Your Holy Spirit and the authority to overcome any obstacle. I fully trust You in this and thank You for filling me with Your presence, granting me the power and authority to overcome the enemy and come out a victor.

Luke 11:13

If you then, though you are evil, know how to give good gifts to your children, how much more will your Father in heaven give the Holy Spirit to those who ask Him!

Thank you, Father, for giving me the Holy Spirit! You do not withhold any good gifts from Your children, and I thank You for giving me the Spirit's power to be an overcomer in this life. Remind me to ask You on a daily basis for Your Spirit to be my source of power and peace. Thank You for giving me the ability to live each day with hope and confidence.

John 3:6

Flesh gives birth to flesh, but the Spirit gives birth to spirit.

I offer myself to You, Holy Spirit, and ask You to expose any way in which my flesh is exerting itself and bringing a spirit of death over my life. I do

not want to live by the flesh but by Your Spirit. Show me the fruit of how I live so that I may pursue living by Your Spirit on a daily basis.

John 7:38-39a
Whoever believes in Me, as Scripture has said, rivers of living water will flow from within them." By this He meant the Spirit, whom those who believed in Him were later to receive.

I ask for living waters to flow through me, Lord. Your Spirit is like a river of life and healing, and I desire for You to flow out of my life into others around me. May I be a conduit of Your presence and a demonstration of the Spirit within, bearing much fruit for Your glory.

John 14:26
But the Advocate, the Holy Spirit, whom the Father will send in My name, will teach you all things and will remind you of everything I have said to you.

Thank You for sending Holy Spirit to teach me and remind me of everything You have said. Help me listen to His counsel and follow His advice so that it will go well with my soul. I ask Your Helper to guide me each day so I can grow in my ability to hear and perceive Your presence.

John 15:26
When the Advocate comes, whom I will send to you from the Father - the Spirit of truth who goes out from the Father - He will testify about Me.

Father, I am listening for Your Spirit to reveal Jesus to me and remind me of the things He has said and done on my behalf. Thank You that I am not alone. I have a Counselor who bears witness to heavenly realities and confirms who Jesus is. I yield to Your Spirit and thank You for the amazing things You want to show me.

Acts 1:8
But you will receive power when the Holy Spirit comes on you; and you will be My witnesses in Jerusalem, and in all Judea and Samaria, and to the ends of the earth.

Holy Spirit, You are here to make me a witness to the life-giving power of Christ in my life. Enable me to boldly testify about Christ and to reach those that no one else can reach. Show me where to go and who to touch. Fill me with Your Spirit so I share the gospel without hesitation to those who haven't yet heard.

Acts 2:4

All of them were filled with the Holy Spirit and began to speak in other tongues as the Spirit enabled them.

Thank You for the heavenly language with which we can communicate with Your Spirit. Thank You for giving me access to Your heart and thoughts through this spiritual language. Enable me to receive this supernatural gift so I can declare the praises of God in other languages, both of men and of angels. Teach me how to use this gift so it will bring the Father all the glory and be a blessing to my life and others around me.

Acts 2:17-18

"In the last days," God says, "I will pour out My Spirit on all people. Your sons and daughters will prophesy, your young men will see visions, your old men will dream dreams. Even on My servants, both men and women, I will pour out My Spirit in those days, and they will prophesy."

Thank You, Lord, for the increase of Your Spirit on the earth! May the fullness of Your Spirit be poured out upon all flesh all across the earth. May Your presence be manifest with dreams, visions, and manifestations of Your power. May there be spontaneous prophetic utterances that declare Your words to a world in desperate need of deliverance. May I be a conduit of this blessing and share it with others.

Acts 2:38

Peter replied, "Repent and be baptized, every one of you, in the name of Jesus Christ for the forgiveness of your sins. And you will receive the gift of the Holy Spirit."

Thank You for the gift of the Holy Spirit! Thank You for giving me the power to overcome sin and live a victorious life. Today, I again surrender my life to You and ask You to fill me with Your Spirit from above. Alert me when any sin gets in the way of this union so that I can be free to walk in the fullness of the Spirit's power and presence.

Acts 8:15-17

When they arrived, they prayed for the new believers there that they might receive the Holy Spirit, because the Holy Spirit had not yet come on any of them; they had simply been baptized in the name of the Lord Jesus. Then Peter and John placed their hands on them, and they received the Holy Spirit.

Thank You for giving us the Helper so that we can accomplish that which You've called us to do as followers of Christ. Thank You for the impartation of Your Spirit that comes when believers agree together and pray for one another to receive Your most wonderful gift! May I be so filled with Your Spirit that others around me are stirred with a greater desire for the same thing!

Romans 8:6

The mind governed by the flesh is death, but the mind governed by the Spirit is life and peace.

Mold my mind, Lord, according to the ways of the Spirit. Show me where my thinking is of the flesh and void of power. Teach me the ways of Your throne. I want my mind established in the Spirit of truth that reflects life and peace in every decision I make.

Romans 8:11

And if the Spirit of Him who raised Jesus from the dead is living in you, He who raised Christ from the dead will also give life to your mortal bodies because of His Spirit who lives in you.

Thank You for resurrection power! I acknowledge that the same power that raised Christ from the dead is the same Spirit that lives inside of me! Remind me to walk in this supernatural power so I can bring dead things back to life and show others the power of Your everlasting Kingdom. There is life after death through the power of Your Spirit!

Romans 8:26-27

In the same way, the Spirit helps us in our weakness. We do not know what we ought to pray for, but the Spirit himself intercedes for us through wordless groans. And He who searches our hearts knows the mind of the Spirit, because the Spirit intercedes for God's people in accordance with the will of God.

Holy Spirit, help me when I don't know how to pray. Instill in me the Father's will and teach me how to know His heart when I come in prayer. Thank You for giving me direct access to the throne. Thank You for the ability to connect with heaven and express the Father's heart more clearly.

1 Corinthians 2:12-13

What we have received is not the spirit of the world, but the Spirit who is from God, so that we may understand what God has freely given us. This is what we speak, not in words taught us by human wisdom but in words taught by the Spirit, explaining spiritual realities with Spirit-taught words.

Thank You, God, for giving me understanding of spiritual matters through the power of Your Spirit. Thank You for giving me the words, both in my mind and in my spirit, that help me pray and understand Your purposes. I receive Your words and insights into the realm of the Spirit. Help me to convey them to others in a way that brings life, hope, peace, and purpose.

1 Corinthians 2:14-16

The person without the Spirit does not accept the things that come from the Spirit of God but considers them foolishness and cannot understand them because they are discerned only through the Spirit. The person with the Spirit makes judgments about all things, but such a person is not subject to merely human judgments, for, "Who has known the mind of the Lord so as to instruct Him?" But we have the mind of Christ.

You have given me the mind of Christ! Through the power of Your Spirit, You help me discern what is true and good and right. What is foolishness to the flesh is actually wisdom in the Spirit! I thank You for granting me access to these spiritual realities and giving me the needed clarity and confirmation of Your presence and Your purpose.

1 Corinthians 6:19-20

Do you not know that your bodies are temples of the Holy Spirit, who is in you, whom you have received from God? You are not your own; you were bought at a price. Therefore, honor God with your bodies.

Father, I acknowledge that my body is not my own, but was bought with a price. Help me to be a good steward of Your temple. I choose to honor You in how I take care of myself, what I feed on, and what I do with my body. Teach me to be a faithful vessel that can manifest Your Spirit's glory without shame or guilt. May I be a worthy reflection of You and the power of the Spirit.

2 Corinthians 3:17

Now the Lord is the Spirit, and where the Spirit of the Lord is, there is freedom.

When Your Spirit is alive within me, I am a carrier of freedom! May I live a life that is free of any fleshly encumbrance or demonic influence and be a conduit of freedom to others. May the Spirit within open windows from heaven to bring freedom to the captives and those bound in sin. Help me to live free and stay free. Let freedom ring!

2 Corinthians 4:18

So we fix our eyes not on what is seen, but on what is unseen, since what is seen is temporary, but what is unseen is eternal.

Lord, help me to look at what is unseen and eternal, and not get distracted by what I see in the natural and is only temporary. Remind me when I get distracted and turn my eyes to things that are lifeless and void of truth. I want to focus on things that really matter and that which will bring lasting change.

2 Corinthians 5:7

For we live by faith, not by sight.

Remind me, Lord, to live by faith in You and not by what I see with my natural eyes. Help me grow in my faith and to strengthen the foundation of Your Word in my life. Help me see the spiritual realities that are far greater than natural perceptions. May I be filled with hope and confidence in what You have planned – regardless of what things look like in the natural.

Galatians 4:6-7

Because you are His sons, God sent the Spirit of His Son into our hearts, the Spirit who calls out, "Abba, Father." So, you are no longer a slave, but God's child; and since you are His child, God has made you also an heir.

Thank You, Holy Spirit, for declaring me a child of God! Because of Your presence within, I am no longer a slave to sin, but am free in Christ. I am an heir of the King and a full recipient of all His promises and provisions – just because I'm His!

Galatians 5:16-18

So I say, walk by the Spirit, and you will not gratify the desires of the flesh. For the flesh desires what is contrary to the Spirit, and the Spirit what is contrary to the flesh. They are in conflict with each other, so that you are not to do whatever you want. But if you are led by the Spirit, you are not under the law.

Help me to walk in Your Spirit, Lord, and to not give in to fleshly temptations. I desire what You desire. Purify and sanctify my emotions and my longings, so that I will follow You out of love and not out of obligation to the flesh. I want to be led by Your Spirit!

Galatians 5:22-25

But the fruit of the Spirit is love, joy, peace, forbearance, kindness, goodness, faithfulness, gentleness, and self-control. Against such things there is no law. Those who belong to Christ Jesus have crucified the flesh with its passions and desires. Since we live by the Spirit, let us keep in step with the Spirit.

Lord, I know that the fruit of the Spirit will only come through a life fully surrendered to You. I lay down my rights and my ways of doing things and ask You to fill me with heaven. Help me to keep in step with You. Alert me when I get off track and bring me back to the altar so You can live through me without hindrance.

1 Thessalonians 5:19
Do not quench the Spirit.

Alert me, Holy Spirit, any time I stop listening to the You. I do not want to refuse Your guidance or ignore Your presence. Help me to follow Your promptings and not diminish Your influence in my daily walk. I give You freedom to move in the way You decide, and surrender my will and my preferences to You.

1 John 3:24
The one who keeps God's commands lives in Him, and He in them. And this is how we know that He lives in us: we know it by the Spirit He gave us.

Keep me faithful to Your word, Lord, so that others will see the Spirit of truth in me. Help me recognize Your voice and obey Your directives. Teach me to align my thoughts and ideas with Yours so that Your blessing will be on my life. Teach me to be one with You!

NOTES

Words for Waiting

Psalms 27:13-14

I remain confident of this: I will see the goodness of the Lord in the land of the living. Wait for the Lord; be strong and take heart and wait for the Lord.

God, You are a good Father and I trust You to fulfill Your plan for my life. You do not delight in prolonging Your promises but are faithful in fulfilling Your Word at the perfect time. I rest in Your perfect plans and will wait for You.

Psalms 37:34

Hope in the Lord and keep His way. He will exalt you to inherit the land; when the wicked are destroyed, you will see it.

While I am waiting for my prayers to be answered, Lord, keep me from messing things up! Help me to stay faithful to Your directives and not look to my own ways of doing things. I know You are going after my spiritual adversary and will bring me justice in due time. I know Your ways are better than mine.

Psalms 130:5-6

I wait for the Lord, my whole being waits, and in His word I put my hope. I wait for the Lord more than watchmen wait for the morning, more than watchmen wait for the morning.

Lord, I know I must remind myself on a daily basis of Your words that bring me hope. Help me to be consistent in looking to You and not my circumstances for the breakthroughs I need. Remind me of the words You have already spoken and renew my faith as I start each day.

Proverbs 3:5-6

Trust in the Lord with all your heart, and do not lean on your own understanding. In all your ways acknowledge Him, and He will make straight your paths.

I lay down my need to understand things, Lord. I admit that I don't like the unknowns! But, I choose to give my circumstances to You, knowing You will direct me where I need to go and establish my steps. Thank You for leading me on this journey and making sure I arrive at the right place at the right time.

Proverbs 20:22

Do not say, "I'll pay you back for this wrong!" Wait for the Lord, and He will avenge you.

Forgive me, Lord, for wanting to take matters into my own hands. I confess that I want to jump in and try to fix things based on what I know. But, You alone know what is needed and are a God of justice. You will deal with matters far better than I ever could. Help me to wait for Your intervention and to rest in Your sovereign solutions.

Isaiah 30:18

Yet the Lord longs to be gracious to you; therefore He will rise up to show you compassion. For the Lord is a God of justice. Blessed are all who wait for Him!

I want Your blessing, Lord. Therefore, I will wait for You, knowing Your justice will prevail and Your goodness become evident.

Isaiah 40:31 (ESV)

But they who wait for the Lord shall renew their strength; they shall mount up with wings like eagles; they shall run and not be weary; they shall walk and not faint.

Your Word states that the strength I need to persevere is only found as I wait on You! It is not accessible if I rush ahead or become impatient. Therefore, God, I place my absolute trust in You to accomplish Your purpose in Your time and not mine. Thank You for empowering me to soar in the Spirit as I wait on You.

Lamentations 3:25-26 (ESV)

The Lord is good to those who wait for Him, to the soul who seeks Him. It is good that one should wait quietly for the salvation of the Lord.

I don't want to miss Your goodness, Lord! I want the very best You have for me and I will wait for Your plans instead of running ahead with mine. I will daily seek Your face and wait quietly and patiently for the outcome You have in mind. Thank You for being such a good God!

Habakkuk 2:3

For the revelation awaits an appointed time; it speaks of the end and will not prove false. Though it linger, wait for it; it will certainly come and will not delay.

You have an anointed and appointed time for Your promises to be fulfilled, Lord. You are never late and always do things right on time. There are aspects of situations that I cannot see, and You are tending to all the details! Help me to stand strong in faith as I wait for Your time of breakthrough and deliverance.

Romans 5:3-5

Not only so, but we also glory in our sufferings, because we know that suffering produces perseverance; perseverance, character; and character, hope. And hope does not put us to shame, because God's love has been poured out into our hearts through the Holy Spirit, who has been given to us.

Even in the waiting, Lord, I can grow and mature to be more like You. You are developing perseverance and character and I thank You for using the waiting process for my good and for Your glory. My hope is in Your love that never fails.

Romans 12:12

Be joyful in hope, patient in affliction, faithful in prayer.

I know I need a good attitude while I wait, God. Alert me when I begin to complain so that I can give thanks, instead. Remind me when I become impatient so I can surrender to Your process. Nudge me when I forget to pray and start becoming anxious. In all these things, Lord, I choose to worship You for being a good and faithful God!

Galatians 5:5

For through the Spirit we eagerly await by faith the righteousness for which we hope.

Thank You for this reminder that I cannot wait properly apart from the power of Your Spirit. It is only by Your Spirit that I can see clearly and hope for the right things. Cleanse my mind and heart from those thoughts and ideas that are counterproductive and not established in faith. Fill me with Your Holy Spirit so that I can have the right perspective in waiting. May I rest in Your grace to bring me through to victory!

Galatians 6:9

Let us not become weary in doing good, for at the proper time we will reap a harvest if we do not give up.

Lord, it's hard to keep doing the right thing but never seeing any results! Forgive me for not trusting in You like I should. I put my faith in Your Word and know that as I continue to water those seeds in prayer, there will come a time of harvest. I will wait for that time with joyful anticipation and continue to be faithful in what You've already shown me.

Philippians 1:6

Being confident of this, that He who began a good work in you will carry it on to completion until the day of Christ Jesus.

Lord, You always finish what You start! You wouldn't call me to do some-thing without giving me the grace and ability to complete it. What You have begun in other areas of my life, I also trust You to finish with great results. Thank You for the daily grace to be patient and steadfast as I wait for You to bring me to the finish line and receive the victor's crown!

James 5:7-8

Be patient, then, brothers and sisters, until the Lord's coming. See how the farmer waits for the land to yield its valuable crop, patiently waiting for the autumn and spring rains. You too, be patient and stand firm, because the Lord's coming is near.

Lord, forgive me for my impatience. I know that any good seeds planted in faith will eventually bring forth good fruit. I know I can't rush the process, so I will wait on You to water the seeds and bring forth the harvest in due time. In the meantime, I rejoice in Your faithfulness to fulfill Your Word.

James 5:11

As you know, we count as blessed those who have persevered. You have heard of Job's perseverance and have seen what the Lord finally brought about. The Lord is full of compassion and mercy.

Even though it can be painful to wait, I trust in Your end result, Lord! I know You are working all things for my good and I will trust You with the timing of my breakthrough. I will not give in to fear or doubt, but trust in Your compassion and mercy to determine the best outcome for all.

2 Peter 3:9

The Lord is not slow in keeping His promise, as some understand slowness. Instead, He is patient with you, not wanting anyone to perish, but everyone to come to repentance.

Lord, You alone know how to reach those who are in the valley of decision. You aim to reach their heart even more than change their mind. Do what only You can do! I trust in Your process with those I am praying for and know that You are working in ways I cannot see.

NOTES

Words for Discerning Truth

1 Samuel 16:7

But the Lord said to Samuel, "Do not consider his appearance or his height, for I have rejected him. The Lord does not look at the things people look at. People look at the outward appearance, but the Lord looks at the heart."

Remind me, Lord, when I judge others based on appearances. Help me to see into the heart and to recognize what You see. May I look with Your eyes and take the time needed to discern rightly. Help me not prematurely judge a situation based merely on my own perceptions. Show me what is true, right, and good, from Your perspective so I can align with Your will and plan.

1 Kings 3:8

So give Your servant a discerning heart to govern Your people and to distinguish between right and wrong. For who is able to govern this great people of Yours?

Give me a discerning heart, Lord, so that I can rightly understand situations and people from a heavenly perspective. Help me to see above and beyond what my own thoughts and ideas perceive. Give me Your heart for others so that I will not only look to my own interests, but to the welfare of those around me.

1 Kings 3:11-12

So God said to him, "Since you have asked for this and not for long life or wealth for yourself, nor have asked for the death of your enemies but for discernment in administering justice, I will do what you have asked. I will give you a wise and discerning heart, so that there will never have been anyone like you, nor will there ever be."

God, You deem discernment to be one of the greatest assets we can have. May I realize the treasure of a discerning heart and seek to grow in using it for good and for the wellbeing of others. Thank You for enlarging my heart to perceive and understand what You are doing so that I can better fulfill Your will for my life. I pray that the wisdom You provide will be a sign to others of how great You truly are.

Psalms 111:10
The fear of the Lord is the beginning of wisdom; all who follow His precepts have good understanding. To Him belongs eternal praise.

I desire to walk in the fear of the Lord and the fullness of Your wisdom! Your Word is what brings insight, and Your truth is what brings life and purpose. I submit myself to Your oversight and give You permission to overshadow me with Your holiness and righteousness. All truth flows from this place and I welcome the daily reminder that I answer to You, first and foremost, in all that I do and say.

Psalms 119:66
Teach me knowledge and good judgment, for I trust Your commands.

It appears that knowledge and good judgment come as the result of trusting Your commands. Forgive me when I have not trusted You, Lord. I declare now that You can be trusted! I will build my faith by planting Your Word in my heart and obeying what You say. Your ways are higher than mine and I know You will give me right discernment as I follow Your lead.

Proverbs 3:5-6
Trust in the Lord with all your heart and lean not on your own understanding; in all your ways submit to Him, and He will make your paths straight.

Forgive me, Lord, when I lean on my own understanding instead of Your Spirit. If I expect You to make my paths straight, I must look to Your guidance and direction instead of my own ideas and preferences. I know that as I trust in You, You will give me the discernment needed to know which way to go.

Proverbs 15:14
The discerning heart seeks knowledge, but the mouth of a fool feeds on folly.

Forgive me, Lord, when I have listened more to my friends and peers than to Your Spirit. Forgive me when I have not sought out godly counsel but looked to my own ways. I do not want to be foolish but wise. I want to have all the information needed so I can make a right decision. Show me where I can go for counsel that will enlarge my understanding and increase my capacity to receive truth.

John 7:17-18
Anyone who chooses to do the will of God will find out whether my teaching comes from God or whether I speak on my own. Whoever speaks on their own does so to gain personal glory, but he who seeks the glory of the one who sent him is a man of truth; there is nothing false about him.

You always look to the heart, God! For those who truly want to do Your will, You grant understanding and greater discernment. I want a heart after Yours! I want to please You in all that I do and say. Thank You for sharpening my discernment as a result of following after You.

John 8:31
To the Jews who had believed Him, Jesus said, "If you hold to My teaching, you are really My disciples. Then you will know the truth, and the truth will set you free."

Faith in Your Word is what brings truth that sets us free! I will hold fast to Your teachings and Your directives, Lord. Thank You for revealing truth to me as I stand fast on Your Word and do not waver in unbelief. Thank You for increasing my ability to understand as I believe in You.

Romans 12:2
Do not conform to the pattern of this world but be transformed by the renewing of your mind. Then you will be able to test and approve what God's will is - His good, pleasing, and perfect will.

Alert me, Holy Spirit, when my thoughts and attitudes align more with the world than with Your truth. Forgive me when I have not known Your Word well enough to stand against the tide of popular opinion. Separate those ideas that come more from my flesh than from the realities of Your Spirit. I want to know Your good, pleasing, and perfect will for my life. Thank You for giving me Your Word that helps me agree with Your plans.

1 Corinthians 2:14

The person without the Spirit does not accept the things that come from the Spirit of God but considers them foolishness, and cannot understand them because they are discerned only through the Spirit.

Without Your Holy Spirit, Lord, I have no comprehension of Your will for my life! I cannot journey on my own apart from Your Spirit. Alert me when I begin to operate in unbelief because I'm looking at things through my human eyes and not my spiritual eyes. Give me even greater faith for the truths of Your Spirit which boggle the human mind and challenge our limited understanding.

1 Corinthians 12:10

To another miraculous powers, to another prophecy, to another distinguishing between spirits, to another speaking in different kinds of tongues, and to still another the interpretation of tongues.

Thank You for the gifts of Your Spirit which enable me to understand Your ways. I ask for this gift of distinguishing between spirits so that I can rightly discern the difference between that which is of the human spirit, the Holy Spirit, or a demonic spirit. Grant me the grace to recognize these differences so I can pray more effectively and respond in a way that brings blessing and good fruit.

Philippians 1:9-10

And this is my prayer: that your love may abound more and more in knowledge and depth of insight, so that you may be able to discern what is best and may be pure and blameless for the day of Christ, filled with the fruit of righteousness that comes through Jesus Christ - to the glory and praise of God.

Thank You for the reminder that all discernment of truth flows out of Your perfect love. Fill me with more of this love so that my perceptions will be filtered through Your heart and not my own understanding. Fix my mind on what You deem good, right, and true, so that fruit will abound and You will receive all the glory for the answers.

Hebrews 4:12

For the word of God is alive and active. Sharper than any double-edged sword, it penetrates even to dividing soul and spirit, joints and marrow; it judges the thoughts and attitudes of the heart.

Thank You for Your Word, Lord! Thank You for this blueprint that gives me proper foundations for sound doctrine. Remind me to fill my mind and spirit with Your Word before trying to judge something I don't understand. May Your Word cut like a knife to my own heart so that I can be sharpened in my discernment and recognize what is true.

Hebrews 5:14

But solid food is for the mature, who by constant use have trained themselves to distinguish good from evil.

Lord, I want to grow and mature in my ability to rightly discern the truth. I know this comes as I practice on a consistent basis. May I learn to know You and Your words so keenly and so intimately that I will immediately recognize those voices and beliefs that are counter to Your truth. Teach me to separate lies and half-truths from the plumbline of Your Word.

James 4:8

Come near to God and He will come near to you. Wash your hands, you sinners, and purify your hearts, you double-minded.

If there is anything that is affecting my ability to discern You, Lord, come and cleanse my heart and mind. Show me if any ungodly belief, offense, misperception, or unresolved sin is keeping me from knowing Your heart and will. Purify my heart of anything that is offensive to You so that I can be rightly focused on Your heart alone.

1 John 4:1-3

Dear friends, do not believe every spirit, but test the spirits to see whether they are from God, because many false prophets have gone out into the world. This is how you can recognize the Spirit of God: Every spirit that acknowledges that Jesus Christ has come in the flesh is from God, but every spirit that does not acknowledge Jesus is not from God. This is the spirit of the antichrist, which you have heard is coming and even now is already in the world.

Jesus, You are the Son of God and yet came to earth in full humanity. Unlike any other spirit that seeks to counterfeit the power of the cross and Your triumph over death, Holy Spirit testifies to this reality that You are fully God and fully human. Help me to recognize the source of any teaching that denies this truth.

NOTES

NOTES

Deuteronomy 15:10
Give generously to them and do so without a grudging heart; then because of this the Lord your God will bless you in all your work and in everything you put your hand to.

Father, I want Your fullest blessing on my life and all that I put my hand to. I desire to give to others out of a free and joyful heart, and not with a grudge or any resentment. Give me Your heart for the needy so that I can give generously without hesitation.

Deuteronomy 28:2, 8, 11-12
All these blessings will come on you and accompany you if you obey the Lord your God... The Lord will send a blessing on your barns and on everything you put your hand to. The Lord your God will bless you in the land He is giving you... The Lord will grant you abundant prosperity - in the fruit of your womb, the young of your livestock and the crops of your ground - in the land He swore to your ancestors to give you. The Lord will open the heavens, the storehouse of His bounty, to send rain on your land in season and to bless all the work of your hands. You will lend to many nations but will borrow from none.

Thank You, Lord, for the blessings of obedience! You promise to bless the work of my hands when I obey Your voice and heed Your Word. Show me if there is any way in which I have not been obedient to You. May I be a faithful doer of Your word, and not a hearer only. Thank You for blessing the fruit of my labors, my family and household, my land and properties, and all that I put my hand to. For the glory of Your name!

Psalms 34:10
The lions may grow weak and hungry, but those who seek the Lord lack no good thing.

I purpose to seek You above all else, Lord – even before seeking my practical needs. Because You are a faithful and loving God, I know You have my best interests in mind and will provide what I need, exactly when I need it. I will put You first, knowing You are always faithful.

Psalms 37:25-26

I was young and now I am old, yet I have never seen the righteous forsaken or their children begging bread. They are always generous and lend freely; their children will be a blessing.

May I live a righteous life, Lord, so that Your blessing will be upon me and my children. Show me if there is anything that is hindering your fullest blessing on my life. I believe that as I follow Your lead and obey Your words, You will provide me with more than enough for my family, and enough left over to give to others.

Psalms 107:9

For He satisfies the thirsty and fills the hungry with good things.

You are a good Father and will always take care of me. You know my practical needs and I thank You for not only providing for me, but giving me the best and not the left-overs. Keep my heart from jealousy or wanting what others have. Show me what You've already done for me so my heart will stay fixed on Your goodness in my life.

Psalms 112:5

Good will come to those who are generous and lend freely, who conduct their affairs with justice.

Lord, make me a good steward of money, so that good will come from my giving. Teach me to be wise with my finances and to handle financial decisions with honor, integrity, and transparency. May the money You give me be used to help others and be a witness of Your eternal Kingdom.

Psalms 145:15-16

The eyes of all look to You, and You give them their food at the proper time. You open Your hand and satisfy the desires of every living thing.

Forgive me, Lord, for my impatience. You have promised to give me what I need - when I need it. I choose to trust in Your perfect timing for my provision. May my desires be aligned with Your purposes and give You honor.

Proverbs 3:9-10
Honor the Lord with your wealth, with the first fruits of all your crops; then your barns will be filled to overflowing, and your vats will brim over with new wine.

It is a joy to honor Your faithfulness in my life, Lord, and share Your blessings with others. Show me where to sow a first fruits gift from what You have provided. I believe that in giving the first fruits of my labors, You will bless the remainder to come and reveal even more of Your abundant provision in my life.

Proverbs 10:4
Lazy hands make for poverty, but diligent hands bring wealth.

Forgive me, Lord, for any laziness on my part that is keeping me in poverty. Give me a greater joy in working for a living and not seeing it as a necessary evil. I believe You want me to prosper, so I purpose to be diligent in what You have gifted me to do. Open the right doors for me to earn a living in a way that blesses others and honors You.

Proverbs 13:11
Dishonest money dwindles away, but whoever gathers money little by little makes it grow.

Teach me how to invest wisely, Lord, and to guard my heart against attaining wealth dishonestly or too quickly. It is for my good that You teach me how to steward wealth little by little so that I learn the valuable lessons. May both my spending and my investments honor You and reflect the wisdom from heaven.

Proverbs 15:27
The greedy bring ruin to their households, but the one who hates bribes will live.

Lord, in my business dealings with others, I purpose to not accept a bribe or receive any personal financial gain at the expense of personal integrity. Remind me to honor You when dealing with others and to be fair and just, even willing to pass on a seeming good deal if it's not done with Your fullest blessing.

Proverbs 21:5
The plans of the diligent lead to profit as surely as haste leads to poverty.

Help me to not be hasty, Lord, when making financial decisions. Help me consider everything necessary to make the best choice. I trust in Your timing and in Your methods so that my financial decisions will bring great blessing and honor to You.

Proverbs 22:1
A good name is more desirable than great riches; to be esteemed is better than silver or gold.

Lord, I do not want to be tempted by money in a way that discredits my testimony. Grant me the courage to say 'No' to any financial gain if it means tarnishing my reputation or Your good name. I want to live a life of honor, especially when it comes to decisions about money. May I be known as one who operates in integrity and can be trusted with finances.

Proverbs 22:7
The rich rule over the poor, and the borrower is slave to the lender.

Lord, give me wisdom in taking out loans and borrowing money. I do not want to be a slave to money or sign contracts I cannot fulfill. Increase my ability to wait on Your timing for the provisions I need and to trust Your ways of releasing them.

Proverbs 28:20
A faithful person will be richly blessed, but one eager to get rich will not go unpunished.

Keep my heart free from greed, Lord! I believe that You reward the faithful. I look forward to the blessings to come as I trust in You for all my provision.

Malachi 3:10

Bring the whole tithe into the storehouse, that there may be food in My house. Test Me in this," says the Lord Almighty, "and see if I will not throw open the floodgates of heaven and pour out so much blessing that there will not be room enough to store it."

All that You have given me, Lord, belongs to You. To give back is nothing because it's all Yours to begin with. I will not horde my provision or be fearful of lack. I believe that as I joyfully give back to You a portion of what is already Yours, Your blessing will continue and even increase. May my heart be more fixed on joyfully giving, than on holding back what is Yours.

Matthew 6:19-21

Do not store up for yourselves treasures on earth, where moths and vermin destroy, and where thieves break in and steal. But store up for yourselves treasures in heaven, where moths and vermin do not destroy, and where thieves do not break in and steal. For where your treasure is, there your heart will be also.

Father, if my heart is too fixed on material possessions or earthly gain, draw me higher into Your eternal purposes. Show me if I am hoarding my provisions or pursuing money. Cleanse my heart so that I will always choose You above any temporal accumulations or possessions.

Matthew 6:24

No one can serve two masters. Either you will hate the one and love the other, or you will be devoted to the one and despise the other. You cannot serve both God and money.

Show me, Lord, if my heart is divided between you and attaining wealth. Show me if I'm too preoccupied with money – either how much I have, or how little I have. I do not want money to be an idol – either by being greedy - or being stingy. You alone are the One I live for and I thank You for showing me how to be a good and faithful manager of my finances.

Matthew 19:21

Jesus answered, "If you want to be perfect, go, sell your possessions, and give to the poor, and you will have treasure in heaven. Then come, follow Me."

Father, I never want my material wealth to become an idol. Help my heart to be so fixed on You, that I could give it all away and still be perfectly happy and content in knowing You. My first and most important treasure is my relationship with You. Help me keep it that way.

Mark 10:29-30

"Truly I tell you," Jesus replied, "no one who has left home or brothers or sisters or mother or father or children or fields for Me and the gospel will fail to receive a hundred times as much in this present age: homes, brothers, sisters, mothers, children, and fields - along with persecutions - and in the age to come eternal life."

Thank You for the rewards of faithfulness, Lord. You have promised to give back whatever has been lost out of obedience to You, not only in the life to come, but in this life now. I trust in this promise, Lord, and choose to fully obey You, even if it means temporary setbacks. Your goodness will manifest in my life and I thank You for the testimonies to come in the days ahead!

Luke 6:35

But love your enemies, do good to them, and lend to them without expecting to get anything back. Then your reward will be great, and you will be children of the Most High, because He is kind to the ungrateful and wicked.

Lord, give me Your heart for my enemies so that I do not despise them, but desire to do good to them. Show me how to express Your unconditional love to them. Show me how to give to them in a way that draws them to You. I lay down any expectation of reward and will joyfully follow Your lead in being kind and generous to those who are against me or don't know You.

Luke 6:38

Give, and it will be given to you. A good measure, pressed down, shaken together and running over, will be poured into your lap. For with the measure you use, it will be measured to you.

Lord, may I always give even more than what I receive. I desire to be a cheerful giver and to reflect Your heart to bless others. I know with the measure I use, it will be measured back. Show me where to give and to do so with a glad and thankful heart.

Luke 12:15

Then He said to them, "Watch out! Be on your guard against all kinds of greed; life does not consist in an abundance of possessions."

Alert me if any greed begins to grip my heart, Lord. Forgive me for coveting possessions or being jealous of others who have much. Do not allow the devil any foothold in my life through my fleshly desires for more. Help me put money in its proper place and not allow it to take center stage.

Luke 12:29-31

And do not set your heart on what you will eat or drink; do not worry about it. For the pagan world runs after all such things, and your Father knows that you need them. But seek His kingdom, and these things will be given to you as well.

Forgive me, Lord, for having any worry or anxiety about my daily needs. You have promised to provide, so I choose to trust You and fix my faith on Your ability to take care of me. My hope in You is greater than my dependency on what I eat or drink. Thank You for Your watchful care.

Luke 14:28-30

Suppose one of you wants to build a tower. Won't you first sit down and estimate the cost to see if you have enough money to complete it? For if you lay the foundation and are not able to finish it, everyone who sees it will ridicule you, saying, "This person began to build and wasn't able to finish."

Give me the needed wisdom and instruction to make good decisions, Lord. Show me the necessary steps and needed components in following through in financial matters so I will not be caught off guard or ill-prepared. Teach me to lay a proper foundation and do the needed work ahead of time to make the right decision for the long haul.

Luke 16:11-12

So if you have not been trustworthy in handling worldly wealth, who will trust you with true riches? And if you have not been trustworthy with someone else's property, who will give you property of your own?

Teach me, Lord, how to be faithful with little so that You can entrust me with more. I will not despise small beginnings, but will trust in the measure You give to me, knowing You will give me more as I am faithful and obedient. Thank You for giving me the opportunity to grow as a good steward!

Romans 13:8

Let no debt remain outstanding, except the continuing debt to love one another, for whoever loves others has fulfilled the law.

You exhort us to live free of debt. Teach me how to handle money in a way that does not make me a servant to another. Help me get free of my debt and to learn how to make wise decisions in the future so I can be fully devoted to You without financial constraints.

2 Corinthians 8:7

But since you excel in everything - in faith, in speech, in knowledge, in complete earnestness and in the love we have kindled in you - see that you also excel in this grace of giving.

May my life reflect an excellent spirit in everything I do, Lord, including my giving. You have been so good to me and I want to express my gratitude in joyfully extending Your blessing to those around me. Increase my capacity to give!

2 Corinthians 9:7-8

Each of you should give what you have decided in your heart to give, not reluctantly or under compulsion, for God loves a cheerful giver. And God is able to bless you abundantly, so that in all things at all times, having all that you need, you will abound in every good work.

Lord, I want to be a cheerful giver and not just give out of duty. I want to know and express Your heart as a generous Father who loves to give to others. Your desire is for us to thrive, not just survive. Renew my heart and mind so that my thoughts and actions will reflect Your huge heart to give.

2 Corinthians 9:13
Because of the service by which you have proved yourselves, others will praise God for the obedience that accompanies your confession of the gospel of Christ, and for your generosity in sharing with them and with everyone else.

Lord, the world desperately needs to see how good You are. May my giving be a demonstration of Your faithful provision and Your desire to bless Your creation. May my giving be a testimony that gives honor and glory to You as the faithful God and consistent Provider.

Philippians 4:19
And my God will meet all your needs according to the riches of His glory in Christ Jesus.

Thank You, Lord, for meeting every one of my needs as I follow You. You are my source and the keeper of my storehouse. I determine to put my trust in You and do what You say, knowing that You will always provide.

1 Timothy 5:8
Anyone who does not provide for their relatives, and especially for their own household, has denied the faith and is worse than an unbeliever.

Lord, give me the wisdom to know how to take care of my family, both in my own household, as well as extended family. Show me when and how to provide for their needs in a way that honors You, blesses them, and is not out of obligation, co-dependency, or fear. May every decision come from a heart of absolute faith and conviction concerning Your long-term purposes for our lives.

1 Timothy 6:10

For the love of money is a root of all kinds of evil. Some people, eager for money, have wandered from the faith and pierced themselves with many griefs.

You are an abundant Provider, Lord. Do not let my heart become enamored with money. I never want to lose my closeness with You by trading it for wealth or riches. Keep me in the center of Your perfect will and teach me how to keep material wealth in its proper place – as a tool for doing good – not for personal satisfaction.

1 Timothy 6:17-19

Command those who are rich in this present world not to be arrogant nor to put their hope in wealth, which is so uncertain, but to put their hope in God, who richly provides us with everything for our enjoyment. Command them to do good, to be rich in good deeds, and to be generous and willing to share. In this way they will lay up treasure for themselves as a firm foundation for the coming age, so that they may take hold of the life that is truly life.

Thank You, Lord, that You desire to give me more than what I need so that I can joyfully share with others. My hope is in You and not in my bank account. I desire to be an extravagant giver and a reflection of Your abundant provision. Keep my heart and mind fixed on the eternal rewards to come and not on how much I can accumulate in this life.

Hebrews 13:5

Keep your lives free from the love of money and be content with what you have, because God has said, "Never will I leave you; never will I forsake you."

Lord, everything I have belongs to You. Keep my heart free from greed or jealousy of others who have wealth. Help me to see money as a currency of exchange and not as the source of my security. I am thankful for what You have given me – be it plenty or just enough. I know You will always provide what I need.

2 Peter 1:3
His divine power has given us everything we need for a godly life through our knowledge of Him who called us by His own glory and goodness.

Lord, You have already given me everything I need to be pleasing in Your eyes. I believe this includes my material needs, as well. Thank You for being more concerned about the issues of my heart than my material possessions. You are more than able to provide exactly what I need so that You will receive the glory as a faithful Father.

NOTES

Words for Establishing Joy

Psalms 16:11

You make known to me the path of life; You will fill me with joy in Your presence, with eternal pleasures at Your right hand.

When I'm with You, God, I have access to heaven's joy! Draw me closer to Your heart so that I can see what You see and rejoice in the days to come. Remind me to get Your perspective on things and to look at things from an eternal perspective and not a temporary one.

Psalms 30:5

For His anger lasts only a moment, but His favor lasts a lifetime; weeping may stay for the night but rejoicing comes in the morning.

Thank You that the trials I face and the pains I feel are only temporary! Thank You for Your mercy and kindness that displaces the darkness and releases joy into my heart. Thank You for each new day that brings the hope of Your light breaking through and Your joy permeating my life!

Psalms 51:12

Restore to me the joy of Your salvation and grant me a willing spirit, to sustain me.

Lord, remind me of what I felt when I first came to know the power of Your love for me. Remind me of the joy of salvation and the gladness I felt when I realized I was Yours and You had a plan for my life. Displace my doubts with this confidence of Your presence and Your intention to finish what You have started.

Psalms 118:24 (ESV)

This is the day that the Lord has made; let us rejoice and be glad in it.

Each new day brings hope! Each new day has been given as an opportunity to see You at work! Open my eyes to see where and how You are moving so I can give You thanks. I rejoice in this day because You are Lord, and You never stop working on my behalf!

Psalms 126:5-6

Those who sow with tears will reap with songs of joy. Those who go out weeping, carrying seed to sow, will return with songs of joy, carrying sheaves with them.

Thank You for the joy that is being sown through my tears, Lord. I know when I carry Your heart, I feel the pain that You do concerning sin, disappointment, and loss. May my prayers and intercession be filled with the fruit of Your presence and joy. Thank You for the blessings to come as a result of my waiting on You and believing in Your promises for breakthrough.

Proverbs 10:28

The prospect of the righteous is joy, but the hopes of the wicked come to nothing.

Lord, You always reward those who are faithful and those who walk according to Your Word. I can fully expect for good things to come when my relationship with You is right. Keep me in the center of Your will so that I can joyfully anticipate the fruit to come.

Proverbs 17:22

A cheerful heart is good medicine, but a crushed spirit dries up the bones.

Lord, I do not want to make myself sick because of disappointment or discouragement. I speak to my soul and say, "Cheer up! God's got you!" I choose joy instead of despair and put my faith in Your ability to bring healing to my spirit, soul, mind, and body. I receive Your joy as the best medicine I can take!

John 15:10-11

If you keep My commands, you will remain in My love, just as I have kept My Father's commands and remain in His love. I have told you this so that My joy may be in you and that your joy may be complete.

Joy comes from obeying You, Jesus! You promise to fill me with joy in Your presence as I follow You and heed Your directives. Your love gets established in my heart when I walk this way. Thank You for replacing my insecurities and doubts with Your supernatural joy!

John 16:24

Until now you have not asked for anything in My name. Ask and you will receive, and your joy will be complete.

Holy Spirit, teach me how to pray with greater accuracy. Show me where I have presumed things and not even bothered to ask You about them! Thank You for the power of Jesus' name and this invitation to receive all that He has provided for me. Help me to ask according to the Father's will so that I can have complete confidence and joy in His answers.

Romans 12:12

Be joyful in hope, patient in affliction, faithful in prayer.

I place my faith and hope in You, Lord. Regardless of the wait time, I trust You to fulfill Your purposes for my life. I will be steadfast in prayer and not get impatient when things don't happen as quickly as I'd like. Stir hope in my heart so I can have joy in the midst of the waiting.

Romans 14:17-18

For the kingdom of God is not a matter of eating and drinking, but of righteousness, peace, and joy in the Holy Spirit, because anyone who serves Christ in this way is pleasing to God and receives human approval.

Forgive me, Lord, for worrying so much about my daily needs. You are more than able to take care of me. I choose, instead, to be thankful for Your presence in my life. I rest in Your care and provision and know that You will lead me through. You will reward my faith and establish me with peace and security.

Romans 15:13

May the God of hope fill you with all joy and peace as you trust in Him, so that you may overflow with hope by the power of the Holy Spirit.

Fill me, Holy Spirit, with hope for the future. I trust in You to take me where I need to go! Remind me of God's promises and intentions for my life so that I can be expectant for the days to come. Thank You for Your joy that sets my heart free and empowers me to run and not faint.

could face the cross because You saw the victory ahead. Clear my own vision of anything that prevents me from seeing the victorious future You have in store for me. Thank You for showing me it's possible to be joyful in the midst of hardship because of the glorious outcome on the other side.

James 1:2-4

Consider it pure joy, my brothers and sisters, whenever you face trials of many kinds, because you know that the testing of your faith produces perseverance. Let perseverance finish its work so that you may be mature and complete, not lacking anything.

Forgive me, Lord, for not seeing the silver lining on the clouds. Even when I have to walk through troubling waters, You always have a plan to bring me out in better condition than when I went in! Thank You for loving me enough to challenge my faith and take me through circumstances that will strengthen my faith and see You in ways I've never seen. I will persevere in the journey and look forward to the blessed outcome!

1 Peter 1:8-9

Though you have not seen Him, you love Him; and even though you do not see Him now, you believe in Him and are filled with an inexpressible and glorious joy, for you are receiving the end result of your faith, the salvation of your souls.

It is my faith that overcomes the world and it is my hope in You that gives me joy! Lord, forgive me for limiting You by only looking at things through my natural eyes. You are always doing things I don't perceive and working in ways I don't fully understand. My joy comes from knowing that Your love is working behind the scenes and bringing me through to victory!

NOTES

NOTES

FAMILY

The Word was...
and the Word was God...

The same was in the beginning
with God. All things were made
by him; and without him was not
any thing made that was made.
In him was life; and the life was
the light of men. And the light
shineth in darkness; and the
darkness comprehended it not.
There was a man sent from God,
whose name was John. The same
came for a witness, to bear witness
of the Light, that all men through
him might believe. He was not that
Light, but was sent to bear witness
of that Light. That was the true Light,
which lighteth every man that
cometh into the world. He was in the
world, and the world was made by him,
and the world knew him not.
He came unto his own, and his own
received him not. But as many as
received him, to them gave he power
to become the sons of God, even to
them that believe on his name:
Which were born, not of blood,
nor of the will of the flesh,
nor of the will of man,
but of God.

Words for Our Families

Genesis 2:24

That is why a man leaves his father and mother and is united to his wife, and they become one flesh.

Lord, if there are any unhealthy apron strings still attached to my own parents or family, please reveal them so I can cut them. I am thankful for my parents, but I do not want to be codependent on them or look to them for help when I should be looking to my spouse and You. I want my marriage to be a powerful union that is free from any obligations, either past or present. May we be one flesh that is totally united and walking in agreement with You.

Genesis 18:19

For I have chosen him, so that he will direct his children and his household after him to keep the way of the Lord by doing what is right and just, so that the Lord will bring about for Abraham what He has promised him.

What an amazing promise, Lord, that You chose and commended Abraham because of his father's heart. You bring blessing, increase, and abundance on fathers and mothers who teach and train their young to know and serve You. Lord, may I walk in blessing and favor as Abraham did, and lead my family in truth and righteousness. May I teach my children, and their children after them, to follow You with all their hearts.

Exodus 20:12

Honor your father and your mother, so that you may live long in the land the Lord your God is giving you.

Lord, you desire for the family unit to be established in honor. As we honor those who have gone before us, that honor is extended to us as we lead our own children. Thank You for choosing my parents for me, and using both their strengths and their weaknesses for my good.

Deuteronomy 6:1-2

These are the commands, decrees, and laws the Lord your God directed me to teach you to observe in the land that you are crossing the Jordan to possess, so that you, your children and their children after them may fear the Lord your God as long as you live by keeping all His decrees and commands that I give you, and so that you may enjoy long life.

Father, I want to be faithful to keep Your Word and teach my children to do the same. May I walk in the fear of the Lord and model this for those who walk after me. May my household see my reverence and awe of You in all that I do and say. May they learn how following You will bring blessing and even long life as they follow in Your paths and precepts.

Joshua 24:15b

But as for me and my household, we will serve the Lord.

I declare that my family will serve the Lord! I declare over my household that the name of the Lord is above every other name and that serving Christ is our number one priority. I declare that my children will follow after God and surrender their lives fully to the King. May our home be a light on a hill and a beacon of hope to all who are looking for answers.

Psalms 27:10

Though my father and mother forsake me, the Lord will receive me.

I am not disqualified from Your blessing, Lord, if my parents or elders don't support me! Thank You for receiving me into Your household of faith and being a good Father. May my own family know the joy of being members of Your everlasting household of faith. May they always know they can count on You, even when others let them down.

Psalms 103:17-18

But from everlasting to everlasting the Lord's love is with those who fear Him, and His righteousness with their children's children - with those who keep His covenant and remember to obey His precepts.

Your blessing and favor rests upon those who follow Your commands and keep Your ways. Lord, may we be faithful to this and teach our children the joy of obeying You. May we teach our sons and daughters the ways of the Lord. May we give them great joy in searching out truth for themselves and discovering the great adventure of walking with You.

Psalms 127:3-5

Children are a heritage from the Lord, offspring a reward from Him. Like arrows in the hands of a warrior are children born in one's youth. Blessed is the man whose quiver is full of them. They will not be put to shame when they contend with their opponents in court.

Thank You, Lord, for the blessing of children. Thank You for the promises and blessings that they will see long after we are gone. May our children, both natural and spiritual, see an increase of Kingdom demonstrations and may our legacy be secure through them. Thank You for the favor You bring on families that seek after You and determine to build a lasting heritage that honors You.

Psalms 133

How good and pleasant it is when God's people live together in unity! It is like precious oil poured on the head, running down on the beard, running down on Aaron's beard, down on the collar of his robe. It is as if the dew of Hermon were falling on Mount Zion. For there the Lord bestows his blessing, even life forevermore.

Father, I want our home to be drenched in the oil of Your presence and blessing. Knowing that it always starts at the head, I declare that our home is under Your Lordship. I declare that I am in submission to You and desire to walk in truth and righteousness. I desire that my relationship with You will flow down into my family and that our home would be filled with peace and joy because of Your supremacy in our lives.

Proverbs 6:20-22

My son, keep your father's command and do not forsake your mother's teaching. Bind them always on your heart; fasten them around your neck. When you walk, they will guide you; when you sleep, they will watch over you; when you awake, they will speak to you.

Lord, bring remembrance of the good seeds You planted in me through my father and my mother. Show me when it was You speaking through them and planting truth in my heart. May I be a conduit of Your love and guidance to my own household. I bless Your voice through both fathers and mothers, knowing that each have their role and purpose from You.

Proverbs 15:27

The greedy bring ruin to their households, but the one who hates bribes will live.

Lord, keep me from greed and a desire for earthly treasures. Keep my heart pure so that I will not look to material wealth for my satisfaction or joy. May I walk in integrity in every financial decision that is made and seek to honor You through how we spend money. May we learn how to be good stewards of Your blessings, trusting You for the increase and fruit of our faithfulness.

Proverbs 22:6

Start children off on the way they should go, and even when they are old they will not turn from it.

Thank You for the chance to sow good seeds into my family from the very beginning. I ask that every good seed that has been sown would reap a harvest of righteousness. I pray that my children will never forget the good that was planted in them. Water those seeds, Holy Spirit, and grow Your truth in their hearts so that they will always come back to You.

Acts 16:31

They replied, "Believe in the Lord Jesus, and you will be saved - you and your household."

It is Your desire, Lord, for entire households to come to faith. You delight in bringing families into Your kingdom and demonstrating the blessings of Your House. I declare that my entire household, and even extended family, will come to know You and surrender their lives to Christ.

Colossians 3:20-21

Children, obey your parents in everything, for this pleases the Lord. Fathers, do not embitter your children, or they will become discouraged.

Lord, as I teach my children the value and blessing of obedience, help me to demonstrate Your mercy and love. May I never express unbridled anger or disappointment towards them, but always lead in a way that stirs their hope and kindles a greater love for their heavenly Father. Make me a good example of parental love, support, and blessing.

1 Timothy 3:5

If anyone does not know how to manage his own family, how can he take care of God's church?

Being a witness to the world always starts at home. Lord, help me be faithful to the charge you have given me as a parent. May my greatest motivation and passion be to raise godly children who passionately pursue You. May our family be a demonstration of what the body of Christ can look like when we put You first in everything we do.

2 Timothy 1:5

I am reminded of your sincere faith, which first lived in your grandmother Lois and in your mother Eunice and, I am persuaded, now lives in you also.

Lord, thank You for generational blessings! I receive the mantles of grace that are upon our family from our forefathers and foremothers. I bless the gifts you bestowed on the generations before me and ask You to fan them into flame. May our family walk in the fullness of these gifts so that You will receive glory and honor, and others will be blessed and encouraged through them.

2 Timothy 3:14-15

But as for you, continue in what you have learned and have become convinced of, because you know those from whom you learned it, and how from infancy you have known the Holy Scriptures, which are able to make you wise for salvation through faith in Christ Jesus.

May our home be a place of learning and a hunger for Your Word, Lord. May I walk in this myself and look forward to all that You want to teach me. Help us to instill in our children that joy of seeking Your heart through Your Word and discovering those hidden treasures that set our hearts and minds free. I pray that every household of faith will walk in this reality so that Your Kingdom will manifest from house to house, city to city, and nation to nation.

1 Peter 4:8
Above all, love each other deeply, because love covers over a multitude of sins.

Lord, may our family learn to love well. May it begin with our relationships with one another. Teach us how to overlook minor offenses and to put on love to believe the best in each other. May we learn to walk in mercy and grace towards one another and find the joy that comes when love leads the way.

NOTES

NOTES

WORDS FOR HUSBANDS

Genesis 2:18

The Lord God said, "It is not good for the man to be alone. I will make a helper suitable for him."

Thank You, Lord, for giving me a partner to do life with! I know I cannot fulfill Your purposes for my life on my own. You have given me a wife in order to bless me, but also to challenge me. As we help one another fulfill our purpose, grant us a greater joy in this journey of discovery.

Genesis 2:24

That is why a man leaves his father and mother and is united to his wife, and they become one flesh.

Lord, if there is any way in which I am still tied to the apron strings of my parents and not giving myself fully to my wife, please show me. I want to give myself fully to her, without any unhealthy attachments from my past. May we be fully united, not only in body, but in heart, soul, and mind. I know this oneness honors You and opens the way for even greater blessing in our marriage.

Deuteronomy 24:5

If a man has recently married, he must not be sent to war or have any other duty laid on him. For one year he is to be free to stay at home and bring happiness to the wife he has married.

Father, teach me how to recognize those seasons in life when I need to focus more on the home front. Don't let me become distracted by my work in any way that detracts from my marriage. Help me keep my priorities straight so that our marriage will be strong and secure, without any competing loyalties. May my wife feel secure in my love and confident in my care for her wellbeing.

Proverbs 18:22
He who finds a wife finds what is good and receives favor from the Lord.

Lord, You say that I will find favor as a married man! I know that You love the bond of marriage and desire to bless it. I pray that You would be seen in our marriage in such a powerful way, it would draw others to salvation and create a greater hunger for a relationship with You. May we do more together than we could ever do alone!

Ecclesiastes 4:9-12
Two are better than one, because they have a good return for their labor: If either of them falls down, one can help the other up. But pity anyone who falls and has no one to help them up. Also, if two lie down together, they will keep warm. But how can one keep warm alone? Though one may be overpowered, two can defend themselves. A cord of three strands is not quickly broken.

Thank You, Lord, for the power of unity! Thank You for giving me a helpmate that makes me stronger and more productive. Thank You for teaching us how to serve one another and draw out the best in each other. May we be a tight knit powerhouse of Your glory that will take ground for the Kingdom!

Jeremiah 29:11
"For I know the plans I have for you," declares the Lord, "plans to prosper you and not to harm you, plans to give you hope and a future."

Thank You for Your plans, Lord! I know You have given us a great future with much hope! I declare Your goodness in this, despite any temporary setbacks or disappointments! Thank You for always looking ahead and making every twist and turn a hidden blessing. I receive Your promise for our future and look forward to the outcome!

Malachi 2:15-16
Has not the one God made you? You belong to Him in body and spirit. And what does the one God seek? Godly offspring. So be on your guard, and do not be unfaithful to the wife of your youth. "The man who hates and divorces his wife," says the Lord, the God of Israel, "does violence to

the one he should protect," says the Lord Almighty. So be on your guard, and do not be unfaithful.

Lord, guard my heart from any faithless attitudes or ideas. I want to be one who protects my wife and the future You have given us. We desire to raise up sons and daughters, both natural and spiritual, who reflect and demonstrate Your power and Your goodness. Keep me from discouragement and renew the purpose and call for which You called us together. May You be glorified in the process!

Matthew 5:28
But I tell you that anyone who looks at a woman lustfully has already committed adultery with her in his heart.

Forgive me, Lord, for wandering eyes. Keep me accountable for what I look at and what I think on. I want to be pure before You and my wife. Give me Your eyes with which to see my wife as beautiful, attractive, and filled with Your glory and wonder. May my desire be only for her.

Romans 12:10-12
Be devoted to one another in love. Honor one another above yourselves. Never be lacking in zeal, but keep your spiritual fervor, serving the Lord. Be joyful in hope, patient in affliction, faithful in prayer.

As the head of my home, Lord, remind me to be devoted to my wife and show love and honor in all that I say and do. Help me to model righteous zeal and a hunger for Your Word that will inspire her own journey. May I exhibit joy, hope, and patience during the hard times. Remind me to faithfully pray for my wife so that she receives all You have for her. Make me a greater leader through serving her.

1 Corinthians 7:14
For the unbelieving husband has been sanctified through his wife, and the unbelieving wife has been sanctified through her believing husband. Otherwise, your children would be unclean, but as it is, they are holy.

Thank You, Lord, for giving me access to Your holiness and righteousness through the power of the cross. Thank You for extending this blessing over my household as I faithfully obey You. Even when my wife does not believe, help me to reflect Your unconditional grace and love in a way that covers, protects, and believes for the best. Thank You for providing this blessing over my family so that they, too, can experience Your love and Your truth.

1 Corinthians 10:13

No temptation has overtaken you except what is common to mankind. And God is faithful; He will not let you be tempted beyond what you can bear. But when you are tempted, He will also provide a way out so that you can endure it.

Lord, when I am tempted to be unfaithful to my vows, or react in my flesh, please step in to remind me of Your presence and purpose. Instill in me the fear of the Lord that will guard me from any trap of the enemy or any trial that seeks to pull me down and destroy my faith. Thank You for always providing a way out of temptations so that my marriage can be a conduit of Your abundant provision, love, and power.

1 Corinthians 11:3

But I want you to realize that the head of every man is Christ, and the head of the woman is man, and the head of Christ is God.

Lord, I submit the headship of my home and marriage to You. You are the one I answer to, and You are the one who can teach me how to love my wife fully and completely. Help me not to rush ahead of You when making decisions and grant me Your wisdom in providing protection and oversight to my home. I desire for Your perfect love to be reflected in how I lead my family.

Ephesians 5:25-28

Husbands, love your wives, just as Christ loved the church and gave Himself up for her to make her holy, cleansing her by the washing with water through the word, and to present her to Himself as a radiant church, without stain or wrinkle or any other blemish, but holy and blameless. In this same way, husbands ought to love their wives as their own bodies. He who loves his wife loves himself.

Jesus, may I love my wife with the same unconditional love that You have for the Church. Fill my heart with more of Your compassion and blessing so that I can joyfully serve my wife and do all I can to help her fulfill her calling and destiny. May I do for her what I desire others to do for me. Show me how to encourage her, bless her, and empower her to be all she can be for the glory of Your name.

Ephesians 5:21

Submit to one another out of reverence for Christ.

Remind me, Lord, to defer to my wife when needed and to give her equal honor and equal respect when making decisions in our home. Show us our differing gifts and perspectives that You designed - on purpose - in order to be a greater blessing to the whole.

Colossians 3:19

Husbands, love your wives, and do not be harsh with them.

Lord, forgive me for any harsh words I have spoken to my wife out of impatience or frustration. Remind me to slow down, take a breath, and consider how You would speak to her in times of stress or turmoil. Cleanse my heart of any bitter attitude so that I can love her as You do.

1 Timothy 5:8

Anyone who does not provide for their relatives, and especially for their own household, has denied the faith and is worse than an unbeliever.

Lord, forgive me if I have put the needs of others outside my household before my own family. Forgive me when I overlook the needs of my wife or dismiss my responsibility in caring for her. I want to be generous to those I love the most. Help me to be a faithful steward of all You've given so that those in my own household will be the first to receive Your provision and Your grace.

Hebrews 13:4

Marriage should be honored by all, and the marriage bed kept pure, for God will judge the adulterer and all the sexually immoral.

Lord, keep my mind and heart pure before You so that I can love my wife with honorable intentions. Keep me from sensual temptations and the traps of the enemy to fill my mind with impure images. I choose to close my eyes and ears to anything that would defile or dishonor the intimacy in our marriage. Alert me when my eyes wander so that I can keep them fixed on You.

1 Peter 3:7
Husbands, in the same way be considerate as you live with your wives and treat them with respect as the weaker partner and as heirs with you of the gracious gift of life, so that nothing will hinder your prayers.

Lord, thank You for my wife and the gift You have given me through her. Help me to show her the honor and respect that pleases You and that demonstrates Your heart towards her. Help me to see any way in which a wrong attitude on my part is hindering our prayers or limiting your blessing on our home and marriage.

1 Peter 3:8-9
Finally, all of you, be like-minded, be sympathetic, love one another, be compassionate and humble. Do not repay evil with evil or insult with insult. On the contrary, repay evil with blessing, because to this you were called so that you may inherit a blessing.

Lord, guard my tongue and keep me from saying things that bring chaos and confusion instead of order and peace. Help me to respond to crises with a gentle but firm spirit that opens the door for You to come as the Prince of Peace into our home and marriage. When accusations or insults come my way, speak into my ears Your words of life that will nullify the darts of the enemy. May our home inherit Your fullest blessing as we steward Your presence faithfully.

1 Peter 4:8
Above all, love each other deeply, because love covers over a multitude of sins.

Lord, when I am discouraged and frustrated about my wife's weaknesses and failings, fill my heart with an even greater love for her. Give me greater grace and greater mercy to extend kindness and patience so that You can reach her in ways I cannot. May my love not be shallow and selfish, but centered in Your unconditional love and unwavering hope for our future.

NOTES

WORDS FOR WIVES

Proverbs 14:1
The wise woman builds her house, but with her own hands the foolish one tears hers down.

Father, may I be a wife that builds up our home through my words and actions. Forgive me for speaking things that are destructive and self-centered. Show me how to strengthen my husband and build up our marriage in practical ways. Give us a united vision for our home and family that is secure for the long haul.

Proverbs 19:14
Houses and wealth are inherited from parents, but a prudent wife is from the Lord.

Regardless of any material blessings or privileges from my past, I desire to walk in wisdom and insight regarding my own home and marriage. Give me the needed skills to manage my household well. Teach me how to steward what You have already given us rather than focus on what we can attain.

Proverbs 31:10-12
A wife of noble character who can find? She is worth far more than rubies. Her husband has full confidence in her and lacks nothing of value. She brings him good, not harm, all the days of her life.

Lord, I desire to be a wife of noble character. I want my husband to have confidence in me because of my relationship with You. Show me how to add goodness and abundance to our home and marriage in a way that makes him feel richly blessed!

Proverbs 31:26
She speaks with wisdom, and faithful instruction is on her tongue.

Lord, give me the right words to speak! Teach me by Your Word how to address the challenges in our home so that I can bring wisdom and insight.

Where I lack understanding, show me Your ways and expand my heart to more fully comprehend Your vision for our home. May I be a conduit of blessing through the things I speak.

Proverbs 31:30
Charm is deceptive, and beauty is fleeting; but a woman who fears the Lord is to be praised.

Father, I desire to walk in the fear of the Lord. I desire my life to exhibit a reverence for Your holiness and a passion for righteousness. Remind me when I place too much emphasis on my body image or how I look. Teach me to pursue that which makes me truly beautiful from the inside out.

Ecclesiastes 4:9-12
Two are better than one, because they have a good return for their labor. If either of them falls down, one can help the other up. But pity anyone who falls and has no one to help them up. Also, if two lie down together, they will keep warm. But how can one keep warm alone? Though one may be overpowered, two can defend themselves. A cord of three strands is not quickly broken.

Thank You, Lord, for the power of unity! Thank You for giving me a helpmate that makes me stronger and more productive. Thank You for teaching us how to serve one another and draw out the best in each other. May we be a closeknit powerhouse of Your glory that will take ground for the Kingdom!

Jeremiah 29:11
"For I know the plans I have for you," declares the Lord, "plans to prosper you and not to harm you, plans to give you hope and a future."

Thank You for Your plans, Lord! I know You have given us a great future with much hope! I declare Your goodness in this, despite any temporary setbacks or disappointments! Thank You for always looking ahead and making every twist and turn a hidden blessing. I receive Your promise for our future and look forward to the outcome!

Luke 6:37

Do not judge, and you will not be judged. Do not condemn, and you will not be condemned. Forgive, and you will be forgiven.

Lord, I choose to walk in forgiveness towards my husband. When he disappoints me, remind me how You've forgiven me for my own mistakes and failures. Thank You for working in his life in ways I can't see. You alone know his heart, and I release any preconceived ideas I have that may limit Your working in his life. Touch him with Your presence and fill him with Your power to overcome!

1 Corinthians 7:14

For the unbelieving husband has been sanctified through his wife, and the unbelieving wife has been sanctified through her believing husband. Otherwise, your children would be unclean, but as it is, they are holy.

Thank You, Lord, for giving me access to Your holiness and righteousness through the power of the cross. Thank You for extending this blessing over my household as I faithfully obey You. Even when my husband does not believe, help me to reflect Your unconditional grace and love in a way that compels him to seek You further. Cover our home with Your presence and protection. Thank You for providing this blessing over my family so that they, too, can experience Your love and Your truth.

Ephesians 4:2-3

Be completely humble and gentle; be patient, bearing with one another in love. Make every effort to keep the unity of the Spirit through the bond of peace.

I desire for our home and marriage to be filled with Your peace, Lord. I know this will only happen as I submit myself to You and love my family as You do. Forgive me for looking to my own interests before the interests of others. Help me to listen more carefully, speak more circumspectly, and pursue the kind of peace that can only come from doing things Your way.

Ephesians 5:21

Submit to one another out of reverence for Christ.

Remind me, Lord, to defer to my husband when needed and to give him equal honor and equal respect when making decisions in our home. Show us our differing gifts and perspectives that You designed - on purpose - in order to be a greater blessing to the whole.

Colossians 3:17

And whatever you do, whether in word or deed, do it all in the name of the Lord Jesus, giving thanks to God the Father through Him.

Keep my heart centered on You, Lord, in all that I do in my home and marriage. May my words and actions be done in love and with an attitude of thankfulness. I desire to serve You and please You in how I conduct myself with my husband and family. Remind when I start serving myself and keep me focused on higher things of eternal value. May my loved ones come to know You more through my service unto You.

1 Thessalonians 5:16-18

Rejoice always, pray continually, give thanks in all circumstances; for this is God's will for you in Christ Jesus.

Alert me when I begin to complain too much, Lord! Remind me to pray about things more than gripe. Grant me a thankful heart and help me to see the good when I start to focus on the bad. May I please You in how I respond to challenges by always exercising my absolute trust in Your providential care for my life.

Titus 2:3-5

Likewise, teach the older women to be reverent in the way they live, not to be slanderers or addicted to much wine, but to teach what is good. Then they can urge the younger women to love their husbands and children, to be self-controlled and pure, to be busy at home, to be kind, and to be subject to their husbands, so that no one will malign the word of God.

Father, I want my life to be a testimony of Your power and faithfulness. May I not follow the ways of the world but be set apart in how I treat my husband and children. May my words about them and my actions towards them draw others to the power of Your love. May my marriage and home be filled with such peace and unity, that others will ask how we do it!

Hebrews 13:4

Marriage should be honored by all, and the marriage bed kept pure, for God will judge the adulterer and all the sexually immoral.

Lord, keep my mind and heart pure before You so that I can love my husband rightly. Keep me from any temptation to compare him with others. I submit my passions to You and ask that my affection be sincere and from the heart. May my passion for him be as strong as when I first fell in love with him.

James 1:19-20

My dear brothers and sisters, take note of this: Everyone should be quick to listen, slow to speak and slow to become angry, because human anger does not produce the righteousness that God desires.

Stop me when I talk too much, Lord! Help me to listen more and not be so defensive when I think my husband doesn't understand me. Quiet my spirit so that I can respond with patience and a desire to understand him, even more than to be understood. Sanctify my desires to want Your way even more than my own.

1 Peter 3:1-2

Wives, in the same way submit yourselves to your own husbands so that, if any of them do not believe the word, they may be won over without words by the behavior of their wives, when they see the purity and reverence of your lives.

I want You to be honored in my marriage, Lord. Even when I don't understand or agree with my husband, I trust You to intervene and speak to him when I can't. May he hear your voice without any interference from mine. I release to You the differences we have and ask that You fill me with love and joy instead of anxiety and stress. Give him all that he needs to be a strong leader in our home and a blessing to our family.

1 Peter 3:8-9

Finally, all of you, be like-minded, be sympathetic, love one another, be compassionate and humble. Do not repay evil with evil or insult with insult. On the contrary, repay evil with blessing, because to this you were called so that you may inherit a blessing.

Lord, guard my tongue and keep me from saying things that bring chaos and confusion instead of order and peace. Help me to respond to crises with a peaceful spirit that opens the door for You to come as the Prince of Peace into our home and marriage. When accusations or insults come my way, speak into my ears Your words of life that will nullify the darts of the enemy. May our home inherit Your fullest blessing as we steward Your presence faithfully.

1 Peter 4:8

Above all, love each other deeply, because love covers over a multitude of sins.

Lord, when I am discouraged and frustrated about my husband's weaknesses and failings, fill my heart with an even greater love for him. Give me greater grace and greater mercy to extend kindness and patience so that You can reach him in ways I cannot. May my love not be shallow and selfish, but centered in Your unconditional love and unwavering hope for our future.

NOTES

NOTES

Words for Our Children

Exodus 20:12

Honor your father and your mother, so that you may live long in the land the Lord your God is giving you.

Lord, may I direct and lead my children in a way that inspires obedience and surrender to You. May they see my love for You in such a way that teaches them the power of honor and submission to godly authority. May they embrace these values and experience the blessing that comes with honoring the fathers and mothers before them.

Deuteronomy 6:5-9

Love the Lord your God with all your heart and with all your soul and with all your strength. These commandments that I give you today are to be on your hearts. Impress them on your children. Talk about them when you sit at home and when you walk along the road, when you lie down and when you get up. Tie them as symbols on your hands and bind them on your foreheads. Write them on the doorframes of your houses and on your gates.

Remind me, Lord, to use every opportunity as a teaching moment for my children. Alert me when You are revealing an aspect of Your heart and character so that I can call their attention to it. Teach me how to make You such an interactive part of our lives that my children will learn the power of Your daily presence. May we be a family that doesn't just talk about Your Word, but lives it and demonstrates it in everything we do.

Psalms 8:2

Through the praise of children and infants you have established a stronghold against your enemies, to silence the foe and the avenger.

Lord, I declare that my children will learn to praise You and worship You in the midst of every trial. May their praise and thanksgiving shatter the lies of the enemy and break every hold of the adversary. Teach them the power of Your praise to silence their accusers and overcome those who stand against them and Your will for their lives, in Jesus' name.

Proverbs 1:8-9

Listen, my son, to your father's instruction and do not forsake your mother's teaching. They are a garland to grace your head and a chain to adorn your neck.

Lord, I want to teach and lead my children well! Help me to impart spiritual truths at every stage of their development that can last them a lifetime. May they seek out godly instruction and counsel and realize the blessing and benefit of wisdom from others.

Proverbs 18:24

One who has unreliable friends soon comes to ruin, but there is a friend who sticks closer than a brother.

Father, give my children good friends. Teach them to recognize who their true friends are and who they can trust. Weed out those people in their lives who are not good for them. Give them friends who will stick together through good times and hard times. May they develop lasting friendships that are based on authentic companionship and not just on personal convenience.

Proverbs 22:6

Start children off on the way they should go, and even when they are old they will not turn from it.

Thank You, Lord, for watching over my children and the seeds that have been planted in their hearts. Show me how to water those seeds of Your love and Lordship in a way that inspires them to know You more as they grow older. I declare that they will seek You with their whole heart and surrender fully to Your will and purpose in order to bring a harvest of righteousness for Your glory. Amen!

Proverbs 29:15

A rod and a reprimand impart wisdom, but a child left undisciplined disgraces its mother.

Teach me how to discipline my children, Lord, in a way that brings fruit and not frustration. Keep my heart from anger and show me how to be firm and loving in how I correct them. May my child learn the blessing of obedience and gain a heart that seeks to please You above all else.

Proverbs 29:17
Discipline your children, and they will give you peace; they will bring you the delights you desire.

Father, it's my desire to raise children that bring You delight and serve You with their whole heart. May I steward their training well and direct them in a firm but loving way. May I teach them how to govern their own heart and emotions in a way that feeds their spirit more than satisfying their own flesh. May we experience Your peace together as we pursue a right relationship with You and with one another.

Isaiah 30:21
Whether you turn to the right or to the left, your ears will hear a voice behind you, saying, "This is the way; walk in it."

I declare that my children will learn to hear Your voice so distinctly, Lord, that they will quickly follow and obey. When facing obstacles or tough decisions, Lord, speak in such a way that they will quickly and instinctively follow. Holy Spirit, direct their paths in unmistakable ways and give them a joy in this journey of daily obedience.

Isaiah 44:3
For I will pour water on the thirsty land, and streams on the dry ground; I will pour out My Spirit on your offspring, and My blessing on your descendants.

Thank You, Holy Spirit, for pouring out Your presence and Your power on my children and their own children. I pray they walk in the fullness of Your gifts and the power of Your Kingdom with signs, wonders, and miracles following them! May the prayers of their forefathers and foremothers bear much fruit in the years to come for the glory of Your name.

Isaiah 54:13

All your children will be taught by the Lord, and great will be their peace.

I declare that my children will hear Your voice and follow it with great joy. May they know Your Word and Your ways and choose to obey You regardless of the cost. May they see that lasting peace can only come when fully surrendered to You. Give them an undivided heart, Lord, so that they will stick to the path You have assigned them and fulfill their destiny in You.

Jeremiah 1:5

Before I formed you in the womb I knew you, before you were born I set you apart; I appointed you as a prophet to the nations.

Father, You have a special purpose for every child you form. Show me the plans and purposes for each of my children so that I can call forth their destiny and prepare them for their journey. May they know they have been set apart from the very moment they were conceived! May they desire to fulfill their purpose and experience the joy of being who You created them to be.

Mark 10:14-15

When Jesus saw this, He was indignant. He said to them, "Let the little children come to Me, and do not hinder them, for the kingdom of God belongs to such as these. Truly I tell you, anyone who will not receive the kingdom of God like a little child will never enter it."

A child-like faith is pleasing to You, Lord. May I not only keep this aspect in my own life, but celebrate this purity of faith in my own children. Help me to encourage their wonder and awe of You. Alert me when I start to dampen their faith with my own doubt and unbelief. May they keep a simplicity of trust in their hearts to always believe for the miraculous and anticipate heaven's highest.

John 10:27

My sheep listen to My voice; I know them, and they follow Me.

May my children learn to know Your voice, Lord. Teach them to listen carefully and discern between Your voice and the voices of their peers or even their enemies. May they have a confidence in hearing from You and trusting what You say. Give them great joy in following You and trusting in Your ability to lead them.

1 Corinthians 15:33
Do not be misled: "Bad company corrupts good character."

Father, watch over my children and all the good seeds that have been planted in their heart. Alert them to those friends who detract from Your truth and lead them astray. Give them a heart that seeks Your highest and Your best. Give them the courage to distance themselves from those who weaken their faith or defile the purity of their love.

Ephesians 6:4
Fathers, do not exasperate your children; instead, bring them up in the training and instruction of the Lord.

Lord, help me to be patient with my children and demonstrate godly restraint. Give me wisdom in dealing with various challenges and give me practical ideas in how to direct them without trying to control them. Forgive me for reacting out of anger. Mold my heart to Yours so they can know the immense loving kindness You have towards them.

2 Timothy 1:5
I am reminded of your sincere faith, a faith that dwelt first in your grandmother Lois and your mother Eunice and now, I am sure, dwells in you as well.

Grow my faith in You, Lord, so that my children will see a living example of absolute trust and confidence in Your truth. May my faith be demonstrated in practical ways so that my children will see Your faithfulness in every situation we bring before You. May faith arise in my children and deepen in the years to come. I declare that their faith will overcome the world!

2 Timothy 1:13-14
What you heard from me, keep as the pattern of sound teaching, with faith and love in Christ Jesus. Guard the good deposit that was entrusted to you - guard it with the help of the Holy Spirit who lives in us.

As I seek to plant Your Word in the hearts of my children, Lord, I pray that the deposit will grow through the years and bring forth much fruit! I pray that they will guard it with all diligence and teach it to their children in the years to come. Remind my children of the words they have heard that will inspire a fresh faith and renewed hope in Your purpose for their lives.

2 Timothy 3:14-15

But as for you, continue in what you have learned and have become convinced of, because you know those from whom you learned it, and how from infancy you have known the Holy Scriptures, which are able to make you wise for salvation through faith in Christ Jesus.

Lord, I want our family to know the power of living Your Word. Keep me steadfast in Your Word and show me how to incorporate it in our daily lives. Help me teach my children to read and study Your Word which is alive and active. Show us the power of revelation and the joy of pursuing Your truth. May Your Word be planted in the hearts of my children so their foundation will be secure and their legacy be lasting.

Hebrews 12:9-10

Moreover, we have all had human fathers who disciplined us and we respected them for it. How much more should we submit to the Father of spirits and live! They disciplined us for a little while as they thought best; but God disciplines us for our good, in order that we may share in His holiness.

Lord, may the discipline I use with my children always come from Your heart of perfect love and never from my own heart of dissatisfaction. Teach me to discipline as You would. Show me how to correct my children in a way that inspires obedience instead of commanding it. May my children know this kind of love that corrects for the future instead of punishing for the past.

1 John 2:1

My dear children, I write this to you so that you will not sin. But if anybody does sin, we have an advocate with the Father - Jesus Christ, the Righteous One.

May my children desire to live a godly life and be free from sin. Lord, create in them a pure heart that desires righteousness and godliness more than the shallow pleasures of the world. When they do stray from Your path, show them the way back. Remind them of the power of the cross and Your readiness to forgive. Reveal to them Your lovingkindness and forbearance so they will always turn back to seeking You.

3 John 1:4
I have no greater joy than to hear that my children are walking in the truth.

It is my greatest desire, Lord, to know that my children walk in Your truth. I lift them before You, asking You to watch over them and draw them to Your heart. May they learn to know Your voice and seek Your ways above and beyond that of their friends or peers. May the Spirit of Truth guide their paths and lead their lives in an unmistakable way.

NOTES

WORDS FOR PRODIGALS

Psalms 18:28
You, Lord, keep my lamp burning; my God turns my darkness into light.

Turn on the light, Lord! As my child walks through the darkness, may Your Spirit shine down upon them and show them the way to freedom. May they see Your love and goodness in the midst of their pain and may their hearts burn with a longing to walk in truth once again. Show them the way back to You!

Psalms 34:8
Taste and see that the Lord is good; blessed is the one who takes refuge in Him.

Show my child Your goodness, Lord. Even when they stray from Your ways, may they have a taste of Your unconditional love and see how much You care for them. May they turn to You in their weakness and know the blessings of Your presence.

Psalms 103:11
For as high as the heavens are above the earth, so great is His love for those who fear Him.

Remind my child, Lord, that You are a gracious and loving Father that never gives up on His own. May they see Your consistent presence in their life. May the fear of the Lord stir their conscience and draw them back to You.

Psalms 138:7
Though I walk in the midst of trouble, You preserve my life. You stretch out Your hand against the anger of my foes; with Your right hand You save me.

Preserve my child's life, Lord. Even when they walk through the fire, be their protection and their safety net. Deal with the adversary who seeks to take them out and show them how much You desire to save them. Release

Your angels to combat the enemy's assignments against my child and bring them into a place of safety and rest.

Psalms 139:7,11-12

Where can I go from Your Spirit? Where can I flee from Your presence? If I say, "Surely the darkness will hide me and the light become night around me," even the darkness will not be dark to You; the night will shine like the day, for darkness is as light to You.

Thank You, Lord, for never leaving my child, even when they are in total darkness. May they realize they cannot outrun You or hide from Your presence. May they realize Your incredible love for them and Your determination to bring them out of captivity. I declare that Your light will shatter their darkness and they will surrender to Your never-failing love.

Isaiah 11:2-3

The Spirit of the Lord will rest on him - the Spirit of wisdom and of understanding, the Spirit of counsel and of might, the Spirit of the knowledge and fear of the Lord - and he will delight in the fear of the Lord.

I declare that my child will know the fear of the Lord! I ask Holy Spirit, that You would fall upon my child and rest upon them with great power and presence. I declare that they will submit to You and walk in the fullness of Your Spirit which brings wisdom, understanding, counsel, and might. I declare that the fear of the Lord will keep them from every trap of the enemy as well as their own flesh. For the sake of Your glory, alone!

Isaiah 42:16

I will lead the blind by ways they have not known, along unfamiliar paths I will guide them; I will turn the darkness into light before them and make the rough places smooth. These are the things I will do; I will not forsake them.

Thank You, Lord, for leading my child through the darkness and into the Light! Regardless of the paths they take, may they meet You at every turn. May they see Your hand of protection and care and Your desire to bring them onto level ground. Thank You for meeting them where no one else can!

Jeremiah 31:16-17

This is what the Lord says: "Restrain your voice from weeping and your eyes from tears, for your work will be rewarded," declares the Lord. "They will return from the land of the enemy. So there is hope for your descendants," declares the Lord. "Your children will return to their own land."

Thank You for keeping Your promises, Lord! Forgive me when I give in to despair and respond without hope. I choose to believe in Your goodness and Your plan to bring my child back to You. I stand on Your Word to bring them back home to the knowledge of salvation and all that You have done for them. I look forward to that day when they declare that You are their Lord!

Ezekiel 11:19-20

I will give them an undivided heart and put a new spirit in them; I will remove from them their heart of stone and give them a heart of flesh. Then they will follow My decrees and be careful to keep My laws. They will be My people, and I will be their God.

Lord, give my child a new heart that is totally devoted to You. May they know that they can have a fresh start and receive all they need in order to move forward in life. Renew their faith and stir fresh hope for their future. I declare that they will desire to do Your will and follow You without hesitation.

Matthew 19:26

Jesus looked at them and said, "With man this is impossible, but with God all things are possible."

Thank You, Lord, that nothing is impossible with You! Regardless of the challenges my child is facing, I know You are more than able to overcome them and bring them out of their bondage. Thank You for defeating the enemies in their life and providing a way of escape. May they know that You will do whatever it takes to bring them home to You – even the impossible!

Luke 15:24

"For this son of mine was dead and is alive again; he was lost and is found." So they began to celebrate.

I look forward to the day of celebration, Lord, when my child returns home to You! I declare that they will not die, but will live and be filled to the fulness of Your love and power! Stir in them a longing for this kind of reality and show them the joy that comes when living a life for You.

John 8:32

"Then you will know the truth, and the truth will set you free."

Lord, I pray that my child will desire truth in the innermost part. I pray that You would use every step in their journey to bring them to what is true, lasting, and eternal. I declare that the truth will set them free from lies, deception, and the waywardness of their flesh. May they cling to Truth as a lifeline towards freedom.

Acts 26:18

To open their eyes and turn them from darkness to light, and from the power of Satan to God, so that they may receive forgiveness of sins and a place among those who are sanctified by faith in Me.

Father, as I lift my child before You, I ask You to open their eyes to the deception and lies of the enemy. I declare that they will recognize the path that leads to destruction and turn from their sin and rebellion. Remind them of Your promise to forgive and pardon. May they know they are loved and accepted by You, and return to the Light with a thankful heart.

Romans 8:38-39

For I am convinced that neither death nor life, neither angels nor demons, neither the present nor the future, nor any powers, neither height nor depth, nor anything else in all creation, will be able to separate us from the love of God that is in Christ Jesus our Lord.

Father, may my child know the immense power of Your unconditional love. Draw them to Your presence and overshadow them with Your mercy and compassion. I declare that no circumstance, setback, or disappointment will separate them from the knowledge of Your love and Your desire to set them free. Open their eyes to see how much You love them!

Romans 12:12

Be joyful in hope, patient in affliction, faithful in prayer.

I commit myself, Lord, to maintain an attitude of joy, hope, and patience as I wait on You. Remind me when to pray for my prodigal and when to give You thanks for the breakthroughs to come. Keep my eyes fixed on Your promises and not the circumstances. May my prayers be filled with faith for the future and joy in the journey.

Philippians 1:6

Being confident of this, that He who began a good work in you will carry it on to completion until the day of Christ Jesus.

Thank You, Lord, for the work You started in my child from the moment of their conception! Your plans are good and they are sure to come to pass. That which You began in my child will be completed and I joyfully declare that You will fulfill Your purposes for them. May they recognize Your call on their life and joyfully embrace their destiny.

Colossians 1:11-14

Being strengthened with all power, according to His glorious might, for all endurance and patience with joy; giving thanks to the Father, who has qualified you to share in the inheritance of the saints in light. He has delivered us from the domain of darkness and transferred us to the kingdom of His beloved Son, in whom we have redemption, the forgiveness of sins.

I declare over my child that they would be strengthened with all power, according to Your glorious might, to endure the trials and overcome the darkness. Remind them of Your promise to deliver them and bring them into freedom from the bondage of their flesh. Reveal to them the amazing plan You have for their life and the transformation that You freely offer.

2 Timothy 2:25-26

Opponents must be gently instructed, in the hope that God will grant them repentance leading them to a knowledge of the truth, and that they will come to their senses and escape from the trap of the devil, who has taken them captive to do his will.

I declare over my child that they will come to their senses and escape the traps of the devil. Lord, lead my child to those who can speak words of life and truth and break the spell of deception. May they be drawn by Your loving kindness and realize the promise of redemption. May they joyfully repent of their disobedience and receive the fullness of Your love and mercy.

Hebrews 12:27-29

The words "once more" indicate the removing of what can be shaken - that is, created things - so that what cannot be shaken may remain. Therefore, since we are receiving a kingdom that cannot be shaken, let us be thankful, and so worship God acceptably with reverence and awe, for our "God is a consuming fire."

Thank You, Lord, for shaking up my child so they can know the reality of who You are! I pray that those things which are robbing them of their destiny and fulfillment in You would be shaken off of them and removed. Use their hardships to strip them of their disobedience and willfulness against You so they can receive Your mantle of mercy and grace. Thank You for giving me the grace to see beyond the shaking and trust in Your redemptive plans.

James 4:7-8a

Submit yourselves, then, to God. Resist the devil, and he will flee from you. Come near to God and He will come near to you.

I declare that my child will submit to God with a thankful heart. I declare that they will have the strength to resist the devil and deny him access to their life. I pray that my child will call upon the name of the Lord with a sincere heart and long to be free from the enemy's grip.

1 John 2:16-17

For everything in the world - the lust of the flesh, the lust of the eyes, and the pride of life - comes not from the Father but from the world. The world and its desires pass away, but whoever does the will of God lives forever.

Open the eyes of my child, Lord, to see the bottomless pit of the world's ways. May they see the consequences of sin and the realities of yielding to the flesh.

Turn their heart, O God, so that they will desire those things that are lasting and good. Show them the choice that is before them so they can make the right decision for eternity. I declare that they will choose life everlasting!

NOTES

WORDS FOR CAREGIVERS

Proverbs 19:17
Whoever is kind to the poor lends to the Lord, and He will reward them for what they have done.

May Your kindness always direct my actions, Lord. Thank You for the chances to give to others what You have given me. As I share my blessings to help those around me, I know You will enrich my own storehouse because that's who You are! Thank You for Your rewards and for reminding me of Your desire to take care of me when I care for others.

Matthew 25:40
The King will reply, 'Truly I tell you, whatever you did for one of the least of these brothers and sisters of mine, You did for Me."

Remind me when I forget Lord – when I serve others, I am really serving You. Help me to see You in the service I provide and to demonstrate love and compassion with a grateful heart. May my words and actions be a constant testimony of Your presence and overshadowing care.

Mark 10:45
For even the Son of Man did not come to be served, but to serve, and to give His life as a ransom for many.

When I forget the privilege of serving others, Lord, remind me of the sacrifices You made for me. Give me a greater joy in helping those I care for, knowing the blessing that will come as a result.

Luke 6:31
Do to others as you would have them do to you.

May the things I do for others be to the same quality and level of excellence that I would wish for myself. Lord, may I not think so highly of myself that I forget to treat others the way that You would. May my actions reflect the abundance of Your grace, love, favor, and blessing. Thank You for the being so good to me – may I pass on that goodness so that You will get all the praise.

John 13:34-35

"A new command I give you: Love one another. As I have loved you, so you must love one another. By this everyone will know that you are My disciples - if you love one another."

I want to reflect Your unwavering love for others, Lord, and not allow frustration to rob me of Your peace. May my words and actions be a living illustration to those I care for and encourage their own faith in You. May I serve in the same way You would. Let me be Your hands and feet to those You have placed in my care.

Romans 12:13

Share with the Lord's people who are in need. Practice hospitality.

Lord, may I go beyond merely doing a service for those I care for, but may I bless them and bring them joy. Show me how to make each day special so they can know You love them and are looking out for them. Remind me of all the blessings You've given me so I can freely share and freely give.

Galatians 1:10

Am I now trying to win the approval of human beings, or of God? Or am I trying to please people? If I were still trying to please people, I would not be a servant of Christ.

Father, I want to be sure that I am caring for my loved ones for the right reasons. I do not want to serve out of compulsion or obligation, but with a joyful heart in response to Your invitation. I want to serve with a glad heart and see the helps I provide as an offering unto You.

Galatians 5:22-25

But the fruit of the Spirit is love, joy, peace, forbearance, kindness, goodness, faithfulness, gentleness, and self-control. Against such things there is no law. Those who belong to Christ Jesus have crucified the flesh with its passions and desires. Since we live by the Spirit, let us keep in step with the Spirit.

Lord, I want my service to others to always reflect the fruit of Your Spirit. Check any negative emotions I have that don't reflect Your love and goodness. Show me any way in which my flesh is trying to rule or control a situation. I lay down any selfish preoccupations and ask for Your Spirit to transform my thinking and attitudes so that You, alone, can be seen.

Galatians 6:9-10

Let us not become weary in doing good, for at the proper time we will reap a harvest if we do not give up. Therefore, as we have opportunity, let us do good to all people, especially to those who belong to the family of believers.

When I am weary, God, empower me with Your Spirit and fill me with added strength and endurance. I believe that as I sow seeds of kindness and care for others, You will water those seeds and there will come a time of great harvest. Remind me of the blessings of family and our collective inheritance that You have waiting for us. I will not quit or give up in the low times, but place my trust in Your ability to keep me and sustain me for the long haul!

Ephesians 4:32-5:1-2

Be kind and compassionate to one another, forgiving each other, just as in Christ God forgave you. Follow God's example, therefore, as dearly loved children and walk in the way of love, just as Christ loved us and gave Himself up for us as a fragrant offering and sacrifice to God.

Lord, give me the patience I need when tested in my relationships with those I care for. Keep my heart tender towards them. Keep me from holding offenses and enable me to settle differences quickly. Show me when to confront an issue and when to walk away. Fill me with Your unconditional love so that when sacrifices are needed, I can do so with a glad and sincere heart.

Colossians 3:12-14

Therefore, as God's chosen people, holy and dearly loved, clothe yourselves with compassion, kindness, humility, gentleness, and patience. Bear with each other and forgive one another if any of you has a grievance against someone. Forgive as the Lord forgave you. And over all these virtues put on love, which binds them all together in perfect unity.

Lord, I need a fresh mantle of Your grace! Thank You for clothing me with Your compassion, kindness, humility, gentleness, and patience. Thank You for the grace to put up with things that frustrate me and to not harbor offense. Show me where and when I need to forgive so that Your presence and blessing can continue to overshadow all that I do. Thank You for helping me to love as You do and not be confined to my human limitations.

1 Timothy 5:3-4

Give proper recognition to those widows who are really in need. But if a widow has children or grandchildren, these should learn first of all to put their religion into practice by caring for their own family and so repaying their parents and grandparents, for this is pleasing to God.

Father, thank You for the parents and elders You have given me. Regardless of their weaknesses and shortcomings, You have used them in my life to grow and mature my faith. Show me how to honor them for their role in my life and for the sacrifices they made for me that I don't even know about. I want to please You by blessing them in the ways that are most meaningful to them in the later stages of their life. Thank You for giving me what I need to be a blessing.

Hebrews 6:10

God is not unjust; He will not forget your work and the love you have shown Him as you have helped His people and continue to help them.

Thank You for watching over what I do, Lord. You know my desire to care for those I love. I want to do this out of love for You, knowing that You will take care of me and provide for my physical and spiritual needs, as well. I pray that the seeds of kindness I am sowing to my loved ones will reap a harvest of blessings and favor in the days to come – not only for them, but for me and my own household.

James 1:27

Religion that God our Father accepts as pure and faultless is this: to look after orphans and widows in their distress and to keep oneself from being polluted by the world.

I want my faith to be more than talk, Lord! I don't want to help others just for what they can give back. Nor do I want to serve others for selfish gain or notoriety. May I see those who are less fortunate with love and compassion and realize the amazing opportunity I have to show Your love in such practical ways.

1 Peter 5:2-4

Be shepherds of God's flock that is under your care, watching over them - not because you must, but because you are willing, as God wants you to be; not pursuing dishonest gain, but eager to serve; not lording it over those entrusted to you, but being examples to the flock. And when the Chief Shepherd appears, you will receive the crown of glory that will never fade away.

Father, give me a willing heart to serve those I care for with true love and sincerity. May I reflect Your concern for them and demonstrate compassion in all that I do and say. Keep me from pursuing dishonest gain and help me to see this as an act of service unto You. Thank You for blessing this service and rewarding my faithfulness.

1 John 3:16-18

This is how we know what love is: Jesus Christ laid down His life for us. And we ought to lay down our lives for our brothers and sisters. If anyone has material possessions and sees a brother or sister in need but has no pity on them, how can the love of God be in that person? Dear children, let us not love with words or speech but with actions and in truth.

Lord, I know I need to have Your heart for others so I can rightly determine what You want me to do. I do not want to be selfish in my desires, but rather follow Your direction because of love. Show me how I can care for my own family in a way that honors and pleases You. Give me specific ways in which I can be a blessing to those I love the most.

Revelation 21:4

He will wipe every tear from their eyes. There will be no more death' or mourning or crying or pain, for the old order of things has passed away.

Thank You for the coming day when all pain and suffering will be gone! It's hard to see my loved one suffer. Give them a joyful anticipation of that day when all pain will be gone and they will live free and full of life for all eternity!

NOTES

NOTES

Words Over Our Properties

Numbers 6:24-26

The Lord bless you and keep you; the Lord make His face to shine upon you and be gracious to you; the Lord lift up His countenance upon you and give you peace.

Father, we declare that Your peace and blessing will rest upon this home and property. Shine upon this house and be gracious in Your dealings with us. We invite and welcome Your peace to come and permeate every inch of this property. Make it a place where You can come and rest and make Yourself known to all who enter.

Joshua 24:15

But if serving the Lord seems undesirable to you, then choose for yourselves this day whom you will serve, whether the gods your ancestors served beyond the Euphrates, or the gods of the Amorites, in whose land you are living. But as for me and my household, we will serve the Lord.

Father, I declare today that my home and property are under the Lordship of Jesus Christ. This home is under the jurisdiction of heaven and protected by the angelic host. I renounce and reject any other spirit or presence here that does not submit to the Lordship of Christ and evict it from this home and property. As for me and my house, we will serve the Lord!

2 Samuel 7:29

Now be pleased to bless the house of Your servant, that it may continue forever in your sight; for You, Sovereign Lord, have spoken, and with Your blessing the house of Your servant will be blessed forever.

Bless this house, Lord, that it will prosper and thrive in the days to come. Bless the ground and the foundations. Bless the water and the well. Bless all the inner workings and structural components so that every part will work properly and efficiently. May this home and property flourish and reflect Your goodness and favor on those who trust in You.

2 Chronicles 7:15-16

Now My eyes will be open and My ears attentive to the prayers offered in this place. I have chosen and consecrated this temple so that My Name may be there forever. My eyes and My heart will always be there.

Lord, we commit our home to be a place where prayer is a priority. As we purpose to seek You every day, may Your eyes be open and Your ears be attentive to our intercession and requests. Come and consecrate our home and set it apart for Your purposes. May Your name be glorified in all that happens here.

Psalms 34:7

The angel of the Lord encamps around those who fear Him, and He delivers them.

We ask that the angel of the Lord encamp around our home and property. We ask that the fear of the Lord would rest upon this property to keep any enemy at bay. Thank You, Lord, for not allowing any intruder, either natural or spiritual, to trespass on our property. Thank You for watching over us and keeping us safe.

Psalms 91:1-2

Whoever dwells in the shelter of the Most High will rest in the shadow of the Almighty. I will say of the Lord, "He is my refuge and my fortress, my God, in whom I trust."

Come, Lord, and rest in the midst of our home and property. We place ourselves under the wings of Your protection. As we acknowledge Your presence here, may You be our stronghold and sure defense against any attack of the enemy. May all who live and visit here encounter Your rest and the peace that comes from Your protective care.

Psalms 91:9-10

If you say, "The Lord is my refuge," and you make the Most High your dwelling, no harm will overtake you, no disaster will come near your tent.

We place ourselves under the protection of the Most High God. He is our Refuge and the stronghold of our lives. We declare that no harm will over-

take us and no disaster will come near this property. Thank You, God, for watching over those who place their trust in You.

Psalms 121:8
The Lord will watch over your coming and going both now and forevermore.

As we come and go from this place, Lord, we ask that Your blessing goes before us. Watch over all who enter through these doors and rest upon them with Your peace. May every doorway become an entrance into the reality of Your presence in our daily lives. May we take Your blessing with us as we leave this place and carry it on to others.

Psalms 127:1
Unless the Lord builds the house, the builders labor in vain. Unless the Lord watches over the city, the guards stand watch in vain.

Lord, I ask that You would establish our home in truth and righteousness so that we can be a blessing to those around us. Watch over us and establish Your presence here on our property to bring protection from our enemies. Teach us how to steward this property well so that it will bring honor to You and become a lighthouse to our neighbors.

Proverbs 3:33
The Lord's curse is on the house of the wicked, but He blesses the home of the righteous.

As I pray a blessing upon our home, I ask that any curse that still lingers from previous tenants would now be nullified and cancelled in the name of Jesus. I declare this to be a dwelling of truth and righteousness from this day onward. I declare that this home will reflect God's heart and character and be filled with His presence and peace. I declare this house is blessed and now under the oversight of heaven.

Proverbs 14:11
The house of the wicked will be destroyed, but the tent of the upright will flourish.

Holy Spirit, come and search through this home to reveal any way in which the enemy has access to our lives. We declare this home to be off limits to any spirit that seeks to steal, kill, or destroy. Our desire is to live upright lives before the Lord so that the abundance of the Father's house can be released in our midst. May we flourish in all we do because You are Lord of this home.

Proverbs 24:3-4

By wisdom a house is built, and through understanding it is established; through knowledge its rooms are filled with rare and beautiful treasures.

We invite the spirit of wisdom and revelation to rest upon this house. Holy Spirit, give us greater understanding in how to conduct our lives for the glory of God. As we take time to seek Your face in our home, come and release the treasures of Your heart and the riches of Your goodness. May every room be a place of meeting with You and a treasure-trove of insight and understanding.

Isaiah 32:18

My people will live in peaceful dwelling places, in secure homes, in undisturbed places of rest.

Thank You for Your promise, Lord, to give us a secure home that is undisturbed by the enemy! Thank You for surrounding this home and property and making it a place of rest and peace.

Isaiah 65:21-22

They will build houses and dwell in them; they will plant vineyards and eat their fruit. No longer will they build houses and others live in them, or plant and others eat. For as the days of a tree, so will be the days of my people; My chosen ones will long enjoy the work of their hands.

Thank You for blessing this property, Lord, and making it thrive under our supervision. May all that we do to increase its value bring much fruit and blessing in the days to come. May we reap the benefits of stewarding this property and making it a blessing for all who come here. Teach us how to invest our time and talents into making this a dwelling place of Your presence for many years to come.

Matthew 7:25

The rain came down, the streams rose, and the winds blew and beat against that house; yet it did not fall, because it had its foundation on the rock.

When the winds and rains come, Lord, watch over us and protect our property from any harm. Place Your angels around this property to guard and protect us from harsh weather or unexpected storms. Secure this dwelling and establish us in Your peace. We declare that our natural and spiritual foundations are intact and able to withstand any adversity because You are Lord of this home.

Luke 10:5

When you enter a house, first say, "Peace to this house."

I declare that the Prince of Peace rules over our home and property. Thank You, Lord, that Your peace permeates our dwelling and that all who enter here will experience it. May our home be a refuge for the weary and a place of safety for those who are anxious.

Acts 2:46-47

Every day they continued to meet together in the temple courts. They broke bread in their homes and ate together with glad and sincere hearts, praising God and enjoying the favor of all the people. And the Lord added to their number daily those who were being saved.

Lord, may this home be a place of fellowship and unity of the Spirit. May we be good hosts of Your presence to those who are hungry, either physically or spiritually. May this place be a portal of heaven that brings salvation to the lost and hope to those discouraged. Thank You for the opportunity to minister to others by creating a safe place to fellowship and grow in our walk with You.

Hebrews 13:2

Do not forget to show hospitality to strangers, for by so doing some people have shown hospitality to angels without knowing it.

Give us hospitable hearts, God. Enable us to be gracious to those visiting and to inspire those who come seeking. Show us how to minister to everyone who comes through our doors so we might be a blessing. We welcome even Your angels to come and visit this place! Open our hearts and our spiritual eyes to joyfully demonstrate heaven's hospitality.

James 4:7
Submit yourselves, then, to God. Resist the devil, and he will flee from you.

We submit this home and property to the Lord. We resist any work of the evil one and reject any unclean or perverse spirit that would seek entrance. Holy Spirit, come and fill this place with the presence of God to overflowing so that no other spirit can reside but Yours alone.

NOTES

NOTES

Words of Protection

Exodus 14:14

The Lord will fight for you; you need only to be still.

Forgive me, Lord, when I try to fight my way out of conflict or trouble. Help me to be still in Your presence and trust You for my deliverance. Thank You for fighting my battles and taking up my cause. Thank You for quieting my heart so I can let You do what only You can do.

Exodus 23:20-21a

See, I am sending an angel ahead of you to guard you along the way and to bring you to the place I have prepared. Pay attention to Him and listen to what He says.

Lord, You have already sent angels ahead of me! Your desire is to lead me and my family to places of protection and promise. I will watch and listen for Your directives and follow where You lead. Thank You for guiding us and covering us with Your presence.

Deuteronomy 31:6

Be strong and courageous. Do not be afraid or terrified because of them, for the Lord your God goes with you; He will never leave you nor forsake you.

I will not give in to fear to anything that is in front of me because the Lord goes before me! I am under divine protection. Thank You, God, for never leaving me or asking me to walk alone. Thank You for the assurance that You go with us, even in the hard times. You are a faithful God and will bring us through to victory!

Joshua 1:9

Have I not commanded you? Be strong and courageous. Do not be afraid; do not be discouraged, for the Lord your God will be with you wherever you go.

You are with me, day in and day out! You never leave me, so I know I have nothing to fear. Lord, remind me of Your abiding presence when I begin to get uneasy or fearful. You are more than enough to protect me from the enemy's ploys.

Psalms 3:3
But You, Lord, are a shield around me, my Glory, the One who lifts my head high.

Lift up my head, Lord, so I can see what You see. Keep me from focusing on myself and limiting my vision because of my own pain and discomfort. Help me to focus on Your greatness and Your ability to guard and protect. May I be fixed on the glories ahead and the breakthroughs to come.

Psalms 4:8
In peace I will lie down and sleep, for You alone, Lord, make me dwell in safety.

I will not let my heart be troubled or afraid. There is no safety or protection in worry! You alone give me rest. You alone help me to sleep and revive my soul and spirit. Thank You for watching over my nighttime hours and keeping me safe.

Psalms 18:30
As for God, His way is perfect: The Lord's word is flawless; He shields all who take refuge in Him.

You promise to protect those who take refuge in You, God. Your protection is perfect! Your Word is a strong shield against anything that comes to rob me of my peace and joy. Remind me of Your words that cause the enemy to tremble. May I declare Your word with absolute assurance in Your ability to deliver Your promises.

Psalms 23:4
Even though I walk through the darkest valley, I will fear no evil, for You are with me; Your rod and Your staff, they comfort me.

Regardless of the seeming darkness around me, You are with me, God! You are my Shepherd and My King and I have diplomatic immunity as your child! I am under Your divine care and nothing the enemy does can take me from Your presence or rob me of Your promises. Thank You for Your peace as I walk through the valleys.

Psalms 27:1-3

The Lord is my light and my salvation - whom shall I fear? The Lord is the stronghold of my life - of whom shall I be afraid? When the wicked advance against me to devour me, it is my enemies and my foes who will stumble and fall. Though an army besiege me, my heart will not fear; though war break out against me, even then I will be confident.

You are the stronghold of my life, Lord! I will not walk in fear but trust in Your overriding power to keep me safe from the enemy's attacks. I declare that no foe or force of evil will advance against me or my household, but will stumble and fall under the weight of Your presence. Regardless of what comes, my ultimate confidence is in Your ability to keep us safe and bring us through to victory.

Psalms 34:7

The angel of the Lord encamps around those who fear Him, and He delivers them.

I do not fear the enemy, but fear You, Lord. Your ways are holy and Your cause is righteous. It's the awareness of Your awesome presence that diffuses every other fear. You deliver us from all the power of the enemy when we realize just how powerful and holy You are! Thank You for the protection that comes in the fear of the Lord.

Psalms 34:19-20

The righteous person may have many troubles, but the Lord delivers him from them all; He protects all his bones, not one of them will be broken.

Your promise is incredible, Lord! You say You will deliver me from ALL my troubles! You will protect me physically and not allow the enemy to harm me. Even in times of trouble, Your promise is to preserve me and keep me. I place my faith in You to guard my body, soul, and spirit from all the schemes of the enemy.

Psalms 91:1-2

Whoever dwells in the shelter of the Most High will rest in the shadow of the Almighty. I will say of the Lord, "He is my refuge and my fortress, my God, in whom I trust."

Lord, You promise protection when we abide in You on a consistent basis. Resting in Your shadow means I'm close enough to touch You! Forgive me for presuming upon Your presence instead of actively pursuing it each and every day. I don't want to simply visit You on occasion, or when I need something. I desire to walk with You every step of the way. Thank You for guarding and preserving my life as I walk in Your shadow!

Psalms 118:6-7

The Lord is with me; I will not be afraid. What can mere mortals do to me? The Lord is with me; He is my helper. I look in triumph on my enemies.

Thank You, Lord, for defending me against my enemies. Thank You for protecting me from those who seek to do me harm. I will not fear what comes against me for You are my Helper and sure defense. Thank You for triumphing over those who hate me!

Psalms 118:8-9

It is better to take refuge in the Lord than to trust in humans. It is better to take refuge in the Lord than to trust in princes.

Forgive me, Lord, when I have placed my trust in others before trusting in You. Forgive me when looking to only natural solutions and not believing that You can provide a miraculous outcome! You are my Deliverer and the one who keeps me secure. You are my greatest source and my greatest joy!

Psalms 121:7-8

The Lord will keep you from all harm - He will watch over your life; the Lord will watch over your coming and going both now and forevermore.

Thank You, Lord, for keeping me from all harm. Thank You for watching over my life and the lives of my family. As we come and go throughout each day, I thank You for Your abiding presence and the angelic assistance which guards and protects our steps.

Proverbs 18:10

The name of the Lord is a fortified tower; the righteous run to it and are safe.

Your name is powerful, Lord! You are like a strong tower that withstands any onslaught of evil. I am running to You, knowing that I am safe in Your care. No other name is able to save and deliver. I declare that Jesus is our stronghold and sure defense against every device of the enemy!

Isaiah 43:2

When you pass through the waters, I will be with you; and when you pass through the rivers, they will not sweep over you. When you walk through the fire, you will not be burned; the flames will not set you ablaze.

Regardless of the trials I must walk through, Lord, Your promise is to always bring me through with blessing! I agree with Your Word that I will not be dismayed or destroyed in the trials that come. Rather, I will come out on the other side with greater strength, greater faith, and a greater awareness of Your awesome power over all the works of the enemy! Thank You for protecting me and keeping me.

Isaiah 54:17

"No weapon forged against you will prevail, and you will refute every tongue that accuses you. This is the heritage of the servants of the Lord and this is their vindication from Me," declares the Lord.

I am a servant of the Lord and I declare that my heritage and my vindication comes from Him! Nothing the enemy has planned to come against me or my family will succeed! No spirit of accusation or threat will penetrate the barrier of protection over my family. God's Word is on my lips and I declare that His will and purpose shall prevail!

2 Thessalonians 3:3

But the Lord is faithful, and He will strengthen you and protect you from the evil one.

You are a faithful God who always strengthens and protects me from the evil one! I declare that You are my shield and my security. You are my divine help against any and every attack that comes against me.

James 4:7

Submit yourselves, then, to God. Resist the devil, and he will flee from you.

There is great power in submitting to You, Lord. As I place myself under Your care, the devil has to flee and stop trying to attack me! I will resist his attempts by reminding him of Your Word and Your Lordship over my life.

2 Peter 2:9

If this is so, then the Lord knows how to rescue the godly from trials and to hold the unrighteous for punishment on the day of judgment.

You are my provision and my protection, Lord. I don't always know how to deal with trials and hardship, but You do! Thank You for watching over me when troubles come. Thank You for Your justice and for dealing with those who seek to hurt me. You are my Redeemer and the one who rescues. I place my trust in You.

NOTES

NOTES

CHALLENGING TIMES

WORDS FOR RELATIONAL CONFLICTS

Proverbs 15:1

A gentle answer turns away wrath, but a harsh word stirs up anger.

Guard my lips, Lord, so that I will not react in my flesh when my buttons get pushed! Give me the right words to say to diffuse any anger or hostility in this conflict. May we seek peace in resolving the issues and relate in a way that invites Your presence and power, bringing us through in unity.

Proverbs 16:7

When the Lord takes pleasure in anyone's way, He causes their enemies to make peace with them.

Lord, may my responses in this conflict be so pleasing to You, that even those who oppose me will desire peace. Keep me close to Your heart so that I will act with love, compassion, and forbearance. Especially for those who attack me, may Your favor and blessing rest upon me with such power and protection, it stops the attacks and dissolves the conflict altogether.

Proverbs 16:28

A perverse person stirs up conflict, and a gossip separates close friends.

Holy Spirit, keep me from spouting out my complaint to others and stirring up even more conflict. Cleanse me of my need to defend myself or make someone else look bad so that I look good. I do not want to lose my friends or cause someone else harm. Increase my capacity to love unconditionally so that my words will bring life and not death.

Proverbs 17:14

Starting a quarrel is like breaching a dam; so drop the matter before a dispute breaks out.

Forgive me, Lord, for wanting to prove my point and defend my case more than to bring resolution. Show me if and when it is time to walk away from a disagreement in order to maintain peace. Help me to know how to respond to conflict in a way that closes the door to the enemy and opens the way for You to bring clarity out of the chaos.

Proverbs 18:13
To answer before listening - that is folly and shame.

Help me keep my mouth shut, Lord! Forgive me when I'm not willing to listen to someone who challenges me. Help me to truly hear their heart before interrupting and shutting them down. Give me a greater ability to care about their perspective just as much as I care about my own.

Matthew 5:9
Blessed are the peacemakers, for they will be called children of God.

Lord, give me Your heart that seeks peace more than retribution. Remind me of the blessings that come from resolving conflicts Your way. Give me wisdom and insight in restoring relationship and inviting You in as the Prince of Peace in this situation.

Matthew 5:23-24
Therefore, if you are offering your gift at the altar and there remember that your brother or sister has something against you, leave your gift there in front of the altar. First go and be reconciled to them; then come and offer your gift.

Thank You, Lord, for reminding me how important it is to be in right relationship with others. I know I cannot be totally clean before You if I am in conflict with someone else. Help me to do my part in bringing resolution and restoring fellowship with a brother or sister so that our worship will be pure and our gifts will be pleasing to You.

Matthew 7:3-5
Why do you look at the speck of sawdust in your brother's eye and pay no attention to the plank in your own eye? How can you say to your brother, "Let me take the speck out of your eye," when all the time there is a plank in your own eye? You hypocrite, first take the plank out of your own eye, and then you will see clearly to remove the speck from your brother's eye.

Show me, Lord, any stronghold or sin in my own life that is blinding me to the truth. Help me to come clean before You so that I can rightly discern how to walk in peace with my brothers and sisters.

Matthew 18:15-16

If your brother or sister sins, go and point out their fault, just between the two of you. If they listen to you, you have won them over. But if they will not listen, take one or two others along, so that 'every matter may be established by the testimony of two or three witnesses.'

Lord, I desire to resolve this conflict honorably. I will not seek personal sympathy by spreading my frustrations to others and creating gossip. Help me in going directly to those who have offended or hurt me to invite resolution. If assistance is needed, guide me to the proper oversight to help mediate the differences. I pray that each of us involved will have a heart of compassion towards one another and pursue peace and restoration for the sake of all.

John 7:24

Stop judging by mere appearances, but instead judge correctly.

Help me to see beyond appearances, Lord. Stop me when I start presuming to understand when there may be things I don't see or comprehend. Give me a heart of wisdom to respond rightly and assume the best and not the worst.

Romans 12:9-10

Love must be sincere. Hate what is evil; cling to what is good. Be devoted to one another in love. Honor one another above yourselves.

Help me to be authentic, Lord, and to be honest with others. Give me Your heart so that I will have a conviction about what is good and hate what is evil. May my love for others reflect Your grace and patience. Show me any ways in which I'm being selfish and not considering the needs of others above my own.

1 Corinthians 6:1

If any of you has a dispute with another, do you dare to take it before the ungodly for judgment instead of before the Lord's people?

Father, help me to take my issues with another brother or sister to proper spiritual oversight. I desire to seek Your counsel and the wisdom from fellow believers first and foremost. Guide my pastors and church leaders in helping me resolve the issues so we can invite the power of Your Spirit to bring peace and unity.

1 Corinthians 13:4-5

Love is patient, love is kind. It does not envy, it does not boast, it is not proud. It does not dishonor others, it is not self-seeking, it is not easily angered, it keeps no record of wrongs.

Thank You for teaching me patience, Lord. Show me practical ways to show Your kindness and to lift others up with encouragement and praise. Show me when I take things the wrong way and harbor offense. Cleanse me of any self-righteous attitudes and help me to give without hesitation and bless without finding fault.

Ephesians 4:26-27

In your anger do not sin: Do not let the sun go down while you are still angry, and do not give the devil a foothold.

Lord, forgive me for harboring ill will towards others. I do not want to be under the oppression of unforgiveness or bitterness of heart. I release my anger to You and ask You to give me a softened heart of compassion and mercy towards those I am in conflict with. I do not want the devil to get a foothold because of my inability to do my part. Help me to pursue restoration quickly and not put it off.

Ephesians 4:31

Get rid of all bitterness, rage and anger, brawling and slander, along with every form of malice. Be kind and compassionate to one another, forgiving each other, just as in Christ God forgave you.

Lord, forgive me for any bitterness or anger against my brother or sister. I choose to forgive them for any offense and release them to You. I know You will honor my obedience and intervene on my behalf. Show me how to move forward with kindness and compassion so that You can resolve our conflicts in a godly way.

Philippians 2:3-4

Do nothing out of selfish ambition or vain conceit. Rather, in humility value others above yourselves, not looking to your own interests but each of you to the interests of the others.

Forgive me, Lord, if I have acted as if my perspective is more important than someone else's. Help me to listen and to graciously consider what others think and feel so that I can be a better reflection of Your unconditional love and mercy. I know that You will back me up as I walk with a right heart and a right spirit towards those I disagree with.

Colossians 3:13-14

Bear with each other and forgive one another if any of you has a grievance against someone. Forgive as the Lord forgave you. And over all these virtues put on love, which binds them all together in perfect unity.

Thank You, Lord, for giving me the grace to forgive and release my offense. I choose to walk in Your perfect love towards those who have hurt me and desire restored fellowship with You and with others. Thank You for giving me the needed patience in this process. Keep my thoughts and emotions centered on Your redemptive plan to get us through our differences.

James 1:19-20

My dear brothers and sisters, take note of this: Everyone should be quick to listen, slow to speak and slow to become angry, because human anger does not produce the righteousness that God desires.

Lord, help me to listen and pay attention to those around me. Forgive me for interrupting or being more focused on my viewpoint than on listening to another perspective. Forgive me when I don't respect the opinions of others and shut down a conversation out of frustration. Give me ears to hear and a heart that desires mutual love and fellowship more than having the last word.

James 4:1

What causes fights and quarrels among you? Don't they come from your desires that battle within you?

Holy Spirit, show me if there is anything in my own heart that is causing offense or bitterness. I want to have a clear conscience before You. I repent of any jealousy or covetousness that is stirring up my frustration. I choose to walk in the Spirit and not according to my flesh. Cleanse my heart and mind and renew my desire to walk in purity of heart and integrity towards others.

James 5:16

Therefore, confess your sins to each other and pray for each other so that you may be healed. The prayer of a righteous person is powerful and effective.

Thank You for the reminder, Lord, that my prayers will be hindered if my heart harbors resentment or unforgiveness towards another. You promise healing when we confess our faults to others and seek right relationship. Lead me to those who can help me find healing and restoration so that our prayers will be powerful and effective.

Hebrews 12:14-15

Make every effort to live in peace with everyone and to be holy; without holiness no one will see the Lord. See to it that no one falls short of the grace of God and that no bitter root grows up to cause trouble and defile many.

Reveal to me, Holy Spirit, if there is any seed of bitterness in my heart towards another that will hinder my walk and poison my testimony. I do not want to miss the grace of God! You have given me access to Your holiness as I obey Your Word. Teach me to live in peace with those I disagree with and to have integrity of heart in how I respond.

1 Peter 2:17

Show proper respect to everyone, love the family of believers, fear God, honor the emperor.

Lord, forgive me if I have had any bias towards others that look or sound different than me. Help me see them the way You do. Teach me how to respect the thoughts and ideas of others that I don't agree with. I pray that my attitude will cause others to see that You alone know all the right answers, and are worthy of trust for those who earnestly seek You.

NOTES

Words for Endurance

Matthew 10:21-23

Brother will betray brother to death, and a father his child; children will rebel against their parents and have them put to death. You will be hated by everyone because of me, but the one who stands firm to the end will be saved.

Lord, I know there is a cost for following You. Help me to stay faithful to Your Word, even when those around me do not understand. Help me to endure and not quit when rejected by those I love. May they see heaven reflected in my responses and Your heart displayed in my words.

Luke 21:17-19

Everyone will hate you because of me. But not a hair of your head will perish. Stand firm, and you will win life.

Thank you, Lord, for backing me up when I honor Your name. May my heart stay tender towards those who hate me. May they see Your providential care as a sign of Your love and Your goodness and may it turn them back to You. Thank You for preserving my life as I stand on Your truth.

Romans 5:3-5

Not only so, but we also glory in our sufferings, because we know that suffering produces perseverance; perseverance, character; and character, hope. And hope does not put us to shame, because God's love has been poured out into our hearts through the Holy Spirit, who has been given to us.

Lord, I determine to thank You for every situation You bring my way as a source of instruction and strengthening of my faith. Grant me the ability to overcome every obstacle and to learn the needed lessons so I may bear even greater fruit for my benefit and for Your glory.

Romans 15:4-6

For everything that was written in the past was written to teach us, so that through the endurance taught in the Scriptures and the encouragement they provide we might have hope. May the God who gives endurance and encouragement give you the same attitude of mind toward each other that Christ Jesus had, so that with one mind and one voice you may glorify the God and Father of our Lord Jesus Christ.

Thank you, Lord, for giving me hope and instruction. Thank You for reminding me of Your faithfulness from times past that are recorded in Your Word. Draw me to others who share in this commission so we may encourage one another and strengthen our resolve to complete what You started.

Romans 15:13

May the God of hope fill you with all joy and peace as you trust in Him, so that you may overflow with hope by the power of the Holy Spirit.

It is through You, Holy Spirit, that I can have the fullness of joy and peace in my life. I choose to trust You in all my ways and pray that I will overflow with a renewed hope that is excited about the future!

Philippians 3:10-11

I want to know Christ - yes, to know the power of His resurrection and participation in His sufferings, becoming like Him in His death, and so, somehow, attaining to the resurrection from the dead.

Lord, I realize that without sharing in Your sufferings, I will never fully know You. I trust You to know what I can handle and give me the needed grace to not only endure, but to overcome. Thank You for drawing even closer to me in the midst of the pain.

Hebrews 10:23

Let us hold unswervingly to the hope we profess, for He who promised is faithful.

Thank You, Lord, for being faithful to Your promises. I will hold fast to Your Word and boldly declare that my hope is fully in You. What You have said - You will do. I stand on that assurance.

Hebrews 10:35-39
So do not throw away your confidence; it will be richly rewarded. You need to persevere so that when you have done the will of God, you will receive what He has promised. For, "In just a little while, He who is coming will come and will not delay." And, "But My righteous one will live by faith. And I take no pleasure in the one who shrinks back." But we do not belong to those who shrink back and are destroyed, but to those who have faith and are saved.

Remind me of Your promises, Lord, that I might continue to stand on them and believe with all hope. Help me not to shrink back, but to keep moving forward. Grant me even greater confidence in Your perfect will so that I will press through to the finish line to receive my reward.

Hebrews 12:1-2
Therefore, since we are surrounded by such a great cloud of witnesses, let us throw off everything that hinders and the sin that so easily entangles. And let us run with perseverance the race marked out for us, fixing our eyes on Jesus, the Pioneer and Perfecter of faith. For the joy set before Him He endured the cross, scorning its shame, and sat down at the right hand of the throne of God.

May I have the same patient endurance that you did, Jesus, so that I may share in Your reward. Thank you for the cloud of witnesses who are cheering me on and reminding me of the goal. Help me to see any weight or hindrance that is slowing me down so that I can run unencumbered by any weakness or sin. Fix my eyes on You so I do not get distracted or discouraged. I will press on to the finish and look forward to Your reward.

Hebrews 12:7
Endure hardship as discipline; God is treating you as His children. For what children are not disciplined by their father?

Thank you for loving me perfectly, Heavenly Father. Thank you for calling me one of Your own and for taking such care in ordering my steps. Even when You correct me, You do it out of great love. I desire to please You in all I do and say and ask that You would continue to mold my heart to reflect all of You and none of me!

James 1:2-4

Consider it pure joy, my brothers and sisters, whenever you face trials of many kinds, because you know that the testing of your faith produces perseverance. Let perseverance finish its work so that you may be mature and complete, not lacking anything.

Lord, I do not want to lack anything, but to be the full representation of Christ Jesus while here on the earth. Forgive me for my impatience and help me to fully trust Your methods of instruction that I know are for my good. Fill me with Your joy so I can become all that You intend and finish what You have started in me.

1 Peter 1:6-7

In all this you greatly rejoice, though now for a little while you may have had to suffer grief in all kinds of trials. These have come so that the proven genuineness of your faith - of greater worth than gold, which perishes even though refined by fire - may result in praise, glory and honor when Jesus Christ is revealed.

Father, help me to see that every trial I go through is being used by You to perfect my faith. Teach me to see You in the midst of my troubles and to receive greater revelation of Your goodness and faithful purposes for my life. Grant me a thankful heart to praise you in the midst of the storms.

1 Peter 4:12-13

Dear friends, do not be surprised at the fiery ordeal that has come on you to test you, as though something strange were happening to you. But rejoice inasmuch as you participate in the sufferings of Christ, so that you may be overjoyed when His glory is revealed.

Lord, thank You for loving me enough to not leave me the way I am. You desire me to be strong and steadfast in faith. I will rejoice in the trials that come because You use every single one of them to do a greater work in me! You are Lord of my tests and Lord of my trials. Nothing will go to waste when I trust in You.

NOTES

NOTES

WORDS FOR OVERCOMING ANXIETY

Psalms 37:8

Refrain from anger and turn from wrath; do not fret - it leads only to evil.

Lord, keep my heart from being angry at people and situations in my life that seem contrary. Worry and anxiety only opens the door to the enemy and causes all kinds of unnecessary strife and misunderstanding. I lay down my frustrations and give my worries to You. I put on peace as my shield and trust You to help me respond in a way that's pleasing to You.

Psalms 139:23-24

Search me, God, and know my heart; test me and know my anxious thoughts. See if there is any offensive way in me and lead me in the way everlasting.

Holy Spirit, search my heart and reveal any thought or mindset that is only feeding worry and anxiety. Help me replace any lies with Your truth so that I do not waste time fretting and giving in to fear. Sanctify my heart so that I am filled with faith and absolute confidence in Your purposes and intentions for my good.

Proverbs 3:5-6

Trust in the Lord with all your heart and lean not on your own understanding; in all your ways submit to Him, and He will make your paths straight.

Forgive me, Lord, for trying to figure things out on my own. Forgive me for using human reasoning to make judgment calls. I acknowledge that You have a plan and a purpose far better than my own and I can trust Your solutions for my problems. Come and clear out the cobwebs of my mind and help me see the steps You have laid out for my good.

Proverbs 12:25

Anxiety weighs down the heart, but a kind word cheers it up.

Lord, my heart gets weighed down by my own thoughts and worries. Please bring me a good word to cheer me up! Bring me a testimony, a conversation, a reading, or other means of communication that will encourage my heart and strengthen my faith. Alert me to those messages so that my heart can be set free from worry.

Isaiah 35:4 (ESV)

Say to those who have an anxious heart, "Be strong; fear not! Behold, your God will come with vengeance, with the recompense of God. He will come and save you."

I say to my heart, "Be strong and do not be anxious!" My God is coming with vengeance against all who oppose Him and will reward those who have remained faithful. God, You are not sitting idle or unwilling to act. You have every intention of intervening on my behalf and dealing with my enemies. Thank You for being my Savior, Redeemer, and Champion of Hosts.

Matthew 6:25-27

Therefore I tell you, do not worry about your life, what you will eat or drink; or about your body, what you will wear. Is not life more than food, and the body more than clothes? Look at the birds of the air; they do not sow or reap or store away in barns, and yet your heavenly Father feeds them. Are you not much more valuable than they? Can any one of you by worrying add a single hour to your life?

Lord, I am wasting valuable time by worrying! Forgive me for allowing my thoughts to wander and my heart to fret. You know every detail of my life and know exactly how to get me through my trials. Help me focus my attention on what You are doing all around me and not fixate on those things I have no control over.

Matthew 6:34

Therefore do not worry about tomorrow, for tomorrow will worry about itself. Each day has enough trouble of its own.

Lord, I admit that I'm worrying about the future and not enjoying today. Help me not miss the ways in which You are speaking and working that are right in front of me. Forgive me for worrying so much about tomorrow, that I don't even see You for today.

Matthew 13:22-23

The seed falling among the thorns refers to someone who hears the word, but the worries of this life and the deceitfulness of wealth choke the word, making it unfruitful. But the seed falling on good soil refers to someone who hears the word and understands it. This is the one who produces a crop, yielding a hundred, sixty or thirty times what was sown.

Lord, I need a fresh infusion of Your Word to choke out the weeds of worry! Forgive me for worrying so much about how things will turn out and how much money I have. They have robbed my heart of Your promises. Till the soil of my heart so that I can receive Your word again in a fresh way and replace worry with absolute faith in Your provision.

Luke 10:41-42

"Martha, Martha," the Lord answered, "you are worried and upset about many things, but few things are needed - or indeed only one. Mary has chosen what is better, and it will not be taken away from her."

Forgive me, Lord, for worrying about the lesser things. I know if my heart was totally fixed on You and Your goodness, I would not be so worried about the details. Help me prioritize my thoughts so that I always think of You first and Your unconditional love and care concerning everything about my life. May I find peace and joy through my relationship with You, knowing You will give me grace to deal with the necessary details.

Luke 12:25-26

Who of you by worrying can add a single hour to your life? Since you cannot do this very little thing, why do you worry about the rest?

Thank You, God, that I'm not in control of things. You are! Forgive me for trying to steer my life because it's only causing anxiety. I'm not helping by my constant worry. I surrender my need to control and understand and give You the reins of my life. Take charge of my life and take me where I need to go – when I need to go! My faith and trust are in You – and You always come through.

Luke 21:13-15

And so you will bear testimony to Me. But make up your mind not to worry beforehand how you will defend yourselves. For I will give you words and wisdom that none of your adversaries will be able to resist or contradict.

Thank You, Holy Spirit, for giving me the right words to say at the right time! I don't have to worry about how I will defend myself or state my case. You will give me what to say as I trust in You. Fill me with Your Spirit so that I will have God's thoughts and words and be a powerful witness for You.

John 14:1-2

Do not let your hearts be troubled. You believe in God; believe also in Me. My Father's house has many rooms; if that were not so, would I have told you that I am going there to prepare a place for you?

Thank You, Father, for preparing a house for me in glory! I don't have to be anxious about things on this side because they are only temporary. Regardless of the seeming darkness, You have already determined the outcome for our good and prepared a glorious future for all who trust in You. I will not give room for anxiety to grow, but look forward to all that You have in store for me!

John 14:27

Peace I leave with you; My peace I give you. I do not give to you as the world gives. Do not let your hearts be troubled and do not be afraid.

Jesus, I want to trade my worry for Your peace. You are always with me and know exactly what I am facing. I receive the assurance that You are working on my behalf and will make things clear to me as I trust in You. I speak to my heart and mind and say, "Peace, be still!"

Philippians 4:6-7

Do not be anxious about anything, but in every situation, by prayer and petition, with thanksgiving, present your requests to God. And the peace of God, which transcends all understanding, will guard your hearts and your minds in Christ Jesus.

Father, I will not be anxious or worried about things but will seek Your heart in every situation. I will not give in to anxiety or fear but trust in You alone who can give me a peace that transcends all understanding. I thank You for listening to my prayers and placing a guard around my heart and mind. In Jesus' name.

Philippians 4:8-9
Finally, brothers and sisters, whatever is true, whatever is noble, whatever is right, whatever is pure, whatever is lovely, whatever is admirable - if anything is excellent or praiseworthy - think about such things. Whatever you have learned or received or heard from me or seen in me - put it into practice. And the God of peace will be with you.

Lord, my thoughts keep wandering and making me anxious. I choose to replace those thoughts with the mind of Christ. Help me to think on Your promises and Your purposes, Your good intentions for me, the ways in which You've already answered my prayers, and that which You are teaching me. Help me to see all the good things You are doing and not fixate so much on the few things that don't seem to be working. Your ways are always higher and always better. Thank You for what You are doing!

Hebrews 11:1
Now faith is confidence in what we hope for and assurance about what we do not see.

Holy Spirit, bring remembrance of God's words to me so that my faith can be built up and strengthened. Help me displace my doubts with the confidence that God is going to come through. Regardless of what I see, I place my trust in what He says about things, knowing He always keeps His Word.

1 Peter 5:5b-7
God opposes the proud but shows favor to the humble. Humble yourselves, therefore, under God's mighty hand, that He may lift you up in due time. Cast all your anxiety on Him because He cares for you.

Forgive me, Lord, for any pride that has kept me from You. I acknowledge that You are the Lord of my life and I humble Myself under Your hand which guides me. I know You will lift me up and meet my needs in Your perfect time. I know You love and care for me and I lay all my worries at Your feet.

1 John 4:18

There is no fear in love. But perfect love drives out fear, because fear has to do with punishment. The one who fears is not made perfect in love.

I admit, Lord, that I'm anxious because of fear. But, fear should have no place in my thoughts or heart! Reveal to me new aspects of Your love that will displace my doubts about Your concern. Nullify the lies I'm believing that You won't come through for me. Give me revelation of Your perfect love to cast out every fear and every anxiety, in Jesus' name.

NOTES

NOTES

Words for Healing

Exodus 15:26

He said, "If you listen carefully to the Lord your God and do what is right in His eyes, if you pay attention to His commands and keep all His decrees, I will not bring on you any of the diseases I brought on the Egyptians, for I am the Lord, who heals you."

Lord, Thank You for Your protection over my physical health. Help me to stay faithful to Your commands by doing what You say. Show me any way in which I have missed Your voice so that I can receive the fullness of the blessing and wholeness You provide.

Exodus 23:25

"Worship the Lord your God, and His blessing will be on your food and water. I will take away sickness from among you."

Father, I desire for everything that I eat and drink to be blessed by You and good for my body. Remove any curses or impurities in my food and teach me to make wise choices in what I consume. I am the temple of Your Spirit and will honor You in what I eat and drink.

2 Kings 20:5(a)

Go back and tell Hezekiah, the ruler of My people, "This is what the Lord, the God of your father David, says: I have heard your prayer and seen your tears; I will heal you."

Lord, You show that my physical health and spiritual health are tied together. If there is any way in which I have disobeyed or dishonored You, please forgive me. Cleanse me of any work of the flesh that is manifesting through sickness in my body. I want to follow Your directives and heed Your commands so that my whole body, soul, mind, and spirit will be whole and healed.

2 Chronicles 7:14

If My people, who are called by My name, will humble themselves and pray and seek My face and turn from their wicked ways, then I will hear from heaven, and I will forgive their sin and will heal their land.

Lord, reveal to me anything in my life that has opened a door to a spirit of infirmity. Forgive me for any wrongdoing or grievance that has given the enemy access to my health. Thank You for cleansing me completely and restoring every area of my life.

Psalms 41:1-3

Blessed are those who have regard for the weak; the Lord delivers them in times of trouble. The Lord protects and preserves them, they are counted among the blessed in the land. He does not give them over to the desire of their foes. The Lord sustains them on their sickbed and restores them from their bed of illness.

Lord, You promise healing to those who have regard for the weak. Forgive me for any offense or bitterness I have towards those I deem unworthy. Cleanse my heart and mind of any bias that has stood in the way of Your healing grace. Thank You for purifying my heart with humility and mercy.

Psalms 103:2-3

Praise the Lord, my soul, and forget not all His benefits - who forgives all your sins and heals all your diseases.

I remember the benefits You provided through Your death and resurrection! You not only forgave all my sins, but You healed all my diseases. Thank You for Your healing power in every part of my life.

Psalms 107:19-20

Then they cried to the Lord in their trouble, and He saved them from their distress. He sent out His word and healed them; He rescued them from the grave.

As I cry out to You for my healing, Lord, I ask for a fresh word from You concerning Your promises. Touch my mind and body with Your healing grace. Thank You for hearing my prayer and sending forth Your word as a reminder of Your faithful promise.

Psalms 147:3
He heals the brokenhearted and binds up their wounds.

Father, please heal my mind and emotions from negative thoughts and attitudes that do not reflect Your heart for me. Heal my heart of disappointments and restore my hope in Your goodness. Expose any way in which the enemy is using my past against me and keeping me in an endless cycle of pain and discouragement. Thank You for healing every part of my being and making me whole!

Proverbs 3:7-8
Do not be wise in your own eyes; fear the Lord and shun evil. This will bring health to your body and nourishment to your bones.

I choose to walk in the fear of the Lord and not according to my own thinking or the influence of others. If there is anything in my life that is unpleasing to You, Lord, show me so that I can turn away to follow You. I yield my human understanding to the Spirit of Truth, knowing that my physical and emotional well-being comes from You alone.

Proverbs 4:20-22
My son, pay attention to what I say; turn your ear to My words. Do not let them out of your sight, keep them within your heart; for they are life to those who find them and health to one's whole body.

As I wait on You, I will continually turn to Your words that bring life and healing to my whole being. Your words have supernatural power to transform and restore! Help me to apply Your truths in practical ways so that even my physical health will be a testimony to the power of Your Word.

Proverbs 16:24
Gracious words are a honeycomb, sweet to the soul and healing to the bones.

Lord, make me more aware of the words I speak and the words I listen to. May my speech reflect my faith and hope in You and not open the door to any fear or doubt. Keep me alert to words spoken to me or over me that are not in accordance with Your will. Stand at the gate of my heart so that only words of life and healing can enter and take residence.

Proverbs 17:22
A cheerful heart is good medicine, but a crushed spirit dries up the bones.

You say the joy of the Lord gives me strength. I choose joy! I yield to You all my disappointments and anxieties and trade them for Your joy which is everlasting. Heal my heart from all that has been broken and restore my trust again. May my physical body reflect the healing of my heart.

Isaiah 38:16-17
Lord, by such things people live; and my spirit finds life in them too. You restored me to health and let me live. Surely it was for my benefit that I suffered such anguish. In Your love You kept me from the pit of destruction; You have put all my sins behind Your back.

Lord, You are the One who brings healing to my body and soul. Even through the hard parts, You teach me lessons that make me stronger and more dependent on You. By Your grace, You have kept me and granted me all that I need to come through on the other side of hardship with healing and restoration from all the attacks of the enemy.

Isaiah 40:31
But those who hope in the Lord will renew their strength. They will soar on wings like eagles; they will run and not grow weary, they will walk and not be faint.

My hope is in You, Lord, for all that I need! Even as You provide me with practical wisdom and proper treatments for my healing, I know that You are the ultimate source of my well-being. I trust You with my life, and praise You for providing everything I need to be whole and full of hope for the future.

Isaiah 53:5

But He was pierced for our transgressions, He was crushed for our iniquities; the punishment that brought us peace was on Him, and by His wounds we are healed.

Thank You, Lord, for providing healing for my soul, spirit, and body, through Your sacrifice on the cross. Thank You for making a way to walk in wholeness and peace. I receive this gift with a thankful heart.

Jeremiah 17:14

Heal me, LORD, and I will be healed; save me and I will be saved, for You are the one I praise.

Lord, I fix my gaze on You and give You all my worship and praise. Fill me with Your presence to overflowing. You are my Healer and Redeemer, and You alone are worthy of honor and glory for transforming my life, restoring my soul, and healing my body.

Malachi 4:2

But for you who revere My name, the sun of righteousness will rise with healing in its rays. And you will go out and frolic like well-fed calves.

I stand in awe of Your goodness, Lord. I desire to walk in the fear of the Lord and not allow any other fear to grip my heart or mind. I will not allow the fear of sickness or disease to rob me of my trust in You. I call forth Your healing grace to overshadow me and renew me completely. I delight in giving You all the honor and praise for every good and perfect gift from above.

Matthew 8:16

When evening came, many who were demon-possessed were brought to Him, and He drove out the spirits with a word and healed all the sick.

Father, if there is any demonic influence affecting my physical or mental well-being, please expose these strongholds and set me free! Your word says You healed ALL who were sick, so I believe in Your goodness to show me the way through. Thank You for loving me completely and giving me the victory over the enemy.

Mark 6:56

And wherever He went, into villages, towns or countryside, they placed the sick in the marketplaces. They begged Him to let them touch even the edge of His cloak, and all who touched it were healed.

Being in proximity to Your presence brings healing to me, Lord! When I touch Your heart and encounter Your truth, I am forever changed! Draw me to that place of consistent relationship with You where I can receive the strength and power I need to be whole and set free.

Mark 9:23

"If you can?" said Jesus. "Everything is possible for one who believes."

Lord, I believe that You desire to heal me and those I care about. Help my unbelief and teach me to trust that You can do the impossible. Bring Your words to my mind when I begin to doubt so that any unbelief will be replaced by Your presence and power.

Mark 10:52

"Go," said Jesus, "your faith has healed you." Immediately he received his sight and followed Jesus along the road.

Lord, if there is any wavering in my heart or lack of conviction concerning Your desire to bring health and healing, expose the lies and help me embrace the truth. I want to be a person of faith and not of doubt. Arm me with Your words of life that will sustain me and firmly establish my trust in You.

Luke 6:18b-19

Those troubled by impure spirits were cured, and the people all tried to touch Him, because power was coming from Him and healing them all.

Jesus, I desire to know not just Your truth, but Your power. You are the Living Word, and all who touch You have access to Your healing grace. Teach me how to establish a place of Your presence in my life that opens the door to miraculous powers and healing virtue.

John 10:10

The thief comes only to steal and kill and destroy; I have come that they may have life, and have it to the full.

Jesus, You promise a full life to all who follow You. I believe Your word and ask that this truth manifests in my soul, mind, and body. I will not accept any limitations from the enemy of my soul, and choose to trust You for every need that I have. I speak to my entire being, "Be filled with the fullness of God's goodness, blessing, and healing grace!" Amen.

Hebrews 12:13

Make level paths for your feet, so that the lame may not be disabled, but rather healed.

As I pray for my healing, establish my steps so that my path will be marked by Your truth. Straighten out any crooked thinking that has steered me away from Your purposes. I acknowledge that I am handicapped without You and desire to walk in total submission to You.

James 5:16

Therefore confess your sins to each other and pray for each other so that you may be healed. The prayer of a righteous person is powerful and effective.

Lord, show me if there is any unforgiveness in my heart towards another that may be blocking my healing. I submit my needs to You and those You have placed in my life for accountability. I will openly confess my faults without shame, knowing that Your righteousness covers my guilt and restores my health. Thank You.

3 John 1:2

Dear friend, I pray that you may enjoy good health and that all may go well with you, even as your soul is getting along well.

Lord, You desire for me to be healed in body, soul, and spirit. Bring me into total alignment so that the fullness of Christ dwells in my whole being. Teach me to care for every aspect of my health as a faithful witness to Your goodness and redemptive purposes.

NOTES

Words for Grieving

Job 1:20-22
At this, Job got up and tore his robe and shaved his head. Then he fell to the ground in worship and said: "Naked I came from my mother's womb, and naked I will depart. The Lord gave and the Lord has taken away; may the name of the Lord be praised." In all this, Job did not sin by charging God with wrongdoing.

God, You never do anything wrong. The enemy will not have his way by getting me to accuse You of a lack of love or care. Even when he comes in to rob, kill, and destroy, Your purposes always prevail! I will not blame You for any loss, but choose to praise You because You are God. I trust in Your promises to bring blessing out of pain and abundance out of loss. I declare that You are a loving Father and merciful God!

Psalms 50:23
Those who sacrifice thank offerings honor Me, and to the blameless I will show My salvation.

Though my heart grieves, I give You thanks, Lord. Your love never fails and even in this time of mourning, I choose to praise You. You always bring blessing out of pain when we trust in You. Show me Your goodness in ways I would have missed otherwise.

Psalms 73:26
My flesh and my heart may fail, but God is the strength of my heart and my portion forever.

God, I do not have the strength to endure this process on my own. I cannot go through this without You. Be my strength and anchor my soul in hope. Take my heart and heal it. Take my thoughts and fill them with Your promises for the future.

Isaiah 26:3

You will keep in perfect peace those whose minds are steadfast because they trust in You.

Lord, help me keep my thoughts focused on You and not on my circumstances or grief. Alert me when my mind wanders into worry and fear. Remind me of Your words that bring hope and life. I know I must guard my heart so that it flows with faith for tomorrow. Help me fix my eyes on You so I can reach the other side of this valley with Your absolute peace.

Isaiah 43:2-3a

When you pass through the waters, I will be with you; and when you pass through the rivers, they will not sweep over you. When you walk through the fire, you will not be burned; the flames will not set you ablaze. For I am the Lord your God, the Holy One of Israel, your Savior.

Lord, as I walk through this painful time, thank You for overshadowing me with Your presence to get me through. I stand on Your promises that the pain will not overwhelm me and the process will not harm me. I trust You to bring me through with even greater understanding of Your love and greater power to overcome all that comes against me.

Isaiah 53:4-5

Surely He took up our pain and bore our suffering, yet we considered Him punished by God, stricken by Him, and afflicted. But He was pierced for our transgressions, He was crushed for our iniquities; the punishment that brought us peace was on Him, and by His wounds we are healed.

Jesus, You experienced the pain of suffering and death, and yet came out victorious over the enemy. You know what I am feeling and are more than able to carry me through to life on the other side of this cross. I receive Your grace to persevere through this trial and receive healing and wholeness for the journey ahead.

Isaiah 61:1b-3

He has sent me to bind up the brokenhearted...to comfort all who mourn and provide for those who grieve in Zion - to bestow on them a crown of beauty instead of ashes, the oil of joy instead of mourning, and a garment of praise instead of a spirit of despair. They will be called oaks of righteousness, a planting of the Lord for the display of His splendor.

Jesus, be my comforter to bind up my broken heart. Take the ashes of my loss and bring me beauty instead of darkness. Anoint me with the oil of joy so that my mourning will produce praise instead of despair. With You, there is always hope for the future. I declare that this process will bring forth good fruit and blessing for Your glory and that many will come to know the goodness of the Lord through it all.

Isaiah 66:13-14
As a mother comforts her child, so will I comfort you; and you will be comforted over Jerusalem. When you see this, your heart will rejoice and you will flourish like grass; the hand of the Lord will be made known to His servants, but His fury will be shown to His foes.

God, Your love for me is zealous and fierce – just as a mother has for her children. Thank You for assuring me of Your compassion and Your determination to bring blessing out of loss. Let me see Your goodness in the midst of heartache and Your favor on those who have endured pain.

Matthew 5:4
Blessed are those who mourn, for they will be comforted.

Father, help me to properly mourn and allow this process of grieving. You say that comfort can be found in the midst of mourning, so I give You the pain and sorrow and ask for this divine exchange. I receive the unique blessings that can only come through this process and thank You for overshadowing me with Your constant presence.

Mark 16:9-11
When Jesus rose early on the first day of the week, He appeared first to Mary Magdalene, out of whom He had driven seven demons. She went and told those who had been with Him and who were mourning and weeping. When they heard that Jesus was alive and that she had seen Him, they did not believe it.

Lord, keep my heart from a spirit of unbelief in this time of mourning. Though I feel the pain of loss and separation, may I never miss Your presence or doubt Your purposes. May I always respond in absolute faith to Your goodness and continue to hope in the midst of disappointment.

John 11:35
Jesus wept.

Jesus, even You wept at the loss of a loved one. Knowing that Your good friend would rise again, You still allowed Yourself to feel the pain of separation. In so doing, it brought forth life and hope. Show me how to mourn in a way that brings forth resurrection hope for those who are watching. May Your deep compassion and love be evident to all.

John 14:1
Do not let your hearts be troubled. You believe in God; believe also in Me.

God, I will not give room to anxiety or distress, for they do not bring me hope. I want to have absolute confidence in Your plans and purposes for my life. In this trial, I place my trust in Your unfailing love. Even in this time of walking through the darkness, I believe in Your goodness and Your plans for a bright tomorrow.

John 14:27
Peace I leave with you; My peace I give you. I do not give to you as the world gives. Do not let your hearts be troubled and do not be afraid.

Lord, I do not want to grieve as the world grieves, without hope or joy for the future. Guard my heart and mind from taking on hopelessness and despair. May Your presence be so strong upon my life that there is no room for anxiety or fear about my future. I receive Your supernatural peace and will walk forward with assurance for the days ahead.

2 Corinthians 1:3-5
Praise be to the God and Father of our Lord Jesus Christ, the Father of compassion and the God of all comfort, who comforts us in all our troubles, so that we can comfort those in any trouble with the comfort

we ourselves receive from God. For just as we share abundantly in the sufferings of Christ, so also our comfort abounds through Christ.

You are my comfort and the One who brings me peace, Lord. You have said there will be sufferings in this life, but that Your comfort will be greater and even more abundant than any pain we feel. Thank You, God, for ministering to my heart and being my source of help and my reason to hope.

2 Corinthians 7:6-7
But God, who comforts the downcast, comforted us by the coming of Titus, and not only by his coming but also by the comfort you had given him. He told us about your longing for me, your deep sorrow, your ardent concern for me, so that my joy was greater than ever.

Father, bring to me those brothers and sisters who can provide additional comfort and assurance in this time of loss. May I recognize their acts of compassion and receive their gestures of love and affection. Don't let my mourning blind me to those You send to help me. Thank You for showing me Your love through the kindness of others.

Philippians 4:7
And the peace of God, which transcends all understanding, will guard your hearts and your minds in Christ Jesus.

Your peace is greater than my understanding, God. Therefore, I lay down my right to understand and comprehend what is taking place. Instead, I receive Your mantle of peace and protection over my mind and soul so that I simply rest in You. You are worthy of being trusted. Your love is greater than death and Your hope is greater than any loss. I trust in You, Lord!

1 Thessalonians 4:13-14
Brothers and sisters, we do not want you to be uninformed about those who sleep in death, so that you do not grieve like the rest of mankind, who have no hope. For we believe that Jesus died and rose again, and so we believe that God will bring with Jesus those who have fallen asleep in Him.

Thank You for life after death! Thank You for receiving my loved one and ushering them into Your glory. There is coming a day when we will see one another again and we will have all eternity to spend together! May this hope fill my soul and give me strength to continue on my own journey until You call me home.

Hebrews 13:15
Through Jesus, therefore, let us continually offer to God a sacrifice of praise - the fruit of lips that openly profess His name.

Jesus, it is a sacrifice to praise You in the midst of sorrow. And yet, it is an offering of which You are worthy. You already bore my pain and suffering on the cross and have provided me with victory over the spirit of death and despair. I glorify Your name and rejoice in the victory that is mine because of what You already sacrificed for me.

Revelation 21:4
He will wipe every tear from their eyes. There will be no more death or mourning or crying or pain, for the old order of things has passed away.

Thank You, Lord, that this life is only temporary and the pain of losing a loved one won't last forever. Thank You for telling us what we can look forward to in eternity. Your presence will be so overwhelming, that every loss and disappointment will melt away in the presence of Your perfect love.

NOTES

NOTES

Words for Loneliness

Genesis 2:18

The Lord God said, "It is not good for the man to be alone. I will make a helper suitable for him."

Father, You never designed for us to be alone. I know You want me to have companions and fellowship with others. Bring me those friends who can help me and inspire me to live better. Connect me with those who follow You like I do. Bring me the fellowship I need so that I can fulfill all Your purposes for my life.

Joshua 1:5

No one will be able to stand against you all the days of your life. As I was with Moses, so I will be with you; I will never leave you nor forsake you.

With You by my side, Lord, I have nothing to fear. When I walk with You, You defend me and guard me from the enemy's attempts to destroy me. You do not leave me to fend for myself, but take me every step of the way to where I need to go. Thank You for being my faithful Guide and Companion.

Psalms 16:8

I keep my eyes always on the Lord. With Him at my right hand, I will not be shaken.

Regardless of how I feel, I acknowledge Your presence, Lord. You are right by my side, walking with me every step of the way. I will not let my emotions rule me to shake my faith in You. Take my hand and lead me where You will.

Psalms 23:4

Even though I walk through the darkest valley, I will fear no evil, for You are with me; Your rod and Your staff, they comfort me.

You never leave me, God! Even in the darkest times, You are by my side and I have nothing to fear. Your Word is my source of hope and Your love brings me comfort. I will not give in to despair because You are bringing me through to something wonderful on the other side of the valley! I will follow Your lead and trust You to provide exactly what I need.

Psalms 27:10

Though my father and mother forsake me, the Lord will receive me.

Lord, You are my greatest source of comfort and my most faithful companion. Thank You for taking me in and watching over me when I feel alone. Even when my own family doesn't understand me and turns aside, You are always there. I receive Your unconditional love and rest in the assurance I am never destitute or forsaken.

Psalms 38:9

All my longings lie open before You, Lord; my sighing is not hidden from You.

You know my heartache, Lord, and my feelings of being alone. You know my longings to love and to be loved. You are not a God without feelings, but the Lover of my soul. I know You understand and are working to bring me to a place of life and fulfillment. My heart is in Your hands!

Psalms 68:5-6

A father to the fatherless, a defender of widows, is God in His holy dwelling. God sets the lonely in families, He leads out the prisoners with singing; but the rebellious live in a sun-scorched land.

Thank You, God, for providing me with a spiritual family that loves and cares for me. Lead me to those that I can connect with as brothers and sisters in the Lord. Help me to see Your provision and recognize those people You have brought into my life for this time. Lead me out of my isolation and bring me to a place of fellowship and joy.

Psalms 139:7-12

Where can I go from Your Spirit? Where can I flee from Your presence? If I go up to the heavens, You are there; if I make my bed in the depths, You are there. If I rise on the wings of the dawn, if I settle on the far side of the sea, even there Your hand will guide me, Your right hand will hold me fast. If I say, "Surely the darkness will hide me and the light become night around me," even the darkness will not be dark to You; the night will shine like the day, for darkness is as light to You.

No matter how I disappoint You; no matter how many mistakes I make; no matter how far I have fallen – You are always there! I can't go through anything without Your presence hovering over me! It doesn't matter what I do or say, You are always with me and fighting for my deliverance and freedom. Thank You, Lord, for Your unfailing love and unending presence in my life.

Psalms 147:3
He heals the brokenhearted and binds up their wounds.

You are the Healer of my heart, Lord. Take these feelings of loneliness and grief and breathe life into my soul. My heart is hurting, and I ask You to come and bring wholeness to my thoughts and emotions. You alone know what I truly need to move forward. I place my hope and my trust in Your care and Your ability to bring me joy once again.

Proverbs 18:24
One who has unreliable friends soon comes to ruin, but there is a friend who sticks closer than a brother.

Forgive me, Lord, if I have placed more hope in my friends than in You. I know that people will let me down, but You never will. Regardless of what others say or do, I know You will stick with me and work with me. Thank You for being a faithful friend when I have no other. Thank You for believing the best in me and not giving up on me. With Your help, I am going to make it!

Matthew 11:28-30
Come to me, all you who are weary and burdened, and I will give you rest. Take My yoke upon you and learn from Me, for I am gentle and humble in heart, and you will find rest for your souls. For My yoke is easy and My burden is light.

When I feel overwhelmed with doubts and fears, You offer me rest and hope. Thank You for this exchange, Lord! I now give You this weight I am carrying. I give You my heartaches and concerns. I do not want to live with this burden of hopelessness! I now trade it in for Your grace and Your peace that will lift me above the darkness and bring me to the light. I receive Your mantle of rest and walk forward with confidence in Your plans to bring me through.

Luke 5:16
But Jesus often withdrew to lonely places and prayed.

Jesus, You know what it is to be lonely. You know what it's like to feel like no one truly understands. And yet, You always drew close to Your Father in prayer. Remind me to do the same. Draw me by Your Spirit to pour out my heart and be real with You. Thank You for the comfort that comes when we spend time in sweet and intimate fellowship with each other.

John 16:32-33
A time is coming and in fact has come when you will be scattered, each to your own home. You will leave Me all alone. Yet I am not alone, for My Father is with Me. I have told you these things, so that in Me you may have peace. In this world you will have trouble. But take heart! I have overcome the world.

Even Your friends left You, Jesus. When You needed them the most, they all ran away. And yet, You knew that You were not alone. Just as Your Father stood by Your side and gave You victory over Your enemies, so I know the Father is with me. I receive His peace and the assurance that all of heaven is working on my behalf.

Romans 8:38-39
For I am convinced that neither death nor life, neither angels nor demons, neither the present nor the future, nor any powers, neither height nor depth, nor anything else in all creation, will be able to separate us from the love of God that is in Christ Jesus our Lord.

Regardless of what the enemy does to make me feel abandoned and alone, You are here and Your love is greater than his lies. Nothing can separate me from You! May Your presence overshadow any pain and override any attack from my adversary. I am never alone and Your love will bring me through!

2 Corinthians 1:3-4

Praise be to the God and Father of our Lord Jesus Christ, the Father of compassion and the God of all comfort, who comforts us in all our troubles, so that we can comfort those in any trouble with the comfort we ourselves receive from God.

You are the God of comfort and compassion. Come and reach deep into my soul and address the needs of my heart. I know our fellowship together will fill me and empower me to move forward. Thank You for always being there and on call 24-7! I can always count on You to listen and empathize with my concerns. Help me to receive Your comfort and be strengthened in my journey.

2 Timothy 4:16-17

At my first defense, no one came to my support, but everyone deserted me. May it not be held against them. But the Lord stood at my side and gave me strength, so that through me the message might be fully proclaimed and all the Gentiles might hear it. And I was delivered from the lion's mouth.

Even when others desert me and I am standing alone, You Lord are by my side! You give me strength when all others fail. I will not resent those who have abandoned me and not defended my cause. I will not be burdened with offense against others. Forgive them, Lord. I place my hope and trust in You to deliver me out of my trials and bring me to a place of joy and fullness.

1 John 4:13-16a

This is how we know that we live in Him and He in us: He has given us of His Spirit. And we have seen and testify that the Father has sent His Son to be the Savior of the world. If anyone acknowledges that Jesus is the Son of God, God lives in them and they in God. And so we know and rely on the love God has for us.

Thank You for Your Holy Spirit that testifies to Your presence in my life. Thank You that, by Your Spirit, I can be assured of Your love for me and Your plans for my life. Fill me again with the awareness of Your love and concern that will dispel any doubt that You are here.

1 John 4:18

There is no fear in love. But perfect love drives out fear, because fear has to do with punishment. The one who fears is not made perfect in love.

Lord, I acknowledge that I have been afraid of being alone. I know this is a lie from the enemy. Forgive me for listening to his lies more than Your truth. Come and sanctify my mind and heart to know Your perfect love that casts out every fear. I want to know the reality of Your love that transcends my own understanding and empowers me to live with greater hope for my future.

NOTES

NOTES

WORDS FOR ADDICTIONS

Proverbs 6:27-28

Can a man scoop fire into his lap without his clothes being burned? Can a man walk on hot coals without his feet being scorched?

Forgive me, Lord, for my presumption in thinking I'm strong enough on my own to withstand temptation. Forgive me for any arrogant attitude that says "I can handle this" when I can't. Stop me when I start playing with fire. Remind me of how much I need Your help so I don't get burned.

Proverbs 20:1

Wine is a mocker and beer a brawler; whoever is led astray by them is not wise.

Lord, addictions only make people look foolish. When serving an appetite of the flesh, it only opens the door to the enemy's influence and destructive patterns. Give me a heart of wisdom to remind me of these traps so I can avoid them. Give me the grace to make wise choices that will bring life and truth, both to myself and to those around me.

Proverbs 23:20-21

Do not join those who drink too much wine or gorge themselves on meat, for drunkards and gluttons become poor, and drowsiness clothes them in rags.

Lord, I desire to be rich in the fruit of the Spirit and works of righteousness, not in deeds of the flesh. Thank You for reminding me that to give in to addiction is to invite a spirit of poverty into my life and make me spiritually sleepy. Keep me from falling into this trap. I choose to live by Your Spirit that brings me to a place of abundance and fruitfulness.

John 8:36

So, if the Son sets you free, you will be free indeed.

It's You, Jesus, that can truly set me free! No one else can remove these temptations and free me from the prison of addiction. I desire to be totally free and know the fullness of Your love and grace. Keep working in my life to deliver me and set me on a course filled with promise and hope for the future.

Romans 5:3-5

Not only so, but we also glory in our sufferings, because we know that suffering produces perseverance; perseverance, character; and character, hope. And hope does not put us to shame, because God's love has been poured out into our hearts through the Holy Spirit, who has been given to us.

Even though this journey is hard, I know it is producing good things! Lord, as I stay faithful in overcoming my weaknesses, I know You are building in my life qualities and characteristics that I need. Thank You for wanting me to be strong and filled with perseverance, hope, and love. Thank You for using these trials and temptations as tools for building me up and making me more like You.

Romans 7:21-25a

So I find this law at work: Although I want to do good, evil is right there with me. For in my inner being I delight in God's law; but I see another law at work in me, waging war against the law of my mind and making me a prisoner of the law of sin at work within me. What a wretched man I am! Who will rescue me from this body that is subject to death? Thanks be to God, who delivers me through Jesus Christ our Lord!

Lord, I am at war with myself! I want to do the right thing, but my flesh keeps vying for control. Holy Spirit, I yield to You and ask You to come and give me the power to say "No" to my flesh and "Yes" to Your Spirit. Thank You, Jesus, for providing the way out of this war for my soul. I place this issue at the foot of the cross and ask for Your resurrection life to fill me and empower me to sin no more. May my life be a testimony and a demonstration of a life set free.

Romans 13:14
Rather, clothe yourselves with the Lord Jesus Christ, and do not think about how to gratify the desires of the flesh.

Holy Spirit, stop me when I start daydreaming and thinking of how I can feed my addiction. Stop me when my thoughts wander and I start giving room to the devil. Bring Your Words of life to my mind so I can be renewed in my purpose and strengthened in my resolve.

1 Corinthians 10:13
No temptation has overtaken you except what is common to mankind. And God is faithful; He will not let you be tempted beyond what you can bear. But when you are tempted, He will also provide a way out so that you can endure it.

Thank You, Lord, for the power of Your Spirit that enables and empowers me to turn away from temptations. I know this is a choice that I make as I draw from the well of Your Spirit. Remind me of the negative consequences when I follow my flesh so that I will turn to You. Give me the strength to say "No" and to see the better outcome by doing things Your way.

1 Corinthians 15:33-34a
Do not be misled: "Bad company corrupts good character." Come back to your senses as you ought and stop sinning; for there are some who are ignorant of God.

Lord, help me to choose my friends wisely. Show me those associations in my life that are leading me astray and weakening my faith. Help me to walk away from those who are leading me down a wrong path. Surround me with friends who will love me enough to tell me the truth when I need to hear it. Bring people into my life who can help me overcome my weaknesses and strengthen my resolve to follow after You.

Galatians 5:16-18
So I say, walk by the Spirit, and you will not gratify the desires of the flesh. For the flesh desires what is contrary to the Spirit, and the Spirit what is contrary to the flesh. They are in conflict with each other, so that

you are not to do whatever you want. But if you are led by the Spirit, you are not under the law.

Thank You, Holy Spirit, for giving me the power to walk in freedom! I know I cannot overcome my addiction through my own willpower. It is only when I am filled with Your Spirit and walk in Your ways that I can make the right choices. I will follow Your lead, knowing that You always direct me away from trouble and onto paths that take me to safety, freedom, and purpose.

Ephesians 4:26-27

In your anger do not sin. Do not let the sun go down while you are still angry, and do not give the devil a foothold.

Lord, forgive me for placing myself in situations where I know I will be tempted. Alert me ahead of time to avoid places and people that will drag me down instead of lift me up. Help me to make wise choices that will bring me life and purpose instead of guilt and shame. Help me stay positive in this process and to keep a clean heart before You.

Ephesians 6:11

Put on the full armor of God, so that you can take your stand against the devil's schemes.

Your Word and Your truth are powerful weapons against temptation! Help me to start each day in Your Word so that I can have a buffer against the enemy's plans. May Your Word be my shield and my protection as I overcome my weakness and renew my mind. Teach me Your ways so I can stand against the schemes of the devil and be victorious in my journey to freedom.

2 Timothy 1:7

For the Spirit God gave us does not make us timid, but gives us power, love, and self-discipline.

Holy Spirit, I need the fruit of self-control! I know this is different than human willpower, so I submit to You and ask You to fill me with power, love, and self-discipline. Enable me to make good choices. Empower me to enjoy this journey of freedom and closing the door to those habits that only bring grief and hardship. Thank You for working in my life and empowering me to do what's right!

James 1:12
Blessed is the one who perseveres under trial because, having stood the test, that person will receive the crown of life that the Lord has promised to those who love Him.

I want to pass this test, Lord, and receive Your rewards! Remind me of the blessing of perseverance and the favor that comes from obedience. Thank You for empowering me by Your Spirit to stay faithful to Your ways. My desire is to please You and love You more fully. Help me to do this, Lord!

James 4:7,8,10
Submit yourselves, then, to God. Resist the devil, and he will flee from you. Come near to God and He will come near to you. Wash your hands, you sinners, and purify your hearts, you double-minded...Humble yourselves before the Lord, and He will lift you up.

I am not the lord of my life, but You are, God! Forgive me for thinking I can do what I want and still serve You. Cleanse my thinking so that my desires will be pure and my choices honorable to You. I know I cannot resist temptation on my own, so I submit myself to Your authority and will do what You say. Where the enemy's lures are always destructive, Your ways always bring life, honor, and peace!

1 Peter 2:11-12
Dear friends, I urge you, as foreigners and exiles, to abstain from sinful desires, which wage war against your soul. Live such good lives among the pagans that, though they accuse you of doing wrong, they may see your good deeds and glorify God on the day He visits us.

Lord, I know that temptations of the flesh wreak havoc in my soul and mind. I do not want this struggle to negatively impact my witness to others. Help me to make the right choices so that those who watch me can see Your power at work. Help me overcome this issue so that Your blessing can be upon my life and I can lead others to Your throne of grace.

1 Peter 5:8-9

Be alert and of sober mind. Your enemy the devil prowls around like a roaring lion looking for someone to devour. Resist him, standing firm in the faith, because you know that the family of believers throughout the world is undergoing the same kind of sufferings.

Open my eyes, Holy Spirit, to see how the devil is playing with me! Remove any filters from my eyes that prevent me from seeing his ploys and schemes to destroy me. Show me the poison that is connected to my addiction so that I will be repulsed instead of tempted. Stir my faith in You as I resist the enemy and run to You for help.

2 Peter 2:19

They promise them freedom, while they themselves are slaves of depravity - for "people are slaves to whatever has mastered them."

Lord, I do not want to be a slave to sin or addiction! Thank You for this reality check that whatever controls me is my master. Do not let my flesh master me! Come, Holy Spirit, and fill me with Your presence and power so I can expel this taskmaster from my life that seeks to steal, kill, and destroy me. I am Yours alone and choose You as my Master and my Lord.

1 John 2:16-17

For everything in the world - the lust of the flesh, the lust of the eyes, and the pride of life - comes not from the Father but from the world. The world and its desires pass away, but whoever does the will of God lives forever.

When temptations come, Lord, remind me of what's going to last. Remind me that any temporary fleshly pursuit is but smoke and mirrors and a trap of the enemy. I want my choices and my journey to matter for eternity. I want to choose that which is spiritually alive and is an investment into my future. Sanctify my passions and desires to please You above all else.

NOTES

NOTES

Words for Overcoming Fear

Joshua 24:14

Now fear the Lord and serve Him with all faithfulness. Throw away the gods your ancestors worshiped beyond the Euphrates River and in Egypt, and serve the Lord.

Lord, show me anything from my past that has taken the place of Your supremacy in my life. Because I desire to walk in the fear of the Lord, remove any idols or false securities that have taken Your place. As You reveal these things, I place them at Your feet and renounce their place in my life. I know that as I walk in the fear of the Lord, every other fear will bow.

2 Chronicles 20:15b

This is what the Lord says to you: "Do not be afraid or discouraged because of this vast army. For the battle is not yours, but God's."

Thank You, Lord, that this battle is not up to me! You have asked me to stand and to give You glory, and You will defend Your own name. I will not fear the size of my problem or the number of my opponents. I place my trust in Your power to defeat my enemies and deal with these battles. In the meantime, I will stand in faith, knowing that You are in charge and will have the final word.

2 Chronicles 32:7-8a

Be strong and courageous. Do not be afraid or discouraged because of the king of Assyria and the vast army with him, for there is a greater power with us than with him. With him is only the arm of flesh, but with us is the Lord our God to help us and to fight our battles.

Hallelujah! Regardless of the seeming opposition in my life, Your power is greater than any army from hell. Though the enemy fights from the flesh, You empower me to walk in the power of Your Spirit. Through You I can overcome all the attacks of the enemy. I will press forward, knowing that Your power is greater and our victory is assured.

Job 3:25-26

What I feared has come upon me; what I dreaded has happened to me. I have no peace, no quietness; I have no rest, but only turmoil.

Lord, I do not want to open a door to the enemy through my fears. Show me how to transform my thinking so that I am not bound to any fear about my life or those I care about. Give me a fresh revelation of Your perfect love that casts out every other fear and establishes me in Your peace.

Psalms 27:1

The Lord is my light and my salvation - whom shall I fear? The Lord is the stronghold of my life - of whom shall I be afraid?

I declare that You are my light and my salvation and there is no other greater than You. You hide me in a fortress of Your presence and keep me safe from predators. Forgive me for being fearful of those who stand no chance against You.

Psalms 34:9-10

Fear the Lord, you His holy people, for those who fear Him lack nothing. The lions may grow weak and hungry, but those who seek the Lord lack no good thing.

I will walk in the fear of the Lord and not let any other fear pervade my thinking. For You are my Provider and the source of all that is good in my life. I rest in Your provision and do not fear any supposed lack. You will provide all that I need as I trust in You.

Psalms 73:26

My flesh and my heart may fail, but God is the strength of my heart and my portion forever.

Praise God! Even when I miss it and my emotions overwhelm me, You still prevail! I don't have to trust in my own ability to be steadfast. You stand in the gap for me and give me what I don't have on my own. Thank You for being the strength in my weakness and the peace in my storm. You are amazing, and I rest in You!

Proverbs 1:32-33

For the waywardness of the simple will kill them, and the complacency of fools will destroy them; but whoever listens to Me will live in safety and be at ease, without fear of harm.

Make me more alert to Your working in my life, Lord. Forgive me for any complacency or apathy in my life or unwillingness to search Your heart. I desire to go deeper with You to understand Your ways more fully. Knowing Your will for my life can keep fear at a distance as I learn to hear Your voice and trust Your directions.

Proverbs 29:25

Fear of man will prove to be a snare, but whoever trusts in the Lord is kept safe.

Forgive me, Lord, for being afraid of what others do or say. Forgive me for trying to live up to the expectations of others and not looking to You for my purpose and meaning. I don't want to walk in the fear of man, but choose to follow You in reverential awe and childlike wonder. You alone are worthy of my focus and attention.

Ecclesiastes 12:13

Now all has been heard; here is the conclusion of the matter: Fear God and keep His commandments, for this is the duty of all mankind.

Show me any way in which I have not followed Your commands and removed Your protection and blessing from my life. You are a holy God and no spirit of fear is greater than You. Teach me to walk in all Your ways so that I can receive Your perfect peace and unwavering confidence in Your goodness.

Isaiah 8:13

The Lord Almighty is the One you are to regard as holy, He is the One you are to fear, He is the One you are to dread.

Father, show me the fears in my life that are keeping me in bondage. Transform my thinking so that I see how small those fears are in comparison to Your holiness and perfect love. Teach me to walk in the reality of Your greatness and the foolishness of fretting over things I cannot control. You are a holy God and Your word will stand, regardless of those who think otherwise.

Isaiah 26:3
You will keep in perfect peace those whose minds are steadfast, because they trust in You.

I receive Your perfect peace, Lord, because I choose to trust in You. Your promise is to give me Your peace according to my faith. Help me to grow my faith by establishing Your word in my life and applying it in every situation. May I overcome every fear that challenges my faith and bear the fruit of Your peace.

Isaiah 32:17
The fruit of that righteousness will be peace; its effect will be quietness and confidence forever.

You say that the fruit of righteousness is peace. Search my heart to see if there is anything that is not right with You or with others in my life that has opened a door to fear. I want to wear the robe of righteousness and walk in absolute confidence of Your supremacy in my life. Thank You for the fruit of righteousness that guards me from anxiety and doubt.

Isaiah 41:10
So do not fear, for I am with you; do not be dismayed, for I am your God. I will strengthen you and help you; I will uphold you with My righteous right hand.

I rest in Your hands, Lord. I know You are with me and are carrying me through this process. Give me the strength I need to persevere and to not give in to doubts or apprehension. Remind me of Your unfailing love and constant watchful presence over my life.

Isaiah 54:10
"Though the mountains be shaken and the hills be removed, yet My unfailing love for you will not be shaken nor My covenant of peace be removed," says the Lord who has compassion on you.

Even when my life is totally shaken and that which I have trusted in is removed, You are still there holding me up! Thank You for having such a tender heart towards me and carrying me when everything else falls apart. I receive Your peace, regardless of the circumstances, and rest in Your unfailing love. You are the anchor of my soul.

Jeremiah 32:27

I am the Lord, the God of all mankind. Is anything too hard for Me?

Transform my thinking, Lord, so that I do not give in to doubt or unbelief. I know nothing is too difficult for You and will fix my thoughts on what You alone can do. Regardless of how things look in the natural, I believe that You are the God of the impossible! Thank You for overcoming!

Luke 12:32

Do not be afraid, little flock, for your Father has been pleased to give you the kingdom.

I will not be afraid of not having enough. You say it is Your pleasure to give me all that I need. The Kingdom of God is within me and every resource I need to succeed is available because I am Yours. Show me how to steward what You have given me so that it will grow and flourish and be a blessing to many.

John 14:27

Peace I leave with you; My peace I give you. I do not give to you as the world gives. Do not let your hearts be troubled and do not be afraid.

I receive Your peace, Lord. Draw me into Your presence where truth resides. Forgive me for being anxious and not trusting in You. Keep me from being a sponge and soaking up the fears of others around me. Alert me when I give way to worldly thinking that is void of power to overcome. You are my Prince of Peace and I submit my worries and doubts to You.

John 14:30

I will not say much more to you, for the prince of this world is coming. He has no hold over Me.

Show me, Lord, if there is anything the devil is holding over my head. Search my heart so I can be cleansed of any hidden offense or sin that is opening a door to fear. I want to say as Jesus did that the devil has no hold over me!

Romans 8:6

The mind governed by the flesh is death, but the mind governed by the Spirit is life and peace.

Teach me to govern my own thoughts, Lord, so I don't give room to a spirit of fear or death. Help me renew my thinking so that I am fully convinced of Your power and Your purpose. I yield any worries to the Spirit of peace and ask You to transform my mind to think like You.

Romans 8:15

The Spirit you received does not make you slaves, so that you live in fear again; rather, the Spirit you received brought about your adoption to sonship. And by Him we cry, "Abba, Father."

I am not a slave to fear, but a child of God! My Heavenly Father looks after me and is passionate about my safety and security. Thank You, Father, for calling me Your own and for watching over my life. Thank You for setting me free from the bondage of fear.

2 Thessalonians 3:3

But the Lord is faithful, and He will strengthen you and protect you from the evil one.

You are always faithful, God, to not only protect me from the evil one, but to strengthen my faith and courage. Renew my trust in You and remind me of Your words of life that will overcome my doubts and worries. Thank You for being my constant source of peace and security.

2 Timothy 1:7 (ESV)

For God gave us a spirit not of fear, but of power and love and self-control.

I choose to walk in the Spirit from which comes power, love, and a sound mind. I will not listen to any voice that incites fear, but rather submit my mind, will, and emotions to the Spirit of God who alone brings me peace. Thank You, Lord, for showing me the difference.

Hebrews 2:14-15

Since the children have flesh and blood, He too shared in their humanity so that by His death He might break the power of him who holds the power of death - that is, the devil - and free those who all their lives were held in slavery by their fear of death.

Thank You, Lord, for freeing me from a fear of death! By Your work on the cross, You have broken any fear of death and I can look forward to the future! You carry resurrection life, not only for eternal life, but for abundant life here and now. I will not allow the devil to rob me of my hope and my future. Thank You for Your freedom!

1 Peter 3:14

But even if you should suffer for what is right, you are blessed. "Do not fear their threats; do not be frightened."

You say I am blessed when I trust in You and do the right thing. Therefore I will not fear the threats and accusations that come against me. I will not be frightened by those who do not understand or comprehend Your goodness. Thank You for filling me with the courage to be bold in my faith and not fearful of those who have yet to understand who You really are.

1 John 4:18

There is no fear in love. But perfect love drives out fear, because fear has to do with punishment. The one who fears is not made perfect in love.

I want to know Your perfect love, Father! I acknowledge that some of my fear is the result of not fully knowing the extent or power of Your love for me. Open my eyes to see Your passion for me and Your determination to see me succeed. Sanctify my faith so that I can rest in Your peace and not be afraid of the future.

NOTES

WORDS FOR HOPE DEFERRED

Job 6:10

Then I would still have this consolation - my joy in unrelenting pain - that I had not denied the words of the Holy One.

Lord, may I not add to my restlessness by denying Your Word. You have established Your truth and settled Your purposes which are always good. I declare that I will not waver in my faith just because circumstances are painful. You have promised to bring joy out of the ashes, so I trust in You as I wait to see the fulfillment of Your Word.

Psalms 1:1-3

Blessed is the one who does not walk in step with the wicked or stand in the way that sinners take or sit in the company of mockers, but whose delight is in the law of the Lord, and who meditates on His law day and night. That person is like a tree planted by streams of water, which yields its fruit in season and whose leaf does not wither - whatever they do prospers.

Forgive me, Lord, when I have listened to the opinions of others who don't even know You or serve You. Forgive me for being swayed by circumstances instead of Your Word. I choose to meditate on Your words that bring me life and hope. Thank You for fruit that will come from listening to You.

Psalms 30:5

For His anger lasts only a moment, but His favor lasts a lifetime; weeping may stay for the night, but rejoicing comes in the morning.

Even when I disappoint You, Lord, Your love for me is stronger! I know Your anger is directed towards my adversary and not towards me. As I follow Your heart and submit to Your plans, Your unconditional love and favor for me is going to be seen. Even though I shed tears in the moment, You have joy waiting for me around the next bend. You will show me just how good You are and how much You have been working on my behalf. Thank You for Your goodness, Lord!

Psalms 34:17-18

The righteous cry out, and the Lord hears them; He delivers them from all their troubles. The Lord is close to the brokenhearted and saves those who are crushed in spirit.

Lord, You promise to deliver me out of ALL my troubles! Thank You for being close to me and never leaving my side. Come and heal my broken heart and crushed spirit. Fill me again with Your Holy Spirit so that I may hope for the days to come.

Psalms 40:2-3

He lifted me out of the slimy pit, out of the mud and mire; He set my feet on a rock and gave me a firm place to stand. He put a new song in my mouth, a hymn of praise to our God. Many will see and fear the Lord and put their trust in Him.

When my steps are faltering and I am unsure of what to believe, Lord, pick me up and set me upon the Rock of my salvation. Remind me of Your Word and Your unchanging truths. Give me a fresh perspective of my life and give me a new song to sing. Replace any thoughts of despair with words of praise. Thank You for showing me the good things You have in store for me!

Psalms 42:11

Why, my soul, are you downcast? Why so disturbed within me? Put your hope in God, for I will yet praise Him, my Savior and my God.

I speak to my soul and my emotions to get in line with God's heart and purposes! I declare over my mind, will, and emotions to be perfectly united with the Father's love, the Spirit's peace, and the mind of Christ. I will not yield to my flesh or the enemy's lies. I place my hope in God for He alone is my Savior and Redeemer.

Psalms 94:18-19

When I said, "My foot is slipping," Your unfailing love, Lord, supported me. When anxiety was great within me, Your consolation brought me joy.

Thank You, Lord, that when everyone and everything else fails me, You are still there. Thank You for Your unconditional love and never-ending support. I lean into Your presence and listen for Your voice which can bring me consolation and joy.

Psalms 143:7-8

Answer me quickly, Lord; my spirit fails. Do not hide Your face from me or I will be like those who go down to the pit. Let the morning bring me word of Your unfailing love, for I have put my trust in You. Show me the way I should go, for to You I entrust my life.

Show me, again, Lord, how much You are working on my behalf. I need a confirmation of Your involvement and Your intention to answer my pleas for help. Bring me songs to sing and scriptures to speak that will keep my heart focused on Your love and Your goodness. Establish my steps so that I will keep going in the right direction and end up where You want me.

Proverbs 12:25

Anxiety weighs down the heart, but a kind word cheers it up.

Lord, bring me a word today that will cheer me up! Speak through a friend or unexpected conversation and let me know You are with me. Use my circumstances to reveal Your purposes and give me greater understanding in Your plans. I will not be weighed down by worry, but will look for Your activity throughout my day. Thank You for revealing Yourself to me.

Proverbs 13:12

Hope deferred makes the heart sick, but a longing fulfilled is a tree of life.

Lord, keep me from making myself sick because of disappointment. Alert me when I let my negative emotions wreak havoc with my physical health. Reveal to me any anger or bitterness that is causing this anxiety so I can lay them down and let You be God. I declare that You are a good God and are always faithful to fulfill Your promises.

Isaiah 40:31

But those who hope in the Lord will renew their strength. They will soar on wings like eagles; they will run and not grow weary, they will walk and not be faint.

I will wait on You, Lord, because You alone know what is best for me. Help me to see what You see. Lift me high above the confusion and disappointment of my flesh and help me to soar with You from a heavenly perspective. May I see the joy set before me so I can continue my journey with renewed strength and hope for the future.

Matthew 11:28-30

Come to me, all you who are weary and burdened, and I will give you rest. Take My yoke upon you and learn from Me, for I am gentle and humble in heart, and you will find rest for your souls. For My yoke is easy and My burden is light.

Lord, I lay down my own ideas of what should happen and the need to control things. I yield my right to even understand what You're doing. It has become a yoke of oppression to me and it is not Your will. I release my cares to You and submit to Your way of doing things. I will not take back the reins, but will trust in Your perfect ability to work things out for my good and for Your glory. Thank You for taking charge of my future.

Luke 18:1

Then Jesus told His disciples a parable to show them that they should always pray and not give up.

Forgive me, Lord, when I have forgotten to pray. Remind me that it's not just the words I say, but the time spent with You that builds my faith and hope. Help me focus my prayers more about talking with You than simply reciting a list of needs. It is the daily fellowship with You that will build my faith and let me know I am not alone. Renew my heart as I draw close to Yours.

Romans 8:5-6

Those who live according to the flesh have their minds set on what the flesh desires; but those who live in accordance with the Spirit have their minds set on what the Spirit desires. The mind governed by the flesh is death, but the mind governed by the Spirit is life and peace.

Forgive me for allowing my flesh to rule instead of Your Spirit, Lord. Separate out those thoughts and emotions that are causing anxiety and distress so I can displace them with Your truth. Forgive me for thinking I know what is best. Help me to govern my own mind so that it dwells on Your love for me and Your desire to bless me. I renounce any spirit of death or depression that is trying to take hold and submit myself to the Spirit of life which brings me peace.

Romans 15:13
May the God of hope fill you with all joy and peace as you trust in Him, so that you may overflow with hope by the power of the Holy Spirit.

Come, Holy Spirit, and fill me with Your presence. I declare that my faith and hope are in Christ Jesus alone. Open my eyes to see Your goodness. I refuse to give room to ungodly beliefs or lies that are causing me turmoil and unrest. May the power of Your Spirit overshadow me with hope for the future and the anticipation of good things to come.

Philippians 4:8-9
Finally, brothers and sisters, whatever is true, whatever is noble, whatever is right, whatever is pure, whatever is lovely, whatever is admirable - if anything is excellent or praiseworthy - think about such things. Whatever you have learned or received or heard from me, or seen in me, put it into practice. And the God of peace will be with you.

I submit to You, Lord, all my negative thoughts and emotions that are dragging me down. I know they do not help me or build my faith in You. Open my eyes so that I can see the things You are doing and not focus merely on what I want. Forgive me for giving room to doubts and fears by letting my emotions rule. Cleanse my mind as I yield to the Spirit's direction and truth to lead me in paths of peace and rest.

Hebrews 6:18-20
God did this so that, by two unchangeable things in which it is impossible for God to lie, we who have fled to take hold of the hope set before us may be greatly encouraged. We have this hope as an anchor for the soul, firm and secure. It enters the inner sanctuary behind the curtain, where our forerunner, Jesus, has entered on our behalf. He has become a high priest forever, in the order of Melchizedek.

Thank You for reminding me, God, that You cannot lie! Your Word is always true and You are always faithful to fulfill it. Thank You for interceding on my behalf as my High Priest. Thank You for providing me victory because of what You did at the cross. Thank You for overcoming the spirits of hopelessness and depression and making way for my breakthroughs to come!

NOTES

NOTES

STRATEGIC SPIRITUAL BATTLES

WORDS FOR THE WAR ON THE MIND

Isaiah 26:3
You will keep in perfect peace those whose minds are steadfast, because they trust in You.

My trust is in You, Lord. I do not place my trust in man's ideas or opinions. Thank You for Your peace that shields me from false information and lies planted by the enemy. Help me to be steadfast and on my guard so that I will submit to Your truth which alone brings clarity and purpose.

Matthew 6:34
Therefore, do not worry about tomorrow, for tomorrow will worry about itself. Each day has enough trouble of its own.

Forgive me, Lord, when I allow my mind to be preoccupied with all kinds of "what if's!" I will not think on all the things that can go wrong, but rather put my trust in You to give me victory - one day at a time! Thank You for teaching me to trust You, little by little. Keep my mind fixed on Your good plans for my success.

Matthew 11:28-30
Come to Me, all you who are weary and burdened, and I will give you rest. Take My yoke upon you and learn from Me, for I am gentle and humble in heart, and you will find rest for your souls. For My yoke is easy and My burden is light.

I will not be distracted by the enemy's attempts to steer me off course and into fear. I refuse to take on an unnecessary burden for tomorrow. Father, I receive Your mantle of peace over my mind and soul. Teach me how to walk with a clarity of mind to recognize the enemy's attempts in stirring up trouble and dissension. Thank You for a sound mind!

Matthew 22:37
Jesus replied: "'Love the Lord your God with all your heart and with all your soul and with all your mind."

Jesus, forgive me for not realizing how powerful our minds are. You have told us to love You in our thinking. Show me how to train my mind unto righteousness. May I see my thoughts as a doorway to Your heart. May I show love to You in how I think and discern truth. May You be glorified through my thinking as I anchor my mind in Your Word.

Luke 21:13-15

And so you will bear testimony to Me. But make up your mind not to worry beforehand how you will defend yourselves. For I will give you words and wisdom that none of your adversaries will be able to resist or contradict.

Thank You, Lord, for giving me the words to say when challenged by Your enemies! Prepare me ahead of time so that I will be ready to take a stand and speak a right word without fear. Thank You for a clarity of mind and purpose that defeats the schemes of the enemy to disqualify or discredit me. Thank You for giving me a sharp mind that receives Your words and insights without hindrance.

John 14:27

Peace I leave with you; My peace I give you. I do not give to you as the world gives. Do not let your hearts be troubled and do not be afraid.

Lord, I will not place my hope in the world's reports and information concerning my future. I will not look to natural means for my peace of mind. Rather, I receive Your peace and presence that overrides every negative circumstance and brings hope and promise. You have already overcome the world! I trust in Your words more than in man's words.

Acts 4:32a

All the believers were one in heart and mind.

Holy Spirit, lead us as believers to Your truth so that we can be perfectly united with one mind and purpose. We know the great power and authority that comes from a oneness of mind and spirit. Empower us to do this to withstand the attacks against Your truth.

Romans 8:6
The mind governed by the flesh is death, but the mind governed by the Spirit is life and peace.

I will not allow my mind to be governed by my flesh or any evil influence. Alert me, Lord, to any thought or idea that seeks entrance into my mind that is destructive and opposed to Your will. Give me greater understanding in interpreting the things I see and hear so that I can know Your good and perfect plans. Holy Spirit, come and be the governor of my mind so that I can walk in the fullness of truth.

Romans 12:2
Do not conform to the pattern of this world but be transformed by the renewing of your mind. Then you will be able to test and approve what God's will is - His good, pleasing, and perfect will.

Lord, I will not conform to what the world tells me to believe. My mind belongs to You. Help me to know and apply Your Word in every situation so that I can think and respond like You. Give me proper discernment to know what You're doing so I can partner with You instead of the latest fad or shocking report. Thank You for Your truth that sets me free!

Romans 15:5-6
May the God who gives endurance and encouragement give you the same attitude of mind toward each other that Christ Jesus had, so that with one mind and one voice you may glorify the God and Father of our Lord Jesus Christ.

Holy Spirit, I pray for the body of Christ to be united in our perspective and one in our purpose. May our collective voice be heard because of the soundness of our minds and the power of Your truths. May we lay aside our differences and determine to defeat our enemies together so that You will be glorified.

1 Corinthians 1:30-31

It is because of Him that you are in Christ Jesus, who has become for us wisdom from God - that is, our righteousness, holiness, and redemption. Therefore, as it is written: "Let the one who boasts boast in the Lord."

Jesus, I receive Your wisdom and the righteousness that comes from obeying Your truth. I will not submit my mind or thoughts to those who oppose You and do not know You. I declare myself under the Lordship of Christ who alone can redeem any and every negative situation. You are the author of all that is true and good, and I place myself in Your care.

1 Corinthians 2:16

For, who has known the mind of the Lord so as to instruct Him? But we have the mind of Christ.

Thank You for giving me Your mind, Lord Jesus! Thank You for giving me access to Your heart, Your ways, Your thoughts, and Your truths. I do not have to depend on my own understanding or the opinions of others. I receive the ability to understand what You're doing through the power of Your Spirit. No adversary has access to this! Thank You for giving me this leverage over my enemies.

1 Corinthians 14:33a

For God is not a God of disorder but of peace.

In Jesus' name, I renounce the spirits of disorder and confusion and declare the peace of God over my life and over my household. Holy Spirit, come and cleanse my heart and mind from scattered thoughts and fragmented ideas that are being stirred up in the spiritual realms. I receive a sound mind that is clear and focused on Your purposes and Your presence. Prince of Peace, come and take up residence here!

2 Corinthians 10:4-5

The weapons we fight with are not the weapons of the world. On the contrary, they have divine power to demolish strongholds. We demolish arguments and every pretension that sets itself up against the knowledge of God, and we take captive every thought to make it obedient to Christ.

Holy Spirit, bring to my attention any and every thought and idea that is contrary to the Father's purpose. As You do, I lay them at the foot of the cross and declare Your victory and truth over them. I declare that Your purposes will prevail. I declare that every attempt to spread lies and untruths about the goodness of God and His plans for my future are null and void. The enemies of God must bow to the Spirit of Truth and submit to His plans for the days ahead!

Ephesians 4:22-24

You were taught, with regard to your former way of life, to put off your old self, which is being corrupted by its deceitful desires; to be made new in the attitude of your minds; and to put on the new self, created to be like God in true righteousness and holiness.

Lord, keep me from falling into the traps of the enemy and the traps of my old ways. Alert me when I begin to go my own way and miss You. Create in me new ways of looking at things through Your Word. I submit my mind to You and desire to be fresh in my thinking for the future. Thank You for renewing my thoughts and ideas so they can be lifegiving and fruitful for Your kingdom!

Philippians 2:2

Then make my joy complete by being like-minded, having the same love, being one in spirit and of one mind.

Holy Spirit, draw us as believers to Your truth so we can think like You. May our mutual love for the Lord bring us to a unity that is unmatched by any demonic agenda. Thank You for giving us clarity of purpose which empowers us to stand against the spirit of deception. Thank You for leading us together and showing us how to be a powerhouse for the Kingdom.

Philippians 4:6-7

Do not be anxious about anything, but in every situation, by prayer and petition, with thanksgiving, present your requests to God. And the peace of God, which transcends all understanding, will guard your hearts and your minds in Christ Jesus.

Forgive me, Lord, for giving in to worry. I come to share my heart with You now and all that concerns me. I declare my faith and trust in You to watch over me and work on my behalf. As I stand on Your promises for breakthrough, I ask for Your peace to wash over me. I choose to rest in Your ability to take care of the things that I can't.

Philippians 4:8-9

Finally, brothers and sisters, whatever is true, whatever is noble, whatever is right, whatever is pure, whatever is lovely, whatever is admirable - if anything is excellent or praiseworthy - think about such things. Whatever you have learned or received or heard from me or seen in me - put it into practice. And the God of peace will be with you.

I put aside those negative thoughts that are warring against my mind. Father, remind me of Your words that bring hope and purpose. Give me songs and scriptures that I can focus on to divert the enemy's attempts in causing anxiety. I receive Your thoughts and desires into my heart to direct my attention to the power of Your presence in all things.

Colossians 2:18-19

Do not let anyone who delights in false humility and the worship of angels disqualify you. Such a person also goes into great detail about what they have seen; they are puffed up with idle notions by their unspiritual mind. They have lost connection with the Head, from whom the whole body, supported and held together by its ligaments and sinews, grows as God causes it to grow.

Guard my heart and mind from counterfeit doctrines and corrupted beliefs. Give me a discernment, Lord, to see past the lies of the enemy and see the source of these delusions. Thank You for giving me the spiritual authority to overcome these ungodly systems of belief. Thank You for clarity of mind with which to recognize false ideologies and stand for the truth.

1 Timothy 6:3-5

If anyone teaches otherwise and does not agree to the sound instruction of our Lord Jesus Christ and to godly teaching, they are conceited and understand nothing. They have an unhealthy interest in controversies and quarrels about words that result in envy, strife, malicious talk, evil suspicions and constant friction between people of corrupt mind, who have been robbed of the truth and who think that godliness is a means to financial gain.

Lord, keep me alert to those who speak from a corrupt mind. Help me recognize thoughts and ideas that take away from Your truth and Your holiness. Give me sound instruction from Your Word so I can firmly stand and not be swayed by those who have no intention of following You.

2 Timothy 1:7 (NKJV)

For God has not given us a spirit of fear, but of power and of love and of a sound mind.

Thank You for giving me a sound mind. I refuse to give in to fear, for that is an evil spirit and I do not want to partner with it! I declare that Your power to bring clarity and truth is greater than any chaos and confusion. I declare that Your love is stronger than the enemy's attempts to steal my peace.

1 Peter 5:8-9

Be alert and of sober mind. Your enemy the devil prowls around like a roaring lion looking for someone to devour. Resist him, standing firm in the faith, because you know that the family of believers throughout the world is undergoing the same kind of sufferings.

Thank You for alerting me to the devil's schemes, Lord! Thank You for the power to resist his attempts at robbing my peace and soundness of mind. I will stay fixed on Your Word and not allow doubts and confusion to cloud my thinking or stir anxiety in my heart. I pray for those around me to also stay on the alert so that we can be united in purpose and fixed in our faith.

NOTES

Words for a God-centered Identity

Genesis 1:27
So God created mankind in His own image, in the image of God He created them; male and female He created them.

Father, thank You for making us into Your likeness. Thank You for Your perfect design from the very beginning. You have made us uniquely male and female to reflect all that Your nature and character possesses. Show me the fulness of Your beauty through my own gender as male or female.

Psalms 139:14-16
I praise You because I am fearfully and wonderfully made; Your works are wonderful; I know that full well. My frame was not hidden from You when I was made in the secret place, when I was woven together in the depths of the earth. Your eyes saw my unformed body; all the days ordained for me were written in Your book before one of them came to be.

Lord, You do not make mistakes or misfits! To criticize myself or complain about how You created me suggests You did it wrong. Forgive me for not recognizing the works of Your hands as good and beautiful. Not only have You created me as a specific expression of Your love and goodness, You already planned for me to be blessed and be a blessing. Show me what's in my book so that I can walk Your paths with great expectancy for my future!

Isaiah 43:1
But now, this is what the Lord says - He who created you, Jacob, He who formed you, Israel: "Do not fear, for I have redeemed you; I have summoned you by name; you are mine."

I do not belong to anyone else but You, Lord. I am not a slave to some task master or lesser god that tells me to bow to their agenda. I will not fear anyone who tells me it's impossible to please You. You have already called me by name and declared that I am Yours. Thank You for redeeming my life and giving me a reason to live.

Jeremiah 1:5a

Before I formed you in the womb I knew you, before you were born, I set you apart.

You've known all along exactly who You created me to be and called it good! You have already marked me with a destiny and a purpose to fulfill. You formed me with all the attributes and characteristics that were needed to succeed in this life and to be a blessing to others. Thank You for creating me and setting me apart as Your own.

Jeremiah 29:11-13

"For I know the plans I have for you," declares the Lord, "plans to prosper you and not to harm you, plans to give you hope and a future. Then you will call on Me and come and pray to Me, and I will listen to you. You will seek Me and find Me when you seek Me with all your heart."

Thank You for already planning my future, God, and giving me a reason to hope. Help me to see Your plans and walk in the path You have set out for me. I call upon You, now, to show me the steps to take so that I can rightly discern Your heart. I'm looking for You! Help me to see where You are taking me and follow with joy and anticipation.

John 1:12

Yet to all who did receive Him, to those who believed in His name, He gave the right to become children of God.

I receive You, Lord. I believe in You and Your plans for my life. I will not listen to any voice that tells me I don't belong. You have given me the right to be called Your child, simply because I said "Yes!"

John 15:14-17

You are My friends if you do what I command. I no longer call you servants, because a servant does not know his master's business. Instead, I have called you friends, for everything that I learned from My Father I have made known to you. You did not choose Me, but I chose you and appointed you so that you might go and bear fruit - fruit that will last - and so that whatever you ask in My name the Father will give you.

You picked me, Jesus! You call me Your friend and have chosen me to do a special work. Thank You for sharing Your heart and revealing the Father's purpose for me. I choose to listen and follow Your lead because You alone will enable me to succeed and do great things in Your name.

Romans 8:14-16

For those who are led by the Spirit of God are the children of God. The Spirit you received does not make you slaves, so that you live in fear again; rather, the Spirit you received brought about your adoption to sonship. And by Him we cry, "Abba, Father." The Spirit Himself testifies with our spirit that we are God's children.

I declare that I am led by the Spirit of God and not my flesh. I will not give in to fears or doubts, but walk by the Spirit who gives me life, hope, and purpose. You are my Father and I belong to a Kingdom that's not of this world. Thank You, Lord, for empowering me to rise above my fears and walk in freedom from my past.

1 Corinthians 6:17-18

But whoever is united with the Lord is one with Him in spirit. Flee from sexual immorality. All other sins a person commits are outside the body, but whoever sins sexually, sins against their own body.

In making You Lord of my life, we are one. I am united with You in body, soul, and spirit. I will not defile this oneness by committing any sexual sin that will destroy our union. Forgive me, Lord, when I have failed in this in either thought or action. I want to keep our relationship pure and holy. Help me stand against any temptation or stronghold that seeks to pervert our relationship. I belong to You and long to know You more than anything or anyone else.

1 Corinthians 6:19-20

Do you not know that your bodies are temples of the Holy Spirit, who is in you, whom you have received from God? You are not your own; you were bought at a price. Therefore, honor God with your bodies.

Lord, You have called my body Your temple. It is Your Spirit that resides within me and gives me life from within. I will take care of this temple and honor You in the choices I make concerning its health and wellbeing. This body does not belong to me, but to You. You created and formed it and I delight in caring for it so I can reflect the best of who You are.

2 Corinthians 1:21-22

Now it is God who makes both us and you stand firm in Christ. He anointed us, set His seal of ownership on us, and put His Spirit in our hearts as a deposit, guaranteeing what is to come.

Thank You for Your Spirit that has marked me and sealed me with hope and promise! Come and fill me with an even greater awareness of Your presence and Your purpose for my life. When I look to You, I have a guarantee that Holy Spirit will work in me to live, and move, and have my being. What I have known of Your Spirit's working up to this point is only a taste of what's to come!

2 Corinthians 5:17

Therefore, if anyone is in Christ, the new creation has come: The old has gone, the new is here!

Transform me, Lord! It doesn't matter what the old version of me looks like. When I met You, You gave me the grace and power to change from the inside out into a completely new and beautiful person. I want to be filled with Your Spirit's power to make this exchange and become everything that You have intended me to be.

Galatians 2:20

I have been crucified with Christ and I no longer live, but Christ lives in me. The life I now live in the body, I live by faith in the Son of God, who loved me and gave Himself for me.

It doesn't matter how I want to live my life because I have died to my flesh. As a follower of Christ, I have laid down my life and surrendered any personal wishes and traded them for the heart and mind of Christ. Come and sanctify my longings and desires, Lord, so that You can live through me without any interference from my flesh!

Ephesians 1:4-6

For He chose us in Him before the creation of the world to be holy and blameless in His sight. In love He predestined us for adoption to sonship through Jesus Christ, in accordance with His pleasure and will - to the praise of His glorious grace, which He has freely given us in the One He loves.

Lord, You declare it is possible to be holy and blameless in Your sight. Because of what You did for me on the cross, I can live free from shame or guilt because I am Your child. Thank You for nailing all my failures to the cross and forever declaring them null and void!

Ephesians 2:10

For we are God's handiwork, created in Christ Jesus to do good works, which God prepared in advance for us to do.

You have placed inside of me the desire to do Your will. You have already determined things for me to do, places to go, and people to meet. You have given me all the tools I need to make a difference in the world and demonstrate who You are to those around me. Lord, help me to be faithful to what You have created me to do. Thank You for what's ahead!

Ephesians 4:22-24

You were taught, with regard to your former way of life, to put off your old self, which is being corrupted by its deceitful desires; to be made new in the attitude of your minds; and to put on the new self, created to be like God in true righteousness and holiness.

Holy Spirit, come and separate out those thoughts and desires that come from my flesh and not Your Spirit. I do not want to listen to my flesh or give in to destructive patterns that do not reflect truth and righteousness. I want to be exactly like You, Lord! I put off those ideas that do not bring life and put on my new self, created in Christ Jesus, to accomplish great things!

1 Peter 2:9-10

But you are a chosen people, a royal priesthood, a holy nation, God's special possession, that you may declare the praises of Him who called you out of darkness into His wonderful light. Once you were not a people, but now you are the people of God; once you had not received mercy, but now you have received mercy.

You have chosen me, Lord. You have called me Your special possession, a member of Your royal court, a holy vessel unto You. I praise You because of this inheritance You have given me. I belong! I belong to You and to Your sons and daughters who share in this Kingdom of light and truth. Thank You for calling me out of the darkness and into Your glorious presence.

1 John 3:1

See what great love the Father has lavished on us, that we should be called children of God! And that is what we are! The reason the world does not know us is that it did not know Him.

I am a child of God! I am loved by my Father in heaven and a part of His household. Those voices that tell me I am insignificant, irrelevant, or incomplete don't know my Dad! He made me out of pure love and marked me as royalty. Thank You, Papa, for calling me Your own!

NOTES

NOTES

WORDS FOR ENDURING PERSECUTION

Psalms 3:3-6

But You, Lord, are a shield around me, my Glory, the One who lifts my head high. I call out to the Lord, and He answers me from His holy mountain. I lie down and sleep; I wake again because the Lord sustains me. I will not fear though tens of thousands assail me on every side.

You are my Shield and my Glory, Lord! You keep my head above the waters and help me to fix my gaze in heavenly places and not on earthly troubles. Thank You for granting me rest and peace of mind. Thank You for sustaining me and offering me safety from those who assail me. I will not fear my circumstances, but put my trust solely in You, for You are mighty!

Psalms 31:15-18

My times are in Your hands; deliver me from the hands of my enemies, from those who pursue me. Let Your face shine on Your servant; save me in Your unfailing love. Let me not be put to shame, Lord, for I have cried out to You; but let the wicked be put to shame and be silent in the realm of the dead. Let their lying lips be silenced, for with pride and contempt they speak arrogantly against the righteous.

I look to You, Lord, to guard and protect my life from those who seek to do me harm. May my desire to please You be evident and may Your love shine through. I will not be ashamed of my testimony or my relationship with You. May the lies be exposed and Your truth be revealed. I release my accusers to You, knowing You will deal with them accordingly.

Psalms 35:1-2

Contend, Lord, with those who contend with me; fight against those who fight against me. Take up shield and armor; arise and come to my aid.

Lord, come and do what only You can do! I cannot fight this battle on my own. I acknowledge Your might and strength to do war with my enemies. Thank You for being the Captain of the Hosts and my Champion in Warfare. I yield to Your lead in this fight and look to You as my Buckler and Shield.

Psalms 35:4-6

May those who seek my life be disgraced and put to shame; may those who plot my ruin be turned back in dismay. May they be like chaff before the wind, with the angel of the Lord driving them away; may their path be dark and slippery, with the angel of the Lord pursuing them.

Lord, I know my greatest enemies are not people, but principalities and powers that are aligned against me. May my spiritual adversaries be put to shame and cut off from my life. Drive them away into the darkness and release Your warring angels to rid them from my path. May those who are aligning with these dark forces be awakened to their deception and repent for their ungodly agreements.

Psalms 138:7-8

Though I walk in the midst of trouble, You preserve my life. You stretch out Your hand against the anger of my foes; with Your right hand You save me. The Lord will vindicate me; Your love, Lord, endures forever - do not abandon the works of Your hands.

Thank You for preserving my life, Lord, and dealing with those who have come against me. I know Your right hand is mighty to save and deliver. Vindicate me and continue to lead me and guide me into the fullness of Your truth so that I will fulfill Your purpose in this hour.

Proverbs 16:7

When the Lord takes pleasure in anyone's way, He causes their enemies to make peace with them.

May I please You so completely, Lord, that Your favor would be tangible to those who oppose me. May my enemies find me faultless and blameless and begin to seek peace and restoration. Thank You for vindicating me before their eyes.

Jeremiah 20:11-12

But the Lord is with me like a Mighty Warrior; so my persecutors will stumble and not prevail. They will fail and be thoroughly disgraced; their dishonor will never be forgotten. Lord Almighty, You who examine the righteous and probe the heart and mind, let me see Your vengeance on them, for to You I have committed my cause.

You are my Hero, Lord! You strengthen me and fill me with Your power to stand against my enemies. As I honor You, uphold me and render Your justice against those who stand against me. Examine my heart so there is nothing that will hinder Your righteousness being established. You alone can bring the needed breakthrough.

Matthew 5:10
Blessed are those who are persecuted because of righteousness, for theirs is the kingdom of heaven.

When I am persecuted, I am blessed! I may be in this world, but I am destined for a higher purpose and live for, and from, another Kingdom. Keep me centered in Your truth when others accuse me so that Your Kingdom will be demonstrated by my responses.

Matthew 5:11-12
Blessed are you when people insult you, persecute you and falsely say all kinds of evil against you because of Me. Rejoice and be glad, because great is your reward in heaven, for in the same way they persecuted the prophets who were before you.

Thank You for rewarding my faithfulness – even when it costs me. I know You will reward my obedience in declaring Your Name. I pray that those who oppose me will eventually see the truth. I count myself as blessed to be in the company of others before me who endured opposition for Your name's sake.

Matthew 5:44
But I tell you, love your enemies and pray for those who persecute you.

Forgive me, Lord, for any bitterness towards those who are coming against me. Help me to love them with Your love and to pray for them in sincerity of heart. Give me Your eyes of love so that I can see them the way You do. May my words and responses draw them closer to Your truth.

Mark 4:16-17

Others, like seed sown on rocky places, hear the word and at once receive it with joy. But since they have no root, they last only a short time. When trouble or persecution comes because of the word, they quickly fall away.

Lord, I do not want my faith to be weak. Lead me to Your words of life so that I can establish them in my heart to sustain me for the long haul. Help me to feed my spirit and my mind with Your Word so that I will not falter when opposed and not apologize when questioned. Thank You for arming me with the Truth that never changes.

John 15:18-19

If the world hates you, keep in mind that it hated Me first. If you belonged to the world, it would love you as its own. As it is, you do not belong to the world, but I have chosen you out of the world. That is why the world hates you.

Thank You for this reminder, Lord! I know that when You live inside of me, those who are opposed to You will not receive me. May the Light that shines in me and through me be a testimony of Your goodness and Your steadfast love to those who desperately need it.

John 17:14-15

I have given them your word and the world has hated them, for they are not of the world any more than I am of the world. My prayer is not that you take them out of the world but that you protect them from the evil one.

Lord, remind me that my enemies are not natural, but spiritual. I know that the devil does not like anyone who serves You or loves You. Help me to remain steadfast in my faith and not be offended by those who oppose me.

Acts 5:41-42

The apostles left the Sanhedrin, rejoicing because they had been counted worthy of suffering disgrace for the Name. Day after day, in the temple courts and from house to house, they never stopped teaching and proclaiming the good news that Jesus is the Messiah.

Remind me to praise You when I am persecuted and even punished for Your name's sake! I know my suffering is nothing compared to what You endured. Empower me to continue declaring Your truth and finding JOY in the life-giving message You've shown me.

Acts 7:60

Then he fell on his knees and cried out, "Lord, do not hold this sin against them." When he had said this, he fell asleep.

Lord, grant me the same unconditional love and mercy that Stephen had – even as he was martyred for his faith. May my zeal for Your kingdom be greater than my need for vindication. I entrust myself into Your care, knowing that You will use my testimony to help others see the light of the gospel.

Romans 8:35-37

Who shall separate us from the love of Christ? Shall trouble or hardship or persecution or famine or nakedness or danger or sword? As it is written: "For Your sake we face death all day long; we are considered as sheep to be slaughtered." No, in all these things we are more than conquerors through Him who loved us.

Your love is stronger than any opposition I face, Lord. I know You are with me and cheering me on as I face my enemies. Regardless of threats or accusations, I pray Your love will shine in me and through me so that even my persecutors will be drawn to Love!

Romans 12:14

Bless those who persecute you; bless and do not curse them.

Forgive me, Lord, for the unkind words I have spoken against those who are cursing me. I know my words have power. Give me Your words to bless them so that it can open the way for them to hear Your voice firsthand. May my words be seasoned with salt to make them thirsty for You.

Romans 12:17-19

Do not repay anyone evil for evil. Be careful to do what is right in the eyes of everyone. If it is possible, as far as it depends on you, live at peace with everyone. Do not take revenge, my dear friends, but leave room for God's wrath, for it is written: "It is mine to avenge; I will repay," says the Lord.

Cleanse my heart, Lord, from any ill will towards those who are being cruel to me. Keep me from a bitter spirit. I release my concerns to You and ask that You would vindicate me and give my mind rest from fears or threats. I release my opposers to You and thank You for reaching them where I can't.

2 Corinthians 12:10
That is why, for Christ's sake, I delight in weaknesses, in insults, in hardships, in persecutions, in difficulties. For when I am weak, then I am strong.

I am depending on Your strength to get me through this, Lord. Thank You for filling in the gaps and standing strong through me. I will not complain about any trial, but rejoice that in the midst of it, Your strength will be perfected and I will come out much stronger because of it!

Philippians 1:12-13
Now I want you to know, brothers and sisters, that what has happened to me has actually served to advance the gospel. As a result, it has become clear throughout the whole palace guard and to everyone else that I am in chains for Christ.

Father, I pray that the trials I am going through will serve as a witness to the gospel of the Kingdom. May my testimony be so powerful, even in the midst of my chains, that You will be glorified. May the fruit of this time serve to advance Your purposes and bring You all the praise.

1 Thessalonians 3:7-8
Therefore, brothers and sisters, in all our distress and persecution we were encouraged about you because of your faith. For now we really live, since you are standing firm in the Lord.

Lord, remind me in these times of persecution, that you establish our faith even more firmly than when we're not under pressure. Remind me how others are being encouraged and strengthened. Show me where You are working so that I can be inspired to continue standing firm in my faith.

2 Timothy 3:12-14a

In fact, everyone who wants to live a godly life in Christ Jesus will be persecuted, while evildoers and impostors will go from bad to worse, deceiving and being deceived. But as for you, continue in what you have learned and have become convinced of.

You have told me to not be surprised at persecution when I pursue a righteous life. Forgive me for comparing myself with those who are not following after You and seeming to live in peace and prosperity. I live for a higher purpose! Remind me of Your truths so that I will continue onward and upward to Your calling on my life.

Hebrews 12:3

Consider Him who endured such opposition from sinners, so that you will not grow weary and lose heart.

Thank You for going before me, Jesus, to grant me the needed grace to sustain me through this trial. You not only endured, but You overcame! I embrace Your victory through the cross and will persevere to finish this race well. Renew my heart so that I can praise You in the midst of it.

James 1:2-4

Consider it pure joy, my brothers and sisters, whenever you face trials of many kinds, because you know that the testing of your faith produces perseverance. Let perseverance finish its work so that you may be mature and complete, not lacking anything.

Let my faith shine in this time of testing, Lord. I thank You for maturing my trust in You and increasing my ability to see Your faithfulness in the midst of opposition. Keep my eyes fixed on the blessings that will come as a result of this season of trial.

1 Peter 3:13-16

Who is going to harm you if you are eager to do good? But even if you should suffer for what is right, you are blessed. "Do not fear their threats; do not be frightened." But in your hearts revere Christ as Lord. Always be prepared to give an answer to everyone who asks you to give the reason for the hope that you have. But do this with gentleness and respect, keeping a clear conscience, so that those who speak maliciously against your good behavior in Christ may be ashamed of their slander.

Lord, teach me how to counter accusations and threats with wisdom and mercy. May my words be life-giving and compel those who oppose You to think twice. May my testimony be filled with salt to make others thirsty for You. I will not fear any suffering but rather see it as an opportunity to lead others to Your throne of grace.

1 Peter 4:14-16

If you are insulted because of the name of Christ, you are blessed, for the Spirit of glory and of God rests on you. If you suffer, it should not be as a murderer or thief or any other kind of criminal, or even as a meddler. However, if you suffer as a Christian, do not be ashamed, but praise God that you bear that name.

Thank You, Lord, for calling me blessed even when I am insulted for bearing Your name! I will not be ashamed to declare Your Truth because it brings honor to Your throne. May my testimony give all glory to You.

Revelation 2:10

Do not be afraid of what you are about to suffer. I tell you, the devil will put some of you in prison to test you, and you will suffer persecution for ten days. Be faithful, even to the point of death, and I will give you life as your victor's crown.

Father, may I have such confidence in Your goodness and the victories ahead that I can face whatever comes my way! I choose to walk in faith and not in fear. I know You will uphold me and empower me from on high to not only survive, but to thrive in the midst of opposition – for the glory of Your name!

NOTES

NOTES

Words for Those Suffering Abuse

The scriptures and prayers listed can be used for personal encouragement as well as targeted intercession for others who are suffering from abuse at the hands of wicked people.

Psalms 10:17-18
You, Lord, hear the desire of the afflicted; You encourage them, and You listen to their cry, defending the fatherless and the oppressed, so that mere earthly mortals will never again strike terror.

Strengthen the hearts of those who are suffering, Lord. You know the wicked acts being done against the weak and the vulnerable. Intervene on behalf of those who are trapped and let them know You are working on their release! Do away with those who bring terror to men's souls and let them know their days are numbered!

Psalms 22:24
For He has not despised or scorned the suffering of the afflicted one; He has not hidden His face from him but has listened to his cry for help.

Forgive me, Lord, when I have doubted Your love and care over those who are suffering. You see everything and know all who have cried to You in their distress. Thank You for working on their behalf in ways I cannot see or understand. I know You are a loving Father and are continually working all things for the good of those who look to You.

Psalms 34:18
The Lord is close to the brokenhearted and saves those who are crushed in spirit.

Thank You, Lord, for Your overshadowing presence in the lives of those who are broken and crushed in spirit. Thank You for saving those who are unable to move forward on their own. May Your presence increase in tangible ways to those who are hurting so that they will know of Your incredible love and desire to redeem and restore.

Psalms 107:19-20

Then they cried to the Lord in their trouble, and He saved them from their distress. He sent out His word and healed them; He rescued them from the grave.

You are more than able to heal and restore all those who have been abused and inflicted, Lord! You can rescue those who have a spirit of death hovering over them and bring them back to life! Your saving power is more than enough to redeem those who have suffered and show them the power of resurrection life.

Isaiah 40:29-31

He gives strength to the weary and increases the power of the weak. Even youths grow tired and weary, and young men stumble and fall; but those who hope in the Lord will renew their strength. They will soar on wings like eagles; they will run and not grow weary, they will walk and not be faint.

For those who are weak and weary, Lord, give them extra strength to persevere. Speak to their hearts and minds and let them know You are with them and watching over them. Show them Your truth and Your ability to turn everything evil into something good for Your glory and for their blessing. Give them a reason to hope again.

Isaiah 43:2

When you pass through the waters, I will be with you; and when you pass through the rivers, they will not sweep over you. When you walk through the fire, you will not be burned; the flames will not set you ablaze.

Thank You, Lord, for walking with us through the valley of the shadow of death. We do not need to fear any evil because You are with us! You enable us to keep walking and not give up. You empower us to rise above the flames and not be burned by the enemy's fires. We will not be overcome by evil but overcome evil with the grace of Your goodness. Thank You for being our Shield and Defender, even when we can't see it.

Isaiah 53:10

Yet it was the Lord's will to crush Him and cause Him to suffer, and though the Lord makes His life an offering for sin, He will see His offspring and prolong His days, and the will of the Lord will prosper in His hand.

Father, for those You have called to be a lifeline for others, Your Word says it may entail some suffering and heartache. But, where the enemy wants to destroy us through these trials, You want to purify us so that we can receive the fullness of Your blessing. Just as Jesus was steadfast through His suffering, help me to remain faithful. Thank You for prolonging my days so I can see the answers to my prayers. Thank You that my victory will impact my children and their children for years to come.

Isaiah 53:11a

After He has suffered, He will see the light of life and be satisfied.

Jesus, You set the perfect example of persevering through suffering and receiving the victor's crown. May I have the same vision to see the light and life that will come as the result of Your sovereign work. Help me to see the good things that will come through these hard times so that I can endure with patience and absolute peace.

Jeremiah 29:11-14

"For I know the plans I have for you," declares the Lord, "plans to prosper you and not to harm you, plans to give you hope and a future. Then you will call on Me and come and pray to Me, and I will listen to you. You will seek Me and find Me when you seek Me with all your heart. I will be found by you," declares the Lord, "and will bring you back from captivity. I will gather you from all the nations and places where I have banished you," declares the Lord, "and will bring you back to the place from which I carried you into exile."

Regardless of how things look, Lord, I trust in Your plans. I reaffirm Your heart to prosper Your children and to give them a hope and a future. I stand on this promise and ask that You answer the cries of those who are suffering and show them Your love and concern. Stir their hope in Your Word and in Your determination to use everything in their life to bring them to a place of blessing and abundance.

Malachi 4:2

But for you who revere My name, the sun of righteousness will rise with healing in its rays. And you will go out and frolic like well-fed calves.

Lord, bring healing to all who have been hurt and abused by the wicked. Your healing power is supernatural and able to touch every part of the human soul, mind, and body. Especially for the most vulnerable, may their healing be so complete that they will regain any years lost and be filled to overflowing with joy and vitality.

Matthew 26:39

Going a little farther, He fell with His face to the ground and prayed, "My Father, if it is possible, may this cup be taken from Me. Yet not as I will, but as You will."

Thank You, Jesus, for showing us Your humanity in the midst of pain and turmoil. There is no shame in wanting a way out of suffering. And yet, You yielded Your will to Your Father, knowing that His love was greater than any temporary pain, and His purposes higher than any earthly plan. I surrender my life to You, Lord, and to Your perfect will. Nothing is greater than to know my life is in Your hands!

John 10:10

The thief comes only to steal and kill and destroy; I have come that they may have life and have it to the full.

For those whose lives have been impacted by evil deeds from the wicked, I pray that they will be fully vindicated and receive full retribution for their suffering. Give them life and life abundant, Lord! Hold back nothing that is good and pure for those You will rescue and redeem. With You, all things are possible!

Romans 5:3-5

Not only so, but we also glory in our sufferings, because we know that suffering produces perseverance; perseverance, character; and character, hope. And hope does not put us to shame, because God's love has been poured out into our hearts through the Holy Spirit, who has been given to us.

Thank You, Lord, for using suffering to purify us and bring us to completion. Thank You for Your perfect love which does nothing without a redeeming purpose. I know I can face various sufferings because You are using all of it to show us Your absolute power over the works of darkness!! My hope is not in the circumstances or in fleshly understanding, but in Your great love which conquers every sin and every form of evil.

2 Corinthians 1:5

For just as we share abundantly in the sufferings of Christ, so also our comfort abounds through Christ.

Pour out Your comfort to the hurting, Lord. To the degree the enemy has inflicted pain and torment on the weak and vulnerable, pour out Your tangible presence and unmistakable compassion and mercy. May all who are suffering experience the power of Your love and a hope for tomorrow that is beyond imagination.

2 Corinthians 4:8-10

We are hard pressed on every side, but not crushed; perplexed, but not in despair; persecuted, but not abandoned; struck down, but not destroyed. We always carry around in our body the death of Jesus, so that the life of Jesus may also be revealed in our body.

No matter how the enemy tries to crush and destroy us, Your love is stronger and Your power is greater. Thank You for the grace to override every kind of hardship and pain with an outcome that reveals Your compassion for the suffering and Your wrath towards the wicked. There is always resurrection life inside of us! I call forth that resurrection live in Jesus' name, to vanquish the spirit of death and destruction in the lives of those suffering from abuse. Reveal Yourself, Jesus, and shine forth the life and healing that comes from You alone.

Philippians 2:8-9

And being found in appearance as a man, He humbled Himself by becoming obedient to death - even death on a cross! Therefore, God exalted Him to the highest place and gave Him the name that is above every name.

Jesus, even You had to be obedient to Your Father in heaven. Even at the cost of Your own life, You trusted Your Father with the outcome. As a result, Your obedience gave You victory over death and made provision for all mankind to defeat the enemy. There is no other name as mighty as Yours! May I follow Your example and be obedient, even when it costs me. I know that You will bring great blessing as a result of my surrender.

Hebrews 5:7
During the days of Jesus' life on earth, He offered up prayers and petitions with fervent cries and tears to the one who could save Him from death, and He was heard because of His reverent submission.

Thank You, Lord, that You hear my cries for help. Thank You for listening to me when I am in anguish and don't know what to do. Thank You for honoring my petitions and showing me the way through difficult times. I trust You with my life and know that my obedience will bring its own good reward.

Hebrews 5:8-10 (ESV)
Although He was a son, He learned obedience through what He suffered. And being made perfect, He became the source of eternal salvation to all who obey Him, being designated by God a high priest after the order of Melchizedek.

Father, I know You are a good God who takes us through hardship for great and mighty purposes. You desire to sanctify us and to mold us into the likeness of Your Son. Even when You lead us through painful times, You are perfecting us and preparing us for great glories to come. Thank You for Your grace to take us through so we can come out the other side with great reward!

Hebrews 10:36
You need to persevere so that when you have done the will of God, you will receive what He has promised.

Give me greater endurance, Lord, to walk through difficult times and painful circumstances. Help me to follow Your lead and trust in Your un-

wavering plan to fulfill Your promises. I receive Your grace to walk through the unknown with the full assurance of Your provision and Your power to overcome. Thank You for the promises that are going to be fulfilled!

Hebrews 12:2-3
Fixing our eyes on Jesus, the Pioneer and Perfecter of faith. For the joy set before Him He endured the cross, scorning its shame, and sat down at the right hand of the throne of God. Consider Him who endured such opposition from sinners, so that you will not grow weary and lose heart.

Give me Your eyes, Jesus, to see the glory ahead. I want to walk in the same joy that You had when You went to the cross. Thank You for showing us how we can have joy in the midst of the pain because of the mighty work You are accomplishing through it. Thank You for the victory ahead when the evil and vile deeds of the enemy will be vanquished and undone. I will not be ashamed or fearful of these trials but praise You in the midst of them.

James 1:2-4
Consider it pure joy, my brothers and sisters, whenever you face trials of many kinds, because you know that the testing of your faith produces perseverance. Let perseverance finish its work so that you may be mature and complete, not lacking anything.

Instead of dreading this process of refinement, Lord, or fearing its outcome, I rejoice in Your overcoming power that's going to be seen through it. Thank You for molding us and shaping us as Your sons and daughters into a pure reflection of You. Rather than being anxious about these trials and testing, I submit to Your sanctifying work. Thank You for loving me enough to challenge my faith and teach me the hard lessons I need to learn.

1 Peter 1:6-7
In all this you greatly rejoice, though now for a little while you may have had to suffer grief in all kinds of trials. These have come so that the proven genuineness of your faith - of greater worth than gold, which perishes even though refined by fire - may result in praise, glory, and honor when Jesus Christ is revealed.

I will not be anxious about these trials, Lord, but yield to Your process of strengthening our faith. Though I do not always understand what You are doing, I believe that You are using everything for our good and for Your glory. I look forward to the future testimonies that will reveal how You brought gold out of the ashes and joy out of the suffering.

Revelation 21:3-4

And I heard a loud voice from the throne saying, "Look! God's dwelling place is now among the people, and He will dwell with them. They will be His people, and God Himself will be with them and be their God. He will wipe every tear from their eyes. There will be no more death' or mourning or crying or pain, for the old order of things has passed away."

Thank You, God, that earthly sorrows are nothing when compared with Your glory to come! Thank You for the coming day when every tear shed, and every pain felt will be overshadowed by the power of Your magnificent presence. Thank You for Your love which will erase any and all damage and trauma experienced here on the earth. The power of Your love is so much greater than any earthly suffering!

NOTES

NOTES

Words Concerning Deliverance

The scriptures and prayers listed here represent a general overview of our authority in Christ over demonic influence. Use them as an invitation for the Holy Spirit to reveal any specific or targeted area in your life that may need further counsel and prayer with the assistance of others.

Exodus 23:22

If you listen carefully to what He says and do all that I say, I will be an enemy to your enemies and will oppose those who oppose you.

Lord, I know obedience is the key to Your sovereign protection and intervention in my life. Help me to stay yielded to Your voice and to do what You say. Show me if there is any way in which I have not followed through with Your directives so I can make it right. Thank You for standing in between me and those demonic forces that seek to take me out.

Exodus 23:27

I will send My terror ahead of you and throw into confusion every nation you encounter. I will make all your enemies turn their backs and run.

I ask that the fear of the Lord would go before me to throw my enemies into confusion! Father, help me reflect Your holiness in my life with such power that demons will flee and run. May I be so filled with Your Spirit and power that no demonic spirit will even dare come close!

Exodus 23:29-30

But I will not drive them out in a single year, because the land would become desolate and the wild animals too numerous for you. Little by little I will drive them out before you, until you have increased enough to take possession of the land.

Lord, my desire is to fully possess all Your promises in my life and see the full manifestation of Your power. Thank You for giving me the grace to walk in freedom one day at a time. Show me how to build a solid founda-

tion of faith in my life to withstand any onslaught of the enemy and keep him out. Show me how to make freedom a lifestyle and not just an event.

Leviticus 26:8

Five of you will chase a hundred, and a hundred of you will chase ten thousand, and your enemies will fall by the sword before you.

Give me back up, Lord. Show me who to partner with in this time of deliverance so that our oneness of heart and spirit will be a powerful force against the enemy. Thank You for the power of agreement and the blessing of defeating the enemy when we stand together. Thank You for the assured victory when we move as one.

Deuteronomy 28:2, 7

All these blessings will come on you and accompany you if you obey the Lord your God...The Lord will grant that the enemies who rise up against you will be defeated before you. They will come at you from one direction but flee from you in seven.

Lord, I commit myself to following Your Word and obeying Your voice. Thank You for Your sovereign protection over my life as I yield my life fully to You. Show me any way in which I have missed Your voice so that I can heed Your directives and stay under the canopy of Your blessing. Thank You for dispersing the demonic interference and scattering those who side with evil.

Psalms 18:17-19

He rescued me from my powerful enemy, from my foes, who were too strong for me. They confronted me in the day of my disaster, but the Lord was my support. He brought me out into a spacious place; He rescued me because He delighted in me.

Thank You for supporting me in the battle, Lord. Thank You for creating safe places for me where the enemy can't attack. Lead me into those places where I can retreat and build up my faith for the days ahead. Thank You for bringing me through to freedom and establishing my faith for the long haul.

Matthew 10:1

Jesus called His twelve disciples to Him and gave them authority to drive out impure spirits and to heal every disease and sickness.

Thank You, Jesus, for giving me authority over demonic spirits. I do not have to yield to their control or buy into their lies. Because I have given my life to You and follow Your ways, I have the right to renounce demonic spirits out of my life. Thank You for giving me this access and the authority to establish Your Kingdom rule in my life.

Matthew 16:23

Jesus turned and said to Peter, "Get behind Me, Satan! You are a stumbling block to Me; you do not have in mind the concerns of God, but merely human concerns."

Lord, I do not want to open any door to demonic influence because of my own presumption and pride. Forgive me for not asking You before I assume to know the answer. Cleanse me of any double-mindedness that tries to sidestep Your perfect will. Reveal any way in which the enemy is trying to steer me off course simply because I have not taken the time to inquire of You.

Mark 3:11

Whenever the impure spirits saw Him, they fell down before Him and cried out, "You are the Son of God."

Thank You, Lord, that Your presence is so strong it causes demons to bow. Holy Spirit, come and fill my life to the full measure and empower me to walk in Your power each and every day. I declare that enemy forces must bow to the Lordship of Christ in my life. Thank You, Holy Spirit, for exposing any demonic intrusion that tries to come against me. I rest in the authority of Christ that reigns supreme over any opposition.

Mark 4:39-40

He got up, rebuked the wind and said to the waves, "Quiet! Be still!" Then the wind died down and it was completely calm. He said to His disciples, "Why are you so afraid? Do you still have no faith?"

I speak above the storms in my life and say, "Peace, be still!" I declare the supremacy of the One who created the winds and the waves and reigns forevermore as my Prince of Peace. I renounce and rebuke those evil forces that are trying to prevent me from getting to the other side of my destiny. I declare calm and stillness over the turbulence and a clear horizon ahead as the God of Peace crushes Satan underneath my feet!

Mark 9:25

When Jesus saw that a crowd was running to the scene, He rebuked the impure spirit. "You deaf and mute spirit," He said, "I command you, come out of him and never enter him again."

Through the authority of Jesus Christ, I speak to any impure spirit hovering over my life to leave and be gone. To any influence that has limited my ability to hear the Father's voice and speak His Word, I say, "Be gone" and never return. I yield my ears and my speech to the Holy Spirit to hear and speak what the Father desires without hindrance. Thank You, Lord, for watching over my life and cleansing my soul.

Mark 16:17

And these signs will accompany those who believe: In My name they will drive out demons; they will speak in new tongues.

I believe in You, Lord Jesus! I believe in Your power over every force of darkness and every demon from hell. I place my trust in You alone for deliverance and thank You for setting me free. I believe You will show me the way through the valleys and lead me into new places where I can declare Your goodness and Your power.

Luke 4:35

Be quiet!" Jesus said sternly. "Come out of him!" Then the demon threw the man down before them all and came out without injuring him.

I declare that the presence of Almighty God will overshadow any and every demonic hindrance in my life. I speak silence to those voices that are in opposition to my Father's purposes and say, "Be quiet!" Father, I ask You to expose these influences and shine Your light on their activity. To every evil spirit that is at work in my life I say, "Come out and be gone in Jesus' name!"

Luke 10:19

I have given you authority to trample on snakes and scorpions and to overcome all the power of the enemy; nothing will harm you.

I embrace this authority to overcome all the power of the enemy in my life! By the power of Jesus' name, I declare my life to be off limits to demonic forces. I declare my mind, soul, and body to be kept safe and free from harm. I have been given the right to stand on the head of the snakes that try to destroy my faith and rob me of my blessings. Thank You, Lord, for giving me the victory!

Luke 11:24-26

When an impure spirit comes out of a person, it goes through arid places seeking rest and does not find it. Then it says, "I will return to the house I left." When it arrives, it finds the house swept clean and put in order. Then it goes and takes seven other spirits more wicked than itself, and they go in and live there. And the final condition of that person is worse than the first.

Holy Spirit, teach me how to keep my deliverance. Show me how to fill those voids in my life with Your presence and Your truth. Help me to establish new patterns and new habits that will keep the enemy out of my life. Thank You for showing me how to build a strong foundation of faith in Your Word so I can see long-lasting fruit in my life.

John 8:32

Then you will know the truth, and the truth will set you free.

Holy Spirit, teach me truth in the innermost places of my soul. Show me the lies I have been believing and reveal the Father's heart of truth. Expose those ungodly beliefs that keep me in bondage to my flesh and the enemy's devices. Give me greater revelation of Your heart for me so I can embrace my destiny and look forward to my future with great anticipation.

Acts 10:38

How God anointed Jesus of Nazareth with the Holy Spirit and power, and how He went around doing good and healing all who were under the power of the devil, because God was with Him.

Thank You, Father, that the same spirit which Jesus had is within me! I ask for Your anointing and Your power on my life. Thank You for giving me the same authority as Jesus when He went around doing good and healing anyone who was under the power of the devil. I want to walk with You like Jesus did and see the captives set free!

Acts 18:10

For I am with you, and no one is going to attack and harm you, because I have many people in this city.

Thank You, Lord, for my spiritual family and the fellow believers in my city. Thank You for the authority we have when we are in agreement with You. I pray that our oneness in spirit would limit and hinder any demonic activity and wicked agenda that tries to encroach in our community. I declare an umbrella of divine protection and safety over my city. I speak blessing to the fellowship of believers and declare that our unity will grow even stronger in the days to come!

James 4:7

Submit yourselves, then, to God. Resist the devil, and he will flee from you.

Lord, I now submit my heart, my mind, and my soul to You and ask You to reveal anything that is not pleasing to You. As I humble myself before You, I trust in the power of Your Word over my life. I stand on Your truth and resist the ways the enemy is trying to tempt me, speak to me, and lead me astray. I declare myself under Your Lordship and rule. No other voice is allowed! I will walk in Your ways as You lead me to victory over the enemy!

NOTES

NOTES

Words for Justice Against the Wicked

Psalms 9:12

For He who avenges blood remembers; He does not ignore the cries of the afflicted.

You, O Lord, are the righteous Judge who hears the cry of the afflicted. For those who shed innocent blood, Your zeal for justice is unwavering and Your determination to bring them to account is without fail! Thank You for the coming day when all who have brought violence to the innocent will meet Your judgment and final pronouncement of their fate.

Psalms 33:5

The Lord loves righteousness and justice; the earth is full of His unfailing love.

When You deliver Your justice, God, may it be the power of Your love that receives the most attention. May we be reminded that it is Your love that compels You to act with justice. It is Your love that defends the weak and punishes those who purposely rebel against the gift You offer them. May the earth be filled with the knowledge of Your goodness and love, even in the midst of severe judgement against those who rebel.

Psalms 37:1-2

Do not fret because of those who are evil or be envious of those who do wrong; for like the grass they will soon wither, like green plants they will soon die away.

Forgive me, Lord, when I worry about those who do evil and wonder if they will prevail. Forgive me when I think they have the upper hand. You see from on high and know that their days are numbered and their fate is secure. Regardless of what they seem to get away with, there is a soon and coming day when they will be gone. They will die away and their deeds will be rendered null and void. They will answer to You, the final Judge of all things, and answer for the crimes they've committed.

Psalms 37:32-34

The wicked lie in wait for the righteous, intent on putting them to death; but the Lord will not leave them in the power of the wicked or let them be condemned when brought to trial. Hope in the Lord and keep His way. He will exalt you to inherit the land; when the wicked are destroyed, you will see it.

Thank You, Lord, for championing our freedom as a nation. You will not allow the wicked to rule Your people. Keep our eyes fixed on You so we can have hope for the time of our deliverance and freedom. You have given us this land as an inheritance and You will surely give it into our hands! Thank You for vindicating us and bringing the wicked to account.

Psalms 55:23

But You, God, will bring down the wicked into the pit of decay; the bloodthirsty and deceitful will not live out half their days. But as for me, I trust in You.

I place my trust in You, God, and not in the news or mainstream reports of the supposed success of evil doers. You have said they will not live out their schemes. Thank You for cutting their days short and stopping the bloodlust they practice. My trust is in You, alone, for You are the rightful Judge.

Psalms 94:18-23

When I said, "My foot is slipping," Your unfailing love, Lord, supported me. When anxiety was great within me, Your consolation brought me joy. Can a corrupt throne be allied with You - a throne that brings on misery by its decrees? The wicked band together against the righteous and condemn the innocent to death. But the Lord has become my fortress, and my God the rock in whom I take refuge. He will repay them for their sins and destroy them for their wickedness; the Lord our God will destroy them.

Your love, O Lord, is greater than any doubt or fear. When my heart becomes anxious, come and overshadow me with Your presence. You grant me joy in knowing that no one who does evil will get away with their plans. You will repay them for their sins and destroy works they have done. Thank You for already determining their fate and sealing their destiny.

Psalms 97:3-6

Fire goes before Him and consumes His foes on every side. His lightning lights up the world; the earth sees and trembles. The mountains melt like wax before the Lord of all the earth. The heavens proclaim His righteousness, and all peoples see His glory.

Your holiness is like a burning fire, Lord, and it consumes all who dare to defy it. May the holiness of Your presence be tangible to those who oppose you and defile Your name through vile and corrupt acts. May all of creation witness how powerful You are and how passionate You are to defend the integrity of Your Word and the validity of Your throne!

Psalms 106:3

Blessed are those who act justly, who always do what is right.

Lord, when You release Your judgments against the wicked, may those who have stood for justice at personal cost be rewarded. May all who have acted in truth, justice, and true compassion, be given favor and blessing as a reward for exercising the courage to do what is right.

Proverbs 1:29-31

Since they hated knowledge and did not choose to fear the Lord. Since they would not accept My advice and spurned My rebuke, they will eat the fruit of their ways and be filled with the fruit of their schemes.

Because they have refused You as God, may the godless reap the fruit of what they have sown. May that which they have done to oppress others come back on their heads as payment for their rebellion. May they know that You alone are God and will not allow them to practice their magic without cost.

Proverbs 5:22

The evil deeds of the wicked ensnare them; the cords of their sins hold them fast.

According to Your Word, sin bears a price. Because the wicked have forsaken Your Word and spun their own web of deceit and corruption, they will get ensnared in their sin and become entangled in their own wrongdoings. God, may they see that this is the cost of deliberately refusing Your Lordship and the price of practicing evil. May they have no one to blame but themselves.

Isaiah 35:4

Say to those with fearful hearts, "Be strong, do not fear; your God will come, He will come with vengeance; with divine retribution He will come to save you."

Thank You, God, for Your plans to avenge the cause of Your children. Your plan to rescue and save those who are being attacked without cause is sure. Not only are You coming to bring down the wicked, You are coming to reward those who have withstood the time of trial. Thank You for Your unwavering commitment to save, heal, and restore!

Isaiah 59:17-18

He put on righteousness as His breastplate, and the helmet of salvation on His head; He put on the garments of vengeance and wrapped Himself in zeal as in a cloak. According to what they have done, so will He repay wrath to His enemies and retribution to His foes; He will repay the islands their due.

You wear the mantle of justice and vindication, Lord, and have already promised to pour out Your wrath on the wicked. You are watching all that they do and are preparing to repay them for all they have done. I will not fret at their agendas or worry about their plans because You have already determined their fate. Thank You that in the midst of suffering, You show us the end result. You are Lord and King and will save Your own, bringing justice and liberty to all who are oppressed.

Matthew 5:43-44

You have heard that it was said, "Love your neighbor and hate your enemy." But I tell you, love your enemies and pray for those who persecute you.

As hard as it is, Lord, I pray for these enemies who do harm to others. I pray that Your presence would overshadow them and cause them to turn from the devil's schemes and follow after You. Guard my heart from a spirit of hatred towards individuals so I can focus my prayers on the works of darkness. Separate the sin from the sinner so my prayers will be effective, and my heart remain pure. Fill me with Your love, even for those who do wrong, so that You can have full sway and do what You alone can do.

Romans 2:8-10

But for those who are self-seeking and who reject the truth and follow evil, there will be wrath and anger. There will be trouble and distress for every human being who does evil: first for the Jew, then for the Gentile; but glory, honor, and peace for everyone who does good: first for the Jew, then for the Gentile.

Father, You do not look lightly on sin. For those who reject Your truth and follow their own ways, Your anger and judgment will fall. Though You do not delight in punishment, Your Word is final. May the consequences of our words and deeds cause all to know the true fear of the Lord.

Romans 12:19

Do not take revenge, my dear friends, but leave room for God's wrath, for it is written: "It is mine to avenge; I will repay," says the Lord.

Keep our hearts from hatred, Lord. Keep our minds free from thoughts of revenge or violence against those who wound our young. You alone have the right to bring judgment upon their acts. You alone will determine their destiny and fate.

Romans 13:4

For the one in authority is God's servant for your good. But if you do wrong, be afraid, for rulers do not bear the sword for no reason. They are God's servants, agents of wrath to bring punishment on the wrongdoer.

Lord, bless all our lawmakers and those in governing authority, that they would use their authority to defend the weak and punish those who do wrong. Raise up godly officials who will bear the sword rightly and have the wisdom in governing with truth and righteousness. Grant them courage and boldness to do the right thing and hold the wicked to account.

Galatians 6:7-9

Do not be deceived: God cannot be mocked. A man reaps what he sows. Whoever sows to please their flesh, from the flesh will reap destruction; whoever sows to please the Spirit, from the Spirit will reap eternal life. Let us not become weary in doing good, for at the proper time we will reap a harvest if we do not give up.

Thank You for Your law of sowing and reaping, Lord. For just as evil people have sown violence and murder in the earth, so will they reap their own destruction. May they see what they are doing and repent of their sins. May those who refuse, experience the consequences of sin and the cost of defying Your name. Even in their demise, may Your name be honored, and the fear of the Lord be manifest.

2 Peter 2:9-10a

If this is so, then the Lord knows how to rescue the godly from trials and to hold the unrighteous for punishment on the day of judgment. This is especially true of those who follow the corrupt desire of the flesh and despise authority.

You say You will deliver the godly from trials and rescue them from their distress. Thank You for the plans You made ahead of time to redeem Your own. I will not give in to any idea that the wicked will win or that their destruction will last. You have already determined their judgment. Thank You for Your sovereign plan that assures us our victory and our validation.

Revelation 19:15-16

Coming out of His mouth is a sharp sword with which to strike down the nations. "He will rule them with an iron scepter." He treads the winepress of the fury of the wrath of God Almighty. On His robe and on His thigh, He has this name written: King of kings and Lord of lords.

There is coming a day, Lord, when You will trumpet that Your Word is the highest and final authority on the earth. It is the power of the Living Word that will strike down every nation that has set itself against You. You alone wear the Champion's crown and have the right to rule over the earth with the scepter of righteousness. There is no enemy that will withstand that day. Thank You, Jesus! Amen.

NOTES

NOTES

Words for Courage and Boldness

Deuteronomy 31:6

Be strong and courageous. Do not be afraid or terrified because of them, for the Lord your God goes with you; He will never leave you nor forsake you.

Lord, show me what our enemies look like in Your eyes. I know they are nothing to You. Grant me the courage to confront these spiritual strongholds with absolute assurance of Your backing and Your ability to defeat them. I acknowledge Your presence and Your angelic assistance in helping me overcome all that comes against me.

Joshua 1:9

Have I not commanded you? Be strong and courageous. Do not be afraid; do not be discouraged, for the Lord your God will be with you wherever you go.

Thank You for going before me, Lord. I will not give in to fear or anxiety because You are with me in this battle. I refuse the voices that tell me to retreat or give up. I will not yield to my flesh that is telling me to stop hoping for victory. You are my Courage and my Strength to go on. Let's do this!

1 Chronicles 28:20

David also said to Solomon his son, "Be strong and courageous, and do the work. Do not be afraid or discouraged, for the Lord God, my God, is with you. He will not fail you or forsake you until all the work for the service of the temple of the Lord is finished."

Thank You for this promise, Lord, that You will not leave me until my assignment is complete. You will be with me to see this through, finishing everything that was started. Thank You for the grace I need to continue on this path, regardless of the opposition, until we have completed this mission together.

Psalms 16:8

I keep my eyes always on the Lord. With Him at my right hand, I will not be shaken.

Help me keep my eyes fixed on You, Lord. I will not go a single step without first conferring with You. You are the One I look to for direction and purpose. I receive Your help and Your overshadowing presence that empowers me to stand strong and not be shaken.

Psalms 27:14

Wait for the Lord; be strong and take heart and wait for the Lord.

As I wait on You, Lord, strengthen my heart and my resolve to do what is right. Help me to not rush ahead but to wait for Your perfect timing. Fine-tune my heart to hear Your directives and follow Your every command.

Psalms 112:6-8

Surely the righteous will never be shaken; they will be remembered forever. They will have no fear of bad news; their hearts are steadfast, trusting in the Lord. Their hearts are secure, they will have no fear; in the end they will look in triumph on their foes.

Lord, may I be counted among the righteous who do not give up hope, but trust in You for the victory. I will not fear bad news or conflicting reports, but will remain steadfast in Your Word. I fix my eyes on the completion of this journey when our enemies will be defeated and our foes be silenced.

Psalms 138:3 (ESV)

On the day I called, You answered me; my strength of soul You increased.

Thank You, Lord, that when I call upon You, I am filled with strength and courage. You increase my capacity to believe for the impossible and my ability to stand strong in adversity. Remind me to call upon You each and every day so that I can see this through to completion.

Psalms 144:1-2

Praise be to the Lord my Rock, who trains my hands for war, my fingers for battle. He is my loving God and my Fortress, my

Stronghold and my Deliverer, my Shield, in whom I take refuge, who subdues peoples under me.

Train me in this battle, Lord! Teach me how to war in the spirit and not in my flesh. Show me how to wield the sword of Your Word with power and accuracy. You are my Champion and Hero of faith. As my Stronghold and Deliverer, empower me to stand strong for the honor of Your name.

Proverbs 28:1
The wicked flee though no one pursues, but the righteous are as bold as a lion.

Forgive me, Lord, for being weak of heart and wanting to run from my troubles. Help me to remain steadfast and trust in You. Give me a boldness that defies the enemy and stands up to my opposition. Take my hesitation and transform it into a holy passion that is backed by heaven. May my voice be as a roar to Your enemies and silence their empty threats.

Matthew 10:19-20
But when they arrest you, do not worry about what to say or how to say it. At that time you will be given what to say, for it will not be you speaking, but the Spirit of your Father speaking through you.

Thank You for giving me the words to say when challenged by my enemies! Thank You for filling me with Your Spirit which empowers me to think clearly and answer my accusers with boldness. May Your presence and power be so evident in my responses, there will be no doubt it is You.

Mark 5:36
Overhearing what they said, Jesus told him, "Don't be afraid; just believe."

Lord, help me to believe for the breakthrough I need. Forgive me for any unbelief or inability to see what You can do. Increase my faith so I can withstand the doubts and nullify the lies that tell me to give up hope. With You, all things are possible!

Acts 4:29-30

Now, Lord, consider their threats and enable Your servants to speak Your word with great boldness. Stretch out Your hand to heal and perform signs and wonders through the name of Your holy Servant, Jesus.

Holy Spirit, speak through me! Fill me with Your righteous zeal with which to answer those who oppose You. May my witness and my testimony demonstrate the supremacy of Your Kingdom and the power of Your Spirit. May signs, wonders, and miracles come as a result of taking a righteous stand for truth.

Acts 4:31

After they prayed, the place where they were meeting was shaken. And they were all filled with the Holy Spirit and spoke the word of God boldly.

Fill me with Your Spirit, Lord, so that I may speak Your Word with boldness. My flesh is not capable of releasing Your power. Fill my mouth with words from heaven so that I can speak without fear and testify without hesitation!

1 Corinthians 16:13-14

Be on your guard; stand firm in the faith; be courageous; be strong. Do everything in love.

I will stand firm in my faith and fixed on Your purposes, Lord. Help me guard my heart and mind from any wavering from Your path. Help me keep a heart a love towards all who misunderstand me and give me greater courage to do what is right in Your eyes.

Philippians 1:14

And because of my chains, most of the brothers and sisters have become confident in the Lord and dare all the more to proclaim the gospel without fear.

Even when the enemy tries to put us in chains, it only serves Your purposes, Lord! Thank You for a fearlessness to proclaim Your truth, regardless of the setbacks or opposition. Thank You for the fear of the Lord which falls upon all who dare to quench the work of Your Spirit.

Philippians 1:27b-28
I will know that you stand firm in the one Spirit, striving together as one for the faith of the gospel without being frightened in any way by those who oppose you. This is a sign to them that they will be destroyed, but that you will be saved - and that by God.

Lord, knit me together with others who are standing for truth and righteousness. We are stronger together! Draw Your people together to strengthen our cause and be filled with greater courage and boldness. May our unity be a powerful sign to those who oppose You that their destruction is near.

Philippians 4:13
I can do all this through Him who gives me strength.

You are the One who gives me the strength to persevere, Lord! I cannot do this on my own. I will not rely on my own understanding or abilities, but will look to You as the source of my strength!

2 Timothy 1:7
For the Spirit God gave us does not make us timid, but gives us power, love, and self-discipline.

I know that any anxiety, fear, or doubt does not come from the Father, but from my flesh and the devil. Therefore, I will not give room for those thoughts to linger. I receive, instead, the Holy Spirit's power, love, and self-discipline to forge ahead. Thank You, Lord, for filling me with Your power and love to make the right decisions and move forward with courage.

NOTES

Words for the Fear of the Lord

Exodus 20:18-20

When the people saw the thunder and lightning and heard the trumpet and saw the mountain in smoke, they trembled with fear. They stayed at a distance and said to Moses, "Speak to us yourself and we will listen. But do not have God speak to us or we will die." Moses said to the people, "Do not be afraid. God has come to test you, so that the fear of God will be with you to keep you from sinning."

I do not fear You, Lord, because of Your wrath or judgment. Rather, I'm in awe of Your greatness. You are a loving Father who wants to keep us from sinning and do the right thing. Thank You for demonstrating Your power and might in ways that remind us of the seriousness of our walk. Thank You for the fear of the Lord that reminds us of Your sovereign purposes and keeps us safe in Your care.

2 Chronicles 17:10

The fear of the Lord fell on all the kingdoms of the lands surrounding Judah, so that they did not go to war against Jehoshaphat.

May the fear of the Lord permeate my city and the surrounding region, Lord! May the power of Your presence be so strong that none of Your enemies dares to war against Your people or Your purposes. May Your tangible presence bring conviction and repentance to those who have not known You. May Your peace bring resolution and healing to our communities as we embrace and honor Your glory.

Psalms 25:14

The Lord confides in those who fear Him; He makes His covenant known to them.

I want to know the secrets of Your heart, God. I want to know Your perfect will and purpose. I pray that the fear of the Lord would direct my thoughts and impressions so I can hear the fullness of what You have planned.

Psalms 33:8-9

Let all the earth fear the Lord; let all the people of the world revere Him. For He spoke, and it came to be; He commanded, and it stood firm.

Lord, everything that exists is by the Word of Your mouth. You alone are Creator and Ruler of everything that lives. Remind Your people of the power of Your voice and the creative reality of Your words. May we walk in holy awe as we listen to what You are speaking. May we stand firm in our resolve knowing that what You say, You will do.

Psalms 33:18-19

But the eyes of the Lord are on those who fear Him, on those whose hope is in His unfailing love, to deliver them from death and keep them alive in famine.

Thank You, Lord, for the protection You provide through the fear of the Lord. As we trust in Your sovereignty and wisdom, You deliver us from the traps of the enemy and provide everything we need. You keep us safe when we look to You instead of giving in to fear or panic. May our hope be in Your unfailing love and supernatural ability to keep us safe and secure.

Psalms 34:9-10

Fear the Lord, you His holy people, for those who fear Him lack nothing. The lions may grow weak and hungry, but those who seek the Lord lack no good thing.

You provide everything that is needed for those who cling to Your holiness, Lord. I do not have to worry about my provision or my future because You watch over all who honor You and seek You first. Your ways are always the best and I place my hope completely in You.

Psalms 103:17-18

But from everlasting to everlasting the Lord's love is with those who fear Him, and His righteousness with their children's children - with those who keep His covenant and remember to obey His precepts.

Father, I ask that my children, both natural and spiritual, would see the power of Your love in the fear of the Lord. May they keep Your Word and follow what You say. May they long to know Your truth and determine to follow You without hesitation. Pour out Your love to them as they obey You and trust You in all they do.

Psalms 145:19

He fulfills the desires of those who fear Him; He hears their cry and saves them.

You have promised, Lord, to answer the prayers of those who worship and revere You. As I walk in the fear of the Lord, You give me Your heart and desires so that I want what You want. Mold me and shape me, Lord, so that my thoughts and ways are always pleasing to You.

Proverbs 1:7

The fear of the Lord is the beginning of knowledge, but fools despise wisdom and instruction.

Lord, forgive me when I have not wanted to listen to Your wisdom or counsel. Forgive me for looking to my own understanding. I want to walk in the fear of the Lord in order to access the knowledge and insight that I need to move forward with favor and blessing. May Your Church also desire to walk in this fear of the Lord that teaches us what we need to know so we can be powerful change agents in our cities and nations.

Proverbs 8:13-16

To fear the Lord is to hate evil; I hate pride and arrogance, evil behavior, and perverse speech. Counsel and sound judgment are Mine; I have insight, I have power. By Me kings reign and rulers issue decrees that are just; by Me princes govern, and nobles - all who rule on earth.

Give me Your heart, God. I want to love what You love and hate what You hate. Increase my sensitivity so that I can easily recognize the lines that You draw between what is good and what is evil. I pray that the leaders in our cities and nations would rule with Your heart and lead us in the fear of the Lord. May the laws they make and the decisions they render be true, right, and good for all Your people.

Proverbs 10:27

The fear of the Lord adds length to life, but the years of the wicked are cut short.

Thank You for the added blessing to those who honor Your Word, Lord. I claim this promise for a long life and added years as I determine to walk in the fear of the Lord. Thank You that I can expect to live longer because I honor Your Name and do what You say.

Proverbs 14:26

Whoever fears the Lord has a secure fortress, and for their children it will be a refuge.

I declare that my entire household is under the protection of the Lord as we walk in the fear of the Lord. We are secure and safe because we have made You Lord and King in our midst. My children are under the shadow of Your wings and I thank You, Lord, for Your overwhelming presence that hems us in.

Proverbs 14:27

The fear of the Lord is a fountain of life, turning a person from the snares of death.

Life only comes from You, Lord. Living Water is what brings us health and vitality in all we do. May You be that fountain of life in my home, my city, and my nation. May Your people worship You and look to You as the source from which all of life flows. Spirit of the Living God, fall afresh on me!

Proverbs 22:4

Humility is the fear of the Lord; its wages are riches and honor and life.

Keep my heart in submission to You, Lord, and expose any pride that would rob me of Your favor. I humble myself before You and acknowledge I can do nothing on my own. Thank You for rewarding the humble in heart with abundance, honor, health, and well-being. May Your Church learn this secret that humility is the pathway to the fear of the Lord.

Isaiah 8:12-13

Do not call conspiracy everything this people calls a conspiracy; do not fear what they fear, and do not dread it. The Lord Almighty is the One you are to regard as holy, He is the One you are to fear, He is the One you are to dread.

Lord, show me if I have become too anxious about what others are saying. Expose any fear in my life that is not of You. You alone bring me safety and security. You alone know what is coming and how to bring us through to victory. May we look to Your holiness and righteousness as the standard of truth and the cause for which You move. May we be in awe at Your supremacy and authority to rule and reign.

Isaiah 33:6

He will be the sure foundation for your times, a rich store of salvation and wisdom and knowledge; the fear of the Lord is the key to this treasure.

I want a sure foundation for my life, Lord. Instill in me a reverence and awe of Your holiness so that I will have access to Your treasury of wisdom and knowledge. May I learn the depths of who You are and walk in Your ways.

Malachi 4:2

But for you who revere My Name, the sun of righteousness will rise with healing in its rays. And you will go out and frolic like well-fed calves.

Thank You, Lord, for releasing healing as I walk in the fear of the Lord. Thank You for Your promise to bring freedom and liberty to those who revere Your Name and pursue righteousness. I praise You for healing my soul, mind, and body as I grow in my faith and pursue all that is good and pure.

Matthew 10:28

Do not be afraid of those who kill the body but cannot kill the soul. Rather, be afraid of the One who can destroy both soul and body in hell.

I will not fear what men might think of me or do to me. I choose to walk in the fear of the Lord and surrender fully to what You ask me to say and do, Lord. When I waver, remind me of what is right for eternity. Stir in the hearts of Your people this revelation of Your preeminence in all things. May we be fearless towards others and worship only You.

Luke 1:50

His mercy extends to those who fear Him, from generation to generation.

True mercy and love can only come from You, Lord. I do not want to love out of my human capacity, but from the endless supply of Your heart. May Your people realize that deep mercy can only come when we walk in the fear of the Lord. May it reach to my children and to their children's children, so that the fullness of Your love will be revealed.

Acts 9:31

Then the church throughout Judea, Galilee and Samaria enjoyed a time of peace and was strengthened. Living in the fear of the Lord and encouraged by the Holy Spirit, it increased in numbers.

Lord, may the Church in my city enjoy the peace that comes from knowing You as Lord. May we be strengthened by Your Word. May we live in the fear of the Lord, recognizing the power it has to bring in the lost and expand Your Kingdom. Enlarge our borders, Lord, through a love for holiness and a pursuit of righteousness.

2 Corinthians 7:1

Therefore, since we have these promises, dear friends, let us purify ourselves from everything that contaminates body and spirit, perfecting holiness out of reverence for God.

Cleanse my heart, Lord, from any compromise or half-truth. Purify my heart and sanctify my mind so that I can honor You in all reverence and holiness. You enable me by the power of Your Spirit to do this work in my life. Teach me to walk in Your truth through a holy life.

Hebrews 11:7

By faith Noah, when warned about things not yet seen, in holy fear built an ark to save his family. By his faith he condemned the world and became heir of the righteousness that is in keeping with faith.

Give me the kind of faith that Noah had! May I so revere Your Word and trust Your commands that I'm willing to take risks and do radical things for You. The fear of the Lord brings this kind of courage and boldness to do the impossible. Help me to walk in this, Lord, to bring greater glory to You and change the world around me.

1 Peter 1:17-19
Since you call on a Father who judges each person's work impartially, live out your time as foreigners here in reverent fear. For you know that it was not with perishable things such as silver or gold that you were redeemed from the empty way of life handed down to you from your ancestors, but with the precious blood of Christ, a lamb without blemish or defect.

Remind me, Lord, of what You did for me at the cross. May I not take Your sacrifice for granted, but realize what it cost You. Give me a fresh revelation of this gift so that I may steward it as a sacred treasure. May all Your followers be in awe at what You have done and realize the commission we've been given to spread this good news.

NOTES

THE ECCLESIA

WORDS FOR THE CHURCH

The scriptures and prayers in this section are focused on the local congregation. Though they can apply to the larger Body of Christ, it is ultimately the local houses of fellowship that carry the greatest spiritual authority in any community.

Psalms 133:1

How good and pleasant it is when God's people live together in unity!

I pray, Lord, that the local body of believers would enjoy one another and pursue even deeper bonds of fellowship with You and with each other. Show us how to work through our differences and resolve our conflicts. Teach us how to defer to one another out of love for You. May we reflect a oneness of heart that reflects heaven and releases an overflow of joy in our midst!

Isaiah 61:8-9

For I, the Lord, love justice; I hate robbery and wrongdoing. In My faithfulness I will reward My people and make an everlasting covenant with them. Their descendants will be known among the nations and their offspring among the peoples. All who see them will acknowledge that they are a people the Lord has blessed.

Lord, may we be a people that the world recognizes as blessed and favored. May we be set apart from those who do not know You or follow Your ways as witnesses to a greater Kingdom and a higher truth. May our lives be a testimony to Your greatness and a compelling reason for others to follow.

Luke 17:20-21

Once, on being asked by the Pharisees when the kingdom of God would come, Jesus replied, "The coming of the kingdom of God is not something that can be observed, nor will people say, 'Here it is,' or 'There it is,' because the kingdom of God is in your midst."

Jesus, may Your Kingdom be fully demonstrated here and now in the Church! I pray that every church in my city would long for this reality of the manifestation of Your kingdom to be seen in real time. May Your presence be felt, Your healing be present, and Your gospel demonstrated with great power. May our churches be filled with hunger for the greater things!

Luke 19:13 (KJV)
And He called His ten servants, and delivered them ten pounds, and said unto them, "Occupy till I come."

You have instructed us to occupy and do business on this earth until You return. May we be faithful to Your charge and not sit on the sidelines. Ignite the Church with a fresh fire to impact all parts of our culture and every part of our city. Show us how to be ambassadors for the Kingdom and effective change agents in our community. May we be good stewards of the treasures of the Kingdom and see an increase of the harvest in our own region.

John 4:23-24
Yet a time is coming and has now come when the true worshipers will worship the Father in the Spirit and in truth, for they are the kind of worshipers the Father seeks. God is spirit, and His worshipers must worship in the Spirit and in truth.

Make us worthy worshippers, Lord! Give us a desire to press into the kind of worship that is full of Your Spirit as well as full of Your truth. May our worship reflect the fullness of Your heart and passion. May people know the power of Your presence as well as the realities of Your Kingdom by the songs we sing and the expressions of our adoration.

John 17:11b
Holy Father, protect them by the power of Your Name, the Name You gave Me, so that they may be one as We are one.

Jesus, may the Church know the same kind of oneness that You have with Your Father. May our hearts be so fully united with Yours that it would bring alignment and agreement in our purpose and plans. Teach us how to share together in a way that builds love and affection along with a sincere desire to do Your will.

Acts 2:42-43

They devoted themselves to the apostles' teaching and to fellowship, to the breaking of bread and to prayer. Everyone was filled with awe at the many wonders and signs performed by the apostles.

As I pray for my church, Lord, I ask to keep us faithful to sound doctrine that secures our spiritual foundations. I pray that our fellowship would be heart-felt and deep. I pray that we would continually celebrate the power of the cross and consistently lift our prayers and intercessions before You in unity. May we be a body that is a conduit of miracles for Your glory that would draw in the lost and the hurting.

Romans 12:16

Live in harmony with one another. Do not be proud but be willing to associate with people of low position. Do not be conceited.

Father, cleanse the Church of selfish ambition and pride. Help us to see where we think less of others and more of ourselves. Give us Your heart towards those who are ill-treated by the world and shunned by society. Show us how to love them well and demonstrate Your kindness towards them.

1 Corinthians 12:20-23a

As it is, there are many parts, but one body. The eye cannot say to the hand, "I don't need you!" And the head cannot say to the feet, "I don't need you!" On the contrary, those parts of the body that seem to be weaker are indispensable, and the parts that we think are less honorable we treat with special honor.

Thank You, Lord, for using every part of the Church in a unique and special way. Forgive me for comparing or complaining about those in the Church that I don't understand. Help me see the value of each brother and sister and the unique role they play in the work of Your Kingdom.

1 Corinthians 12:25-26

So that there should be no division in the Body, but that its parts should have equal concern for each other. If one part suffers, every part suffers with it; if one part is honored, every part rejoices with it.

Increase my capacity to love, Lord! Show me how to pray for and care for others in the Church that are hurting. Forgive me for any undue judgments I have placed on those I don't really know, and show me how to demonstrate Your kindness to them. May I be more sensitive to the needs of those around me so that we can walk together in a way that honors You.

2 Corinthians 13:11

Finally, brothers and sisters, rejoice! Strive for full restoration, encourage one another, be of one mind, live in peace. And the God of love and peace will be with you.

Thank You, Lord, for giving us what is needed to restore one another and bring transformation in our midst. Do not let discouragement take root, but teach us to strengthen one another through the hard times. May Your Word be alive and powerful within us to break bonds of despair and bring healing and deliverance to those in bondage. May we experience a supernatural rest and peace as we bring restoration to those parts of the Body that are broken.

Ephesians 4:3-6

Make every effort to keep the unity of the Spirit through the bond of peace. There is one Body and one Spirit, just as you were called to one hope when you were called; one Lord, one faith, one baptism; one God and Father of all, who is over all and through all and in all.

I pray for a greater unity of Your Spirit in the Church, Lord. Draw us higher in Your presence to see what we have in common more than those things that divide us. Keep us focused on the things that matter. Remind us of the power of unity and agreement so that we would pursue this bond that is unbreakable in the Spirit.

Ephesians 4:13

Until we all reach unity in the faith and in the knowledge of the Son of God and become mature, attaining to the whole measure of the fullness of Christ.

Our desire, Lord, is to be fully united with You in our faith, in our knowledge, and in our demonstrations of Your kingdom. Help us to mature towards the fullness You have in mind. Help me to do my part in growing and learning all I can about Your Word. May I know Your presence in my life that can be a sign to others of Your matchless power and love.

Ephesians 4:15-16

Instead, speaking the truth in love, we will grow to become in every respect the mature Body of Him who is the Head, that is, Christ. From Him the whole Body, joined and held together by every supporting ligament, grows and builds itself up in love, as each part does its work.

Show us how to build each other up, Lord. Help us to share the truth with others in a way that brings hope and joy. Help me to do my part in building others up around me. Show me where I can assist and share my gifts and talents in a way to strengthen our church family and grow together as one.

Ephesians 5:25b-27

Christ loved the Church and gave Himself up for her to make her holy, cleansing her by the washing with water through the word, and to present her to Himself as a radiant Church, without stain or wrinkle or any other blemish, but holy and blameless.

Jesus, just as You love the Church and gave Your life so that she could be holy and radiant, give me a greater love for the Body of Christ. May my words and prayers reflect Your heart for her. Bless and strengthen the Church as she becomes more and more like You. I declare that the Body of Christ will fully prepared to meet the Bridegroom in the fullness of Your glory!

Ephesians 5:29-30

After all, no one ever hated their own body, but they feed and care for their body, just as Christ does the Church - for we are members of His Body.

Father, forgive me for any wrong attitude I've had towards the Church. Replace any bitterness or disappointment from past experiences with a compassion and love for all my brothers and sisters in Christ. Teach me how to care for others in my spiritual family with a sincere desire to meet their needs, just as I meet my own.

Philippians 2:2-4

Then make my joy complete by being like-minded, having the same love, being one in spirit and of one mind. Do nothing out of selfish ambition or vain conceit. Rather, in humility value others above yourselves, not looking to your own interests but each of you to the interests of the others.

Make us one, Lord! May our church be fully united in spirit and oneness of heart. May we so value our unity that personal needs and desires would be placed aside in favor of serving one another out of brotherly affection and love. Draw our hearts and minds to the same revelations and plans You have for us so we can move forward with power and effectiveness for the Kingdom.

NOTES

NOTES

WORDS FOR PASTORS AND SPIRITUAL LEADERS

Psalms 25:14
The Lord confides in those who fear Him; He makes His covenant known to them.

Bless my leaders with Your presence, Lord, and overshadow them with an awe of Your holiness. May they desire to walk in the fear of the Lord. Open their hearts and eyes to the depth of Your promises. Give them a greater vision of Your heart and purpose for us as believers and as the Body of Christ.

Psalms 128:1-4
Blessed are all who fear the Lord, who walk in obedience to Him. You will eat the fruit of your labor; blessings and prosperity will be yours. Your wife will be like a fruitful vine within your house; your children will be like olive shoots around your table. Yes, this will be the blessing for the man who fears the Lord.

Father, I ask that our leaders delight in following after You. May they see the abundant blessings you release when they walk in obedience to Your Word. May their entire household reflect Your goodness. May their provisions be met, and may Your favor bring them increase as they faithfully follow Your call on their lives.

Psalms 119:66
Teach me knowledge and good judgment, for I trust Your commands.

Teach our pastors and leaders the knowledge they need to lead well, Lord. Meet them in the quiet place and grant them greater insight into the truths You reveal to them. Give them sound judgment and the ability to rightly distinguish between what is of God, what is of man, and what is of the enemy. May their faith grow as they see the power of Your Word at work in their own lives.

Proverbs 1:7

The fear of the Lord is the beginning of knowledge, but fools despise wisdom and instruction.

Father, I pray that the leaders in my church would operate in the fear of the Lord and not the wisdom of men. May their understanding come from the awe of Your holiness and not the opinions of others. May they pursue the truth and be willing to change if it pleases You.

Proverbs 2:6-8

For the Lord gives wisdom; from His mouth come knowledge and understanding. He holds success in store for the upright, He is a shield to those whose walk is blameless, for He guards the course of the just and protects the way of His faithful ones.

Grant my pastor and leaders increased wisdom and insight as they study Your Word and listen for Your heart. Show them the blessings and sovereign protection that comes from being faithful to Your truth and walking in Your ways. Cover them with Your wings and overshadow them with peace and security.

Proverbs 4:25-27

Let your eyes look straight ahead; fix your gaze directly before you. Give careful thought to the paths for your feet and be steadfast in all your ways. Do not turn to the right or the left; keep your foot from evil.

Guard and protect our pastors, Lord, from temptation and sin. Holy Spirit, speak into their ears the way to go when confronted with challenging choices. Keep their hearts pure and their walk holy. May they desire to have a right relationship with You through a clear conscience and a life of integrity. Anoint their eyes to pursue only that which will bring blessing and honor to Your Name.

Proverbs 29:25

Fear of man will prove to be a snare, but whoever trusts in the Lord is kept safe.

Lord, give our pastors a conviction of Your truth and a determination to follow You at all costs. May they not be lured away by men's praise or bow to men's complaints. May they have a heart to please You above all else and have the grace to deal with those who misunderstand them and oppose them. Keep them safe from the darts of the enemy and strengthen their resolve to finish their race with integrity.

Isaiah 11:2-3a

The Spirit of the Lord will rest on him - the Spirit of wisdom and of understanding, the Spirit of counsel and of might, the Spirit of the knowledge and fear of the Lord - and he will delight in the fear of the Lord.

I pray that pastors and church leaders would be filled to overflowing with the power of Your Spirit. May they operate in the spirit of wisdom and understanding, the spirit of counsel and of might, and the spirit of the knowledge and fear of the Lord. May our leaders receive much joy in walking in Your Spirit and experience, firsthand, the blessing that comes from walking in Your ways.

1 Corinthians 2:4-5

My message and my preaching were not with wise and persuasive words, but with a demonstration of the Spirit's power, so that your faith might not rest on human wisdom, but on God's power.

Bless our pastors as they teach Your Word and declare the truths of the Kingdom. May they go beyond merely teaching the principles to demonstrating these realities with Your power and presence. I ask for signs, wonders, and miracles to follow the teaching of Your Word so that people would be drawn to You above any minister. Encounter pastors and teachers with the power of Your Spirit, Lord, so they will preach a Kingdom of power and not just words.

2 Corinthians 9:8

And God is able to bless you abundantly, so that in all things at all times, having all that you need, you will abound in every good work.

I pray that the leaders in my church would have all their needs met so they would not be hindered in fulfilling their call. May they see, first-hand, the blessings of Your provision as they trust in You. I pray a blessing on the work of their hands and the service that comes from the grace on their lives. May they bear much fruit for Your glory.

Ephesians 6:16-17

In addition to all this, take up the shield of faith, with which you can extinguish all the flaming arrows of the evil one. Take the helmet of salvation and the sword of the Spirit, which is the word of God.

I pray that our pastors would know Your Word with great insight and understanding. May their knowledge of Your Word shield their hearts from doubt and distress. May they be strong in their faith and able to deflect the threats and accusations of the enemy. May they be overshadowed with the confidence that comes from knowing Your heart and trusting in Your providential care.

Philippians 1:9-11

And this is my prayer: that your love may abound more and more in knowledge and depth of insight, so that you may be able to discern what is best and may be pure and blameless for the day of Christ, filled with the fruit of righteousness that comes through Jesus Christ - to the glory and praise of God.

Lord, grant our pastors and church leaders an even greater love and compassion for those they serve. May they know, first and foremost, how much You love them and how committed You are to fulfilling Your purpose for them. Encourage their hearts when they are frustrated with others and weary of dealing with people. May they see the fruit of their labors and know that You smile on their faithful ministry unto You.

Colossians 2:8

See to it that no one takes you captive through hollow and deceptive philosophy, which depends on human tradition and the elemental spiritual forces of this world rather than on Christ.

Keep our pastors and leaders centered in the truth of Your Word, Lord. Guard their hearts and minds from the opinions of men and any teaching which strays from Your truth. As they pursue the work of Your Spirit, grant them a discerning heart to distinguish between what is real and what is counterfeit. Free them from the constraints of religion and center their hearts in the Living Word which alone brings life.

1 Timothy 6:11-12

But you, man of God, flee from all this, and pursue righteousness, godliness, faith, love, endurance, and gentleness. Fight the good fight of the faith. Take hold of the eternal life to which you were called when you made your good confession in the presence of many witnesses.

Give our pastors a passion for purity, Lord. Give them an undivided heart that seeks You above all else. Stir their heart with a hunger for righteousness and all that is holy. Encourage their hearts to stand against the enemy's attacks and reward their diligence in being faithful to their charge.

Hebrews 5:14

But solid food is for the mature, who by constant use have trained themselves to distinguish good from evil.

Give those who preach Your Word a perseverance to study the scriptures and dig deeper into the truth. Give them a joy as they receive revelation and share these insights in a way that calls everyone else deeper. Show our leaders the fruit that comes when they practice what they preach. Through their diligence in studying Your Word, give us greater spiritual perception and depth of insight to overcome evil and pursue what is good.

Hebrews 12:14-15

Make every effort to live in peace with everyone and to be holy; without holiness no one will see the Lord. See to it that no one falls short of the grace of God and that no bitter root grows up to cause trouble and defile many.

Lord, give our pastors and leaders increased grace to settle disputes and bring resolution to conflicts within the Body. May their pursuit of holiness bring clarity and integrity in the way they manage the household of God. Alert them to any spirit of offense that would seek to divide and discourage. May they empower the Church to rise above our differences and find a unity of heart and oneness of purpose for Your glory.

James 3:17-18
But the wisdom that comes from heaven is first of all pure; then peace-loving, considerate, submissive, full of mercy and good fruit, impartial and sincere. Peacemakers who sow in peace reap a harvest of righteousness.

Grant our church leaders the wisdom that comes from above, Lord. Give them keen discernment in making decisions and dealing with the daily challenges of ministry. Give them the right measure of grace and truth in order to uphold the standards of Your Word and yet show tender mercies to the young in faith. May they love well and reap a great harvest through their service unto You.

1 Peter 4:7-8
The end of all things is near. Therefore, be alert and of sober mind so that you may pray. Above all, love each other deeply, because love covers over a multitude of sins.

Father, I pray that our pastors and leaders would have a rich prayer life that is filled with Your presence and power. Alert them when they forget to spend time with You and give them a heart that diligently pursues the quiet place. May their prayers be directed by Your Spirit and inspired by Love. Grant them the ability to love without hesitation and overlook those things that are not priority to You. Give them the wisdom they need to inspire others in overcoming sin and pursuing You above all else.

2 Peter 1:10-11
Therefore, my brothers and sisters, make every effort to confirm your calling and election. For if you do these things, you will never stumble, and you will receive a rich welcome into the eternal kingdom of our Lord and Savior Jesus Christ.

Lord, when the enemy tries to discourage our pastors from their call and make them question their journey, overshadow them and remind them of the destiny You have for them and the rewards that await them. Reaffirm Your purpose for their life and grant them a renewed joy in their call. Give them the clarity they need and establish their steps so they can walk forward with confidence and conviction.

NOTES

Genesis 11:6

The Lord said, "If as one people speaking the same language they have begun to do this, then nothing they plan to do will be impossible for them."

We have no idea of the possibilities there are when we are in agreement! Thank You for giving us the same language of Your Spirit with which to communicate with You and learn Your heart. May we come into unity about the things that really matter so we can be powerful change agents in our communities, states, and nation. Thank You for giving us everything we need to succeed when we truly learn how to work together.

Judges 6:16 (ESV)

And the Lord said to him, "But I will be with you, and you shall strike the Midianites as one man."

Remind us of the authority we have in the spirit when we are united! By the power of Your Spirit, You enable us to be one in heart, mind, thought, and purpose. The enemy has no power against this kind of agreement! May Your Church be so united in our purpose that we would be AS ONE.

Psalms 133

How good and pleasant it is when God's people live together in unity! It is like precious oil poured on the head, running down on the beard, running down on Aaron's beard, down on the collar of his robe. It is as if the dew of Hermon were falling on Mount Zion. For there the Lord bestows His blessing, even life forevermore.

Lord, I want blessing and life to flow out of our church! Draw us into greater unity so that Your Spirit can flow freely. Bless our leaders with a firsthand revelation of Your love and power. May the presence of Holy Spirit in their own lives pour out through them and into the entire Body. May the unity of Your Spirit create an atmosphere that breathes life and blessing to all who come.

Amos 3:3

Do two walk together unless they have agreed to do so?

Lord, give us a greater desire to walk together as a spiritual family and not give up or quit. Give us greater understanding in the part that each one of us plays. Give us a clear vision of where we're going so we can walk in complete harmony and agreement.

Matthew 18:19-20

Again, truly I tell you that if two of you on earth agree about anything they ask for, it will be done for them by My Father in heaven. For where two or three gather in My name, there am I with them.

Holy Spirit, bring us into agreement in our prayers and intercession. Sift out all our personal opinions so that we can be totally focused on Your heart and Your priorities. Consecrate our minds so that we will discern together what is Your good, pleasing, and perfect will. Thank You for responding so quickly when we learn to agree.

John 4:23-24

Yet a time is coming and has now come when the true worshipers will worship the Father in the Spirit and in truth, for they are the kind of worshipers the Father seeks. God is spirit, and His worshipers must worship in the Spirit and in truth.

Thank You for the power of Your Spirit to bring us together! Father, I ask that You bring all believers into an encounter with Holy Spirit that radically transforms their life. I pray that all would pursue Your truth and learn to worship You with their whole heart. May we all walk in the realities of Your Spirit and experience a bond and fellowship that is unbroken.

John 17:21

That all of them may be one, Father, just as You are in Me and I am in You. May they also be in Us so that the world may believe that You have sent Me.

The world is watching the Church, Lord. They are looking to see if we agree and are unified in our purpose. May we demonstrate the same kind of unity that You have with the Father and Holy Spirit. May we as believers find a joy in walking together and working towards the same goal. Make us one as You are one.

Acts 2:1-4

When the day of Pentecost came, they were all together in one place. Suddenly a sound like the blowing of a violent wind came from heaven and filled the whole house where they were sitting. They saw what seemed to be tongues of fire that separated and came to rest on each of them. All of them were filled with the Holy Spirit and began to speak in other tongues as the Spirit enabled them.

Your Spirit moves powerfully when we are in agreement! Just like on the day of Pentecost, Lord draw us together for the common purpose of seeking Your face. May we so long for Your presence that we would not give up meeting together but pursue You with our whole heart. May Your Spirit meet us as we seek You together and may we be filled with power from on high as a result.

Acts 2:42-43

They devoted themselves to the apostles' teaching and to fellowship, to the breaking of bread and to prayer. Everyone was filled with awe at the many wonders and signs performed by the apostles.

I pray that my church family would be devoted to those things that really matter for eternity. Give us good teachers to understand and apply Your Word. Draw us in fellowship with a greater joy in doing life together. Remind us to pray consistently for one another and for our city. May our city see the Kingdom of God at work through our witness and be in awe of Your love and power.

Acts 4:32-34a

All the believers were one in heart and mind. No one claimed that any of their possessions was their own, but they shared everything they had. With great power the apostles continued to testify to the resurrection of the Lord Jesus. And God's grace was so powerfully at work in them all that there were no needy persons among them.

May we have the same testimony as the early Church, Lord! May we be of one heart and mind to help those around us and be a blessing to our community. Shake us from our isolation and self-preoccupation and help us find joy in serving one another. May we freely give away what You have given us and demonstrate the abundance of Your house to others!

Romans 12:4-8

For just as each of us has one body with many members, and these members do not all have the same function, so in Christ we, though many, form one body, and each member belongs to all the others. We have different gifts, according to the grace given to each of us. If your gift is prophesying, then prophesy in accordance with your faith; if it is serving, then serve; if it is teaching, then teach; if it is to encourage, then give encouragement; if it is giving, then give generously; if it is to lead, do it diligently; if it is to show mercy, do it cheerfully.

Open my eyes, Lord, to see the unique gifts of each of my brothers and sisters. Rather than comparing ourselves with each other, may we see our unique contributions as gifts from You. May we recognize the grace on one another's life and champion one another's call. Help us celebrate our differences as pieces of a larger picture. May we honor and glorify You as each one does their part.

Romans 12:16

Live in harmony with one another. Do not be proud, but be willing to associate with people of low position. Do not be conceited.

If there is any way that I have looked down on others because of their position in life, please forgive me Lord! Cleanse my heart of any entitlement and give me Your compassion for those who are different than me. Help me to see them as You do and speak blessing and promise over their life. May I see the hidden treasure within to call out their purpose and destiny.

Romans 14:19-21

Let us therefore make every effort to do what leads to peace and to mutual edification. Do not destroy the work of God for the sake of food. All food is clean, but it is wrong for a person to eat anything that causes someone else to stumble. It is better not to eat meat or drink wine or to do anything else that will cause your brother or sister to fall.

When we have differences among us, Lord, help us to see how we affect those around us. Show us how to walk out our faith in a way that compels others to know You and doesn't become a stumbling block to the weak. Give me a greater sensitivity to those around me as I share my convictions. Show me how to share in such a way that invites change and doesn't demand it.

1 Corinthians 1:10

I appeal to you, brothers and sisters, in the name of our Lord Jesus Christ, that all of you agree with one another in what you say and that there be no divisions among you, but that you be perfectly united in mind and thought.

Lord, give us the kind of unity that comes from thinking like You. You have given us the mind of Christ so we can access Your wisdom and counsel. May we find that kind of oneness of thought so that we can move forward in our purpose and in Your plans. When there are disagreements, show us how to access Your heart and mind so that we can prioritize our ideas and yield them to Your direction.

1 Corinthians 12:18-20

But in fact, God has placed the parts in the Body, every one of them, just as He wanted them to be. If they were all one part, where would the Body be? As it is, there are many parts, but one Body.

Thank You for the diversity within the Church! Thank You for giving each of us a unique part to play and a specific role to fulfill. May we all see these differences as a strength and not a weakness. Give me and my brothers and sisters the grace to recognize the blessing of one another and learn to walk and work together towards Your purposes with joy.

1 Corinthians 12:25-27

So that there should be no division in the Body, but that its parts should have equal concern for each other. If one part suffers, every part suffers with it; if one part is honored, every part rejoices with it. Now you are the Body of Christ, and each one of you is a part of it.

Forgive me, Lord, for comparisons and expectations that I have placed on others in the Church. Show me the unique blessing that each one is to Your plan and purposes. I want to embrace their part with joy and encourage them in their walk. Give me greater empathy towards those I don't understand or are hurting, and sensitivity towards those who need more encouragement.

Ephesians 4:3-6

Make every effort to keep the unity of the Spirit through the bond of peace. There is one Body and one Spirit, just as you were called to one hope when you were called; one Lord, one faith, one baptism; one God and Father of all, who is over all and through all and in all.

Father, forgive us for all the ways we divide over things. Remind us of those things that unite us and make us one. Separate out those opinions and ideas that are counterproductive to Your purposes in this hour and help us to focus on that which is eternal. Strengthen our resolve to fulfill our call and agree on that which will make a lasting difference.

Ephesians 4:11-13

So Christ Himself gave the apostles, the prophets, the evangelists, the pastors and teachers, to equip His people for works of service, so that the Body of Christ may be built up until we all reach unity in the faith and in the knowledge of the Son of God and become mature, attaining to the whole measure of the fullness of Christ.

Thank You for giving us everything we need to grow up and become a mature Ecclesia! Bless the leaders who are called and anointed to teach us and empower us to be a mighty force in this world. Help us see those whom You have called to this task so we can benefit from all their gifts. Help us receive from the grace on their lives so we can be more effective in our own call and purpose.

Ephesians 5:25-27

Husbands, love your wives, just as Christ loved the Church and gave Himself up for her to make her holy, cleansing her by the washing with water through the word, and to present her to Himself as a radiant Church, without stain or wrinkle or any other blemish, but holy and blameless.

Jesus, may we as believers have the same passion and concern for the Church as You do. Help us see what You see and pursue holiness and righteousness with anticipation of our future. May we be united in our desire to be all that You intend. May we encourage one another to do our part in fulfilling Your call and preparing for Your return.

Ephesians 5:29

After all, no one ever hated their own body, but they feed and care for their body, just as Christ does the Church.

Forgive us, Lord, for our offenses and divisions within the Church. Forgive me for my frustration towards others and a lack of love for their wellbeing. Give me Your heart for my brothers and sisters so that I can embrace any differences with grace, patience, and kindness. Show me how to encourage others, especially those that rub me the wrong way. May my words and actions show Your love and care towards all of my spiritual family.

Philippians 2:2-4

Then make my joy complete by being like-minded, having the same love, being one in spirit and of one mind. Do nothing out of selfish ambition or vain conceit. Rather, in humility value others above yourselves, not looking to your own interests but each of you to the interests of the others.

Purify our love for one another, Lord. Forgive us for being self-centered and only thinking of our own needs and desires. Help us to truly care for one another with a sincere love and concern. Replace my own self preoccupation with an increased compassion and empathy for others. May we demonstrate such love for one another that it gets the world's attention and draws others to You.

Colossians 1:3-4

We always thank God, the Father of our Lord Jesus Christ, when we pray for you, because we have heard of your faith in Christ Jesus and of the love you have for all God's people.

I know it is our unified faith in You, Lord, that gives us oneness of heart. I pray that we would grow in our faith by seeking You above all else, knowing that this is what will bring us common purpose and unity. May we embrace one another, and all those who call You Lord, with equal love and concern.

Colossians 1:9

For this reason, since the day we heard about you, we have not stopped praying for you. We continually ask God to fill you with the knowledge of His will through all the wisdom and understanding that the Spirit gives.

Holy Spirit, remind us to keep praying for one another. Alert me when I forget to pray for those who are struggling and need greater understanding in Your purposes for their life. I pray that my spiritual family would grow in wisdom and depth of insight from Your Word. I pray that they would be filled to the full measure of the Spirit of God with great joy and anticipation of their future.

NOTES

NOTES

Words for Spiritual Awakening

Psalms 35:23-24

Awake, and rise to my defense! Contend for me, my God and Lord. Vindicate me in Your righteousness, Lord my God; do not let them gloat over me.

As we wake up to our great need of You, Lord, we ask You to come and contend for us against our enemies. We have been overrun by threats and intimidation. Do not let our enemies have their way! Vindicate us and defend us so that we may rise up as one and declare the greatness of Your Name.

Psalms 80:2b-3

Awaken Your might; come and save us. Restore us, O God; make Your face shine on us, that we may be saved.

Lord, we need to be awakened to the promise of salvation and the power of restoration. Come, Holy Spirit, and move mightily on our behalf to awaken a slumbering Church. Shine Your light upon us to separate out the lies from the truth. We cannot do this on our own, so we ask You to come and manifest the might and power of the Kingdom among us.

Psalms 119:148-149

My eyes stay open through the watches of the night, that I may meditate on Your promises. Hear my voice in accordance with Your love; preserve my life, Lord, according to Your laws.

Lord, I want to have my eyes wide open to what You are doing on the earth today. Keep me alert in intercession and help me to be a faithful watchman in prayer. As I plant Your Word in my heart, may I see things as You do and interpret rightly the activities of Your Spirit. Grant me even greater grace to stay awake and to call others to watch through the night.

Proverbs 6:20-22

My son, keep your father's command and do not forsake your mother's teaching. Bind them always on your heart; fasten them around your neck.

When you walk, they will guide you; when you sleep, they will watch over you; when you awake, they will speak to you.

Father, I pray that You will draw Your people to feed on Your Word and plant Your truth in their hearts and minds. As You awaken us to the power of Your Kingdom, may Your Words come alive in fresh ways and direct us in the transformation to come. Speak to us through Your Words so we can stir the fires of revival and release fresh revelation from Your heart.

Isaiah 44:3-4

For I will pour water on the thirsty land, and streams on the dry ground; I will pour out My Spirit on your offspring, and My blessing on your descendants. They will spring up like grass in a meadow, like poplar trees by flowing streams.

Thank You, Holy Spirit, for pouring out upon our children and their children's children! Thank You for blessing our descendants with the power of Your Spirit to bring abundance and life in all they do. We declare that the generations to come will experience the fruit of our prayers and the manifestation of Your promises. May they see the realities of the earth being covered with the knowledge of Your glory.

Isaiah 52:1-2

Awake, awake, Zion, clothe yourself with strength! Put on your garments of splendor, Jerusalem, the holy city. The uncircumcised and defiled will not enter you again. Shake off your dust; rise up, sit enthroned, Jerusalem. Free yourself from the chains on your neck, Daughter Zion, now a captive.

To the Church in this hour I say, "Wake up from your slumber and clothe yourself with strength! Shake off the failures of the past and the limitations of the flesh. Shake off the chains that have bound you to doctrines of man and clothe yourself with the Spirit's power! Wake up, Ecclesia, to the destiny that is before you!"

Isaiah 64:1-2

Oh, that You would rend the heavens and come down, that the mountains would tremble before You! As when fire sets twigs ablaze and causes water to boil, come down to make Your Name known to Your enemies and cause the nations to quake before You!

Lord, we look to that time when all of heaven will manifest Your glory on the earth. We ask for demonstrations of Your power that would touch all of Your creation. May the rocks cry out Your Name and may Your enemies fall to their knees in the light of Your presence and power. Rend the heavens and come down, Lord! Come and shake the earth with Your glory and might!

Joel 1:5-6
Wake up, you drunkards, and weep! Wail, all you drinkers of wine; wail because of the new wine, for it has been snatched from your lips. A nation has invaded My land, a mighty army without number; it has the teeth of a lion, the fangs of a lioness.

Holy Spirit, I send forth this declaration to all who are spiritually asleep, "Wake up and see the enemies at your gates! Wake up and see the threats that are before us! Wake up to see the devil crouching at your doors!" Father, I ask that Your Spirit stir the hearts of those who are apathetic to Your ways and alert them to the dangers ahead. May the fear of the Lord fall upon those who have yet to see the battles at hand!

Matthew 24:42
Therefore, keep watch, because you do not know on what day your Lord will come.

Keep us alert, Holy Spirit, to the movements and activities of heaven. Remind us to stay awake and watch for what You are doing on the earth. Help us to be ready at any time to welcome Your presence and engage with Your Spirit.

Luke 9:32
Peter and his companions were very sleepy, but when they became fully awake, they saw His glory and the two men standing with Him.

Lord, forgive us for falling asleep on our watch and not realizing what You are doing! Help us to shake off the slumber and clear our eyes of sleepiness. May we see the fullness of Your glory and all that You are doing right in front of our eyes. Awaken Your Church to the glories of Your presence.

Luke 21:36 (ESV)

But stay awake at all times, praying that you may have strength to escape all these things that are going to take place, and to stand before the Son of Man.

May I be faithful in prayer, Lord, in order to stay awake to Your plans and Your purposes. May I continually fill myself with Your truth so I can recognize what is happening. Thank You for strengthening me in avoiding the traps of the enemy and maintaining my righteousness before You.

Acts 2:6-7

When they heard this sound, a crowd came together in bewilderment, because each one heard their own language being spoken. Utterly amazed, they asked: "Aren't all these who are speaking Galileans?"

Holy Spirit, fall upon us with a fresh fire that will alert and awaken a deaf and dumb culture. May they hear the sound of awakening! May they hear You speak to them in supernatural ways! May Your Spirit be released in fresh ways to capture the attention of onlookers and those who have never heard of Your saving grace and power. May we, Your people, be conduits of the sounds of heaven to break the bondages of men!

Acts 2:46-47

Every day they continued to meet together in the temple courts. They broke bread in their homes and ate together with glad and sincere hearts, praising God and enjoying the favor of all the people. And the Lord added to their number daily those who were being saved.

Draw Your people together, Lord, to be so hungry for fellowship with the Spirit and with one another, that revival fire would spread from house to house. May we learn a new joy in being a community that is on fire for You. May we model to our city the kind of love and power that can only come when fully surrendered to You. May salvation come and revival spread as we pursue You together each and every day.

Acts 3:19

Repent, then, and turn to God, so that your sins may be wiped out, that times of refreshing may come from the Lord.

Lord, we need times of refreshing to renew our faith and strengthen our resolve. Show us any areas of our lives that are not clean before You so that we can repent and make things right. We want to be clear of any sin or compromise that would limit the outpouring of Your Spirit. Thank You for this work of Your Spirit to refresh, renew, and revitalize our faith for the days to come.

Acts 12:7

Suddenly an angel of the Lord appeared and a light shone in the cell. He struck Peter on the side and woke him up. "Quick, get up!" he said, and the chains fell off Peter's wrists.

Holy Spirit, I ask for angelic encounters and supernatural interruptions to wake people up from their sleep! Just as Peter was awoken by an angel, so awaken Your people to that which You are doing. May we partner with heaven in fulfilling Your words and seeing prayers answered. Poke us if You need to! Get our attention so we can break off our chains and walk through the enemy's camp, free from constraints and covered by Your presence. Thank You for waking us up to the freedom ahead!

Acts 16:27-30

The jailer woke up, and when he saw the prison doors open, he drew his sword and was about to kill himself because he thought the prisoners had escaped. But Paul shouted, "Don't harm yourself! We are all here!" The jailer called for lights, rushed in and fell trembling before Paul and Silas. He then brought them out and asked, "Sirs, what must I do to be saved?"

Thank You for supernatural signs to wake us up, Lord! May You continue to shake everything that needs to be shaken in order to wake people from their spiritual slumber and call upon Your Name. Do what You must to open people's eyes to see the power of Your Kingdom and the transformation You want to bring. I declare that many will be awakened to their need for salvation and the power of Your Name to break off every chain of the enemy.

Romans 13:11-12

And do this, understanding the present time: The hour has already come for you to wake up from your slumber, because our salvation is nearer now than when we first believed. The night is nearly over; the day is almost here. So let us put aside the deeds of darkness and put on the armor of light.

Awaken us, God, to the realities of Your Kingdom that are here and now. Help us to not only see the works of darkness, but expose them and displace them with demonstrations of Your power. May we be Your light bearers and the ones to bring reformation and transformation to our land. For those still sleeping, I say, "WAKE UP! Today is the day of salvation and the manifestation of God's Kingdom on the earth!"

Ephesians 5:13-14

But everything exposed by the light becomes visible - and everything that is illuminated becomes a light. This is why it is said: "Wake up, sleeper, rise from the dead, and Christ will shine on you."

Holy Spirit, awaken us to the truth and all that brings light. As the darkness comes into the light, may we wake up, rise up, and displace the darkness with Your glory and power. May we shine and reflect Your goodness and power for all the world to see.

1 Thessalonians 5:6-8

So then, let us not be like others, who are asleep, but let us be awake and sober. For those who sleep, sleep at night, and those who get drunk, get drunk at night. But since we belong to the day, let us be sober, putting on faith and love as a breastplate, and the hope of salvation as a helmet.

Set apart Your people, Lord, to stay on the alert and not fall asleep in the dark. Convict us of our tendency to waste our time and get distracted with lesser thing of the flesh. Remind us of our future so we will remain vigilant in keeping watch and preparing for Your glory to come. Fill us with Your Spirit so we will be motivated by love, fueled with Your faith, and expectant in hope.

Revelation 3:2-3

Wake up! Strengthen what remains and is about to die, for I have found your deeds unfinished in the sight of my God. Remember, therefore, what you have received and heard; hold it fast, and repent. But if you do not wake up, I will come like a thief, and you will not know at what time I will come to you.

Wake up Your Church, Lord! May your people look to their foundations to examine what they are standing on. Strengthen our resolve to build upon Your Word and establish truth and righteousness for the generations to come. Wake us up to the cracks and holes in our belief systems that are weakening our faith and causing us to miss Your purposes. May we finish the work You have begun and be faithful in our commission.

NOTES

Words for Reaching the Lost

Psalms 139:7-12

Where can I go from Your Spirit? Where can I flee from Your presence? If I go up to the heavens, You are there; if I make my bed in the depths, You are there. If I rise on the wings of the dawn, if I settle on the far side of the sea, even there Your hand will guide me, Your right hand will hold me fast. If I say, "Surely the darkness will hide me and the light become night around me," even the darkness will not be dark to You; the night will shine like the day, for darkness is as light to You.

Father, for those who think You have abandoned them, give them a revelation of Your presence. Break through the darkness and show them how You have never left them but have been with them the entire time. Break off the blinders of guilt and condemnation and open their eyes to see You standing right in front of them. Show them the love in Your eyes and surround them with Your comfort. I declare that Your light will shine and Your love will penetrate, no matter how far they think they've fallen!

Ezekiel 34:15-16

"I Myself will tend My sheep and have them lie down," declares the Sovereign Lord. "I will search for the lost and bring back the strays. I will bind up the injured and strengthen the weak, but the sleek and the strong I will destroy. I will shepherd the flock with justice."

Thank You, Lord, for being the Good Shepherd who goes after His lost sheep. Thank You for searching them out and bringing back those who have strayed from Your paths. Bring healing to those who have been wounded and strengthen those who have been weakened by trials. May they lie down in peace and know the safety of Your fields once again.

Matthew 5:16

In the same way, let your light shine before others, that they may see your good deeds and glorify your Father in heaven.

Lord, remind me when I get lost in my own world and forget to turn my attention to those who don't know You. I want others to know who You are and the incredible things You have done for me. Give me the words to say and the things to do that will demonstrate the power of Your love to those who are lost. May my relationship with You be more than just talk, but actions that will compel others to want to know the reason for my hope.

Matthew 9:37-38

Then He said to His disciples, "The harvest is plentiful but the workers are few. Ask the Lord of the harvest, therefore, to send out workers into His harvest field."

Lord, use me to bring in the harvest! Empower me to be a witness to Your incredible grace and power to those who don't know. Open my eyes to see who is ready to hear. Give me words to say that will penetrate hearts. Fill my heart with Your love to reach into the darkest places and pull out those who are trapped. Stir Your workers into action so the lost can be found!

Matthew 28:19-20

Therefore, go and make disciples of all nations, baptizing them in the name of the Father and of the Son and of the Holy Spirit, and teaching them to obey everything I have commanded you. And surely I am with you always, to the very end of the age.

Teach us, Holy Spirit, how to mentor and disciple those who come to salvation. Empower Your Church to be not just soul winners, but teachers and coaches to those who are new to the faith. Help us to disciple our young so that our spiritual foundations will be secure. May we bring such transformation to those around us that entire nations will declare You as Savior and Lord.

Luke 15:4-6

Suppose one of you has a hundred sheep and loses one of them. Doesn't he leave the ninety-nine in the open country and go after the lost sheep until he finds it? And when he finds it, he joyfully puts it on his shoulders and goes home. Then he calls his friends and neighbors together and says, "Rejoice with me; I have found my lost sheep."

Father, I ask You to go after that one lost sheep! Thank You for not only caring for them but pursuing them! Thank You for Your love which is passionate and relentless in bringing Your lost sheep home. Thank You for working in ways I cannot see. Thank You for knowing exactly how to find those who have wandered.

John 3:16-17
For God so loved the world that He gave His one and only Son, that whoever believes in Him shall not perish but have eternal life. For God did not send His Son into the world to condemn the world, but to save the world through Him.

Thank You, Jesus, for coming to the earth and providing the way for salvation. Thank You for giving us eternal life through Your death and resurrection. Thank You for not condemning us because of our sins, but saving us. May all who are lost come to know the amazing gift You offer.

John 6:44a
No one can come to Me unless the Father who sent Me draws them.

Father, draw the lost to You and compel them to seek that which is true. Holy Spirit, hover over those who are wandering and shine Your light on the right paths for them to take. Bring them to the cross and the power of a life laid down. Whisper in their ears, Jesus, so they hear Your voice and know that it is You that longs to meet with them and set them free.

John 14:6
Jesus answered, "I am the Way and the Truth and the Life. No one comes to the Father except through Me."

Lord, I pray for those who have lost their way and have no purpose in life. May they have a revelation that Jesus is who they are looking for! Displace the lies about religion and awaken their hearts to a personal relationship with You. May all the paths they take eventually wind their way to Your heart, Your will, and Your unconditional love.

Acts 1:8

But you will receive power when the Holy Spirit comes on you; and you will be My witnesses in Jerusalem, and in all Judea and Samaria, and to the ends of the earth.

Fill me with Your Spirit, Lord, so my testimony will reflect the power of Your love and Your miraculous grace. Enable Your sons and daughters to be demonstrations of heaven on earth so that the lost will see there is a God who loves them and who is supreme over all. Empower Your Church to be that shining light on a hill and set apart for Your purposes.

Acts 2:38

Peter replied, "Repent and be baptized, every one of you, in the name of Jesus Christ for the forgiveness of your sins. And you will receive the gift of the Holy Spirit."

Lord, I pray that every soul that makes a decision for you will be immediately baptized in the power of Your Spirit. May they know the fullness of Your Spirit from the very beginning. May they have the power needed to walk out their salvation and know Your voice. Enable Your servants to bring the lost to Father, Son, and Holy Spirit with a tangible demonstration of heaven on earth.

Romans 2:4

Or do you show contempt for the riches of His kindness, forbearance and patience, not realizing that God's kindness is intended to lead you to repentance?

Lord, forgive me for my frustrations concerning those in my life who are blinded by sin. Help me to keep a good attitude and look for ways to show them kindness instead of contempt. Help me look past their flesh and pull out the good inside of them. Help me to be an encourager and one who gives others hope and vision for their future. May they be overwhelmed by Your kindness, Lord, and melted by Your mercy.

Romans 5:5

And hope does not put us to shame, because God's love has been poured out into our hearts through the Holy Spirit, who has been given to us.

Renew our hope, Lord, so that we will not give up or give in. For those who feel it's too late to turn their lives around, stir in them a fresh vision for their future and a longing to be free. For those in darkness, turn a light on so they can see the promises You have waiting for them. I declare that hope will break through the bondage and call the lost into liberty.

Romans 5:8

But God demonstrates His own love for us in this: While we were still sinners, Christ died for us.

When I share with others who are trapped in sin, Lord help me to demonstrate Your unconditional love to them. May they realize that You forgive any and all who call on Your name. May they see the incredible grace You offer so they can be free from shame and guilt. Reach into their hearts and set them free from condemnation so they can receive the gift of salvation and freedom from sin.

2 Corinthians 5:17

Therefore, if anyone is in Christ, the new creation has come: The old has gone, the new is here!

For those who are weighed down with guilt and shame about their past, I declare the truth of Your resurrection life that makes all things new! May they see the gift You offer and the grace You extend to all who call on Your Name. May they encounter Your love in such a profound way that their weaknesses and failures would no longer be limitations, but doorways for Your grace, redemption, and restoration.

2 Timothy 2:15

Do your best to present yourself to God as one approved, a worker who does not need to be ashamed and who correctly handles the word of truth.

Help me to be a student of Your Word. Teach me to understand Your principles and laws so that I can empower others to do the same. When sharing my faith with others, enable me to present Your Word with simplicity, accuracy, and power. May I represent You well, Lord!

1 John 4:8
Whoever does not love does not know God, because God is love.

Lord, I pray for those around me who are trapped in pain and brokenness. I ask that Your Spirit overwhelm them with the reality of Your love for them. May they have a revelation of Your love that goes beyond anything humanly possible. Open their eyes and hearts to what true love looks like.

NOTES

NOTES

POSSESSING THE LAND

2 Chronicles 7:14

If My people, who are called by My Name, will humble themselves and pray and seek My face and turn from their wicked ways, then I will hear from heaven, and I will forgive their sin and will heal their land.

Make us a people that desire to walk in Your holiness, Lord. Show us where we have fallen away from Your truth so that we can repent and start doing the right things. Keep our hearts humble and free from pride. Remind us to always seek Your face and ask for Your counsel so that our nation will be healed, restored, and set free to worship You.

Nehemiah 2:6

Then the king, with the queen sitting beside him, asked me, "How long will your journey take, and when will you get back?" It pleased the king to send me; so I set a time.

Father, it is Your desire for the earth's leaders to honor Your people. Give us leaders who look favorably upon those called to preach Your Word and establish Your truth. Give us leaders who will support and champion believers in Christ and those called to build Your kingdom.

Job 12:23

He makes nations great, and destroys them; He enlarges nations, and disperses them.

God, You are the one who has the final authority over nations. For those nations that follow after You, bless them and increase their influence on the earth. For those nations that oppose You, disperse their leadership and nullify their impact. May those nations which honor and obey You be exalted on the earth to give You glory.

Psalms 22:27-28

All the ends of the earth will remember and turn to the Lord, and all the families of the nations will bow down before Him, for dominion belongs to the Lord and He rules over the nations.

I declare that all the families of the nations will bow down before You and call You King! For You rule over every nation and are Supreme over all. Even those who defy You and serve other gods have no other choice but to eventually acknowledge You as King. Draw them to Your throne, Lord, that all may remember and turn to You as God of all.

Psalms 33:12

Blessed is the nation whose God is the Lord, the people He chose for His inheritance.

I want to live in a blessed nation, God. I declare that this nation will follow after You and walk in Your truth. May all the people come to know You as Lord and desire to live for You. May we receive the inheritance You have prepared for us as a nation and reflect the fullness of Your glory.

Psalms 47:8-9

God reigns over the nations; God is seated on His holy throne. The nobles of the nations assemble as the people of the God of Abraham, for the kings of the earth belong to God; He is greatly exalted.

You alone, Lord, sit over all the nations of the earth as the rightful King and Ruler. May all men know that You have supreme authority over the affairs of men. May all come to know You as the Father of all nations and the source of all that is good and right.

Psalms 75:7

It is God who judges: He brings one down, He exalts another.

God, You are the final Judge and the One who determines the times and seasons of men's rule. I ask You to remove any government leader that is opposed to Your truth and leading us astray. Open doors for the righteous leaders and close the doors for the rebels. Put in place those men and women who are called and anointed by You so they can bring blessing to this nation.

Psalms 115:16
The highest heavens belong to the Lord, but the earth He has given to mankind.

You have given us the responsibility to rule here on the earth, Lord. You have invited us to reign on the earth as Your sons and daughters. May we be faithful in this charge and show the world the power of Your Kingdom as we follow the ways of the Your throne.

Proverbs 11:11
By the blessing of the upright a city is exalted, but by the mouth of the wicked it is overthrown.

Lord, remind us as believers to bless our city, our state, and our nation. May the words we speak about our government open doors for Your blessing and favor. Forgive us for curses we have spoken out of frustration. May we not come into agreement with negative words and criticisms aimed at destroying what You are doing. May the promises of God overturn the curses of the wicked!

Proverbs 14:34
Righteousness exalts a nation, but sin condemns any people.

May living a good and honorable life become the standard in this nation. May those who relish sin see the negative impact of their lifestyle and turn from their compromise. Pour out Your favor on those who are faithful to do what is right and may others see the blessing and honor that comes from obedience to Your Word.

Proverbs 21:15
When justice is done, it brings joy to the righteous but terror to evildoers.

Father, show our leaders the power of Your justice to bring peace and stability to the land. May the results be evident when the fear of the Lord is established in our nation to discourage the evildoers from practicing their rebellion. May the people of this nation rejoice in just laws and righteous rule and be glad for a government that honors You. May those who oppose You be limited and bound by the weight of Your righteous rule.

Proverbs 29:2

When the righteous thrive, the people rejoice; when the wicked rule, the people groan.

For those who still question the validity of Your throne, show them the blessing and favor that rests upon the righteous. May our obedience and commitment to Your Word be tangible to those who are wondering. May the ways of the wicked be evident and the fruit of their disobedience be a deterrent for those on the fence. May we be a nation that exhibits joy and blessing as a result of Your righteous rule.

Isaiah 2:4

He will judge between the nations and will settle disputes for many peoples. They will beat their swords into plowshares and their spears into pruning hooks. Nation will not take up sword against nation, nor will they train for war anymore.

God, You are the final arbiter of nations and the final Judge over men. You hold entire countries accountable for the choices they've made and the seeds they have sown. As Your people, You have given us responsibility and stewardship in our nation to elect righteous rulers so that our nation will be blessed. Remind us of our charge so we can be faithful in this commission as one nation under God.

Isaiah 9:6-7a

For to us a child is born, to us a Son is given, and the government will be on His shoulders. And He will be called Wonderful Counselor, Mighty God, Everlasting Father, Prince of Peace. Of the greatness of His government and peace there will be no end.

Thank You, Lord, for carrying the governments of this world on Your shoulders. Your Kingdom is the highest of all kingdoms and Your authority supersedes all others. Though other kingdoms will rise and fall, Yours is eternally growing and expanding, bringing lasting peace and promise to all who acknowledge Your reign.

Isaiah 26:9-10

My soul yearns for You in the night; in the morning my spirit longs for You. When Your judgments come upon the earth, the people of the world learn righteousness. But when grace is shown to the wicked, they do not learn righteousness; even in a land of uprightness they go on doing evil and do not regard the majesty of the Lord.

Father, I pray that this nation will learn obedience and the necessity of following Your counsel. When bad decisions are made and we turn aside from Your plans, correct us and get us on track again. May those who oppose You see the consequences of straying from Your truth and turn aside from their wicked ways. May we see the mercy of Your judgments as good and right for us as a people.

Acts 10:34-36

Then Peter began to speak: "I now realize how true it is that God does not show favoritism but accepts from every nation the one who fears Him and does what is right."

God, You are no respecter of persons. You will accept and bless all who believe what You say and do what You do. Those who walk in the fear of the Lord will bless their nation and receive Your favor. May every nation be touched by Your power and drawn by Your Spirit to acknowledge You as Lord.

1 Timothy 2:1-4

I urge, then, first of all, that petitions, prayers, intercession, and thanksgiving be made for all people - for kings and all those in authority, that we may live peaceful and quiet lives in all godliness and holiness. This is good, and pleases God our Savior, who wants all people to be saved and to come to a knowledge of the truth.

Father, I lift up all our leaders and those in positions of authority in our government. I pray that they will follow You with zeal and seek to make wise decisions that honor Your truth and Your word. May their rule help establish peace and prosperity in our land. May the laws they establish open doors for the gospel to be preached and Your truths to be known.

1 Peter 2:9-10

But you are a chosen people, a royal priesthood, a holy nation, God's special possession, that you may declare the praises of Him who called you out of darkness into His wonderful light. Once you were not a people, but now you are the people of God; once you had not received mercy, but now you have received mercy.

Lord, may this nation be a chosen people and royal priesthood. May we walk in holiness and truth and bear the fruit of righteous rule. Make us into a unified people – one nation under God. May we shine brightly for all the world to see.

1 Peter 2:16-17

Live as free people, but do not use your freedom as a cover-up for evil; live as God's slaves. Show proper respect to everyone, love the family of believers, fear God, honor the emperor.

You have called us as a holy people, Lord. Your desire is for us to demonstrate the freedom that comes from living a righteous life. May we be faithful in our nation to use our freedoms for good and not for evil. Lead us to make laws that maintain the standard of Your Word so that all people can have the opportunity to know the joy of following You. May there be honor, respect, and a fear of the Lord in our nation that will bring Your favor and blessing.

NOTES

NOTES

Exodus 23:6-8

Do not deny justice to your poor people in their lawsuits. Have nothing to do with a false charge and do not put an innocent or honest person to death, for I will not acquit the guilty. Do not accept a bribe, for a bribe blinds those who see and twists the words of the innocent.

God, I pray that those executing justice would do so with honor and respect for Your laws. I pray that judges and lawmakers would not show favoritism or bias, but seek to treat each one fairly based on the merits of each case. Stop those who accept bribes and manipulate their position for personal gain. May your truth be revealed in our justice system so that confidence can be restored and our lawmakers esteemed.

Psalms 2:10-12

Therefore, you kings, be wise; be warned, you rulers of the earth. Serve the Lord with fear and celebrate His rule with trembling. Kiss His son, or He will be angry and your way will lead to your destruction, for His wrath can flare up in a moment. Blessed are all who take refuge in Him.

May the fear of the Lord rest upon all our governing leaders. May they know the supremacy of Your authority and the power of Your rule. May they willingly and gladly submit to Your truths and precepts for the sake of the people. May they be reminded of the consequences of unjust decisions so that they will stay within the boundaries of the authority You have given them.

Psalms 24:3-6

Who may ascend the mountain of the Lord? Who may stand in His holy place? The one who has clean hands and a pure heart, who does not trust in an idol or swear by a false god. They will receive blessing from the Lord and vindication from God their Savior. Such is the generation of those who seek Him, who seek Your face, God of Jacob.

Lord, I speak to those in governing positions to have clean hands and a pure heart. Convict them of any idols in their lives and compel them to renounce any allegiance to counterfeit gods or corrupted organizations. Give them a heart for purity and a right standing with You. Protect those who have taken this stand and vindicate their cause for Your glory.

Psalms 128:1-2

Blessed are all who fear the Lord, who walk in obedience to Him. You will eat the fruit of your labor; blessings and prosperity will be yours.

Father, bless those in governing positions who walk in obedience to Your truths. May they see the fruit of their faithfulness, even in the midst of opposition. May their homes and families be blessed and covered with protection and peace. Distinguish those who honor Your Word with such blessing and favor, it will convict the rebels and draw the lost to seek Your face.

Proverbs 8:14-16

Counsel and sound judgment are Mine; I have insight, I have power. By Me kings reign and rulers issue decrees that are just; by Me princes govern, and nobles - all who rule on earth.

Father, show us those leaders who have been called and anointed by You to lead in our government. Distinguish those who honor Your truth and have determined to make just laws and righteous rules. Set apart those who have sound judgment and seek godly counsel so that our nation can thrive and be a blessing.

Proverbs 10:29

The way of the Lord is a refuge for the blameless, but it is the ruin of those who do evil.

God, may those leaders who follow Your ways be found blameless and pure in heart. May they experience Your sovereign protection and grace because of their faithfulness to Your truth. May those who do not follow Your ways see the folly of disobedience and reap the results of their destructive decisions.

Proverbs 11:14
For lack of guidance a nation falls, but victory is won through many advisers.

Be with our leaders so that they will seek right counsel and clear discernment in the decisions they make. Draw together those who honor Your Word so they can be unified in their leadership and one in their purpose. Raise up true leaders with anointing to guide us into the fullness of Your blessing. May all others see the fruit of righteous rule.

Proverbs 21:1
In the Lord's hand the king's heart is a stream of water that He channels toward all who please Him.

For those leaders who are straying from Your truth, draw them back to You, Lord! Direct the thoughts and ideas of our leaders so they will walk in the paths that will bring the greatest blessing on our nation. Establish the steps of those in positions of authority so they will make laws that please You and bring us peace and prosperity.

Proverbs 24:5-6
The wise prevail through great power, and those who have knowledge muster their strength. Surely you need guidance to wage war, and victory is won through many advisers.

Give our governing leaders the confidence they need to make the hard calls. When faced with opposition, give them wise counsel and accurate information with which to make the right decision. Cover them with Your peace and clarity so they can prevail in times of warfare and strife. Bring our leaders into oneness of heart concerning Your purposes so they can move forward with heaven's authority.

Proverbs 29:25
Fear of man will prove to be a snare, but whoever trusts in the Lord is kept safe.

May our governing authorities look to You for counsel and the wisdom to make right decisions. Keep our leaders from bowing to the fear of man and the need for approval. *Expose the counterfeits and false information that would lead them astray. Show our leaders the fruit of right decisions and the protection that comes when following Your lead and not the opinions of men.*

Isaiah 1:17

Learn to do right; seek justice. Defend the oppressed. Take up the cause of the fatherless; plead the case of the widow.

Lord, may our leaders do what is right to seek justice for all who live within our borders. May they have compassion on the oppressed and take up the cause of those without a home or family. May they seek creative ways to meet the needs of the people so that all can have the same opportunity to thrive and succeed in this life.

Isaiah 11:2-3a

The Spirit of the Lord will rest on him - the Spirit of wisdom and of understanding, the Spirit of counsel and of might, the Spirit of the knowledge and fear of the Lord - and he will delight in the fear of the Lord.

I pray that our governing leaders would experience the presence of the Lord upon their lives. I pray they would operate under the power of Holy Spirit with wisdom and understanding, with good counsel and strength of character, and with the knowledge and fear of the Lord. I pray that they would be grateful for the fear of the Lord on their lives and experience great joy in seeing the amazing results from abiding in You.

Isaiah 32:1-4

See, a king will reign in righteousness and rulers will rule with justice. Each one will be like a shelter from the wind and a refuge from the storm, like streams of water in the desert and the shadow of a great rock in a thirsty land. Then the eyes of those who see will no longer be closed, and the ears of those who hear will listen. The fearful heart will know and understand, and the stammering tongue will be fluent and clear.

Bless our leaders with such wisdom from above that people will feel safe, secure, and unafraid to face the future. Give them increased understand-

ing to make right judgment calls concerning our destiny as a nation. May their leadership give us clear vision for the days ahead, filled with hope and expectation.

Isaiah 61:8

For I, the Lord, love justice; I hate robbery and wrongdoing. In My faithfulness I will reward My people and make an everlasting covenant with them.

Lord, may our lawmakers love what You love and hate what You hate. May there be an increased conviction of righteous rule and the necessity of following Your ways. You have made a covenant with Your people to bring us into our inheritance and fulfill Your promises for the generations to come. Establish the foundations in our nation to reflect Your love for justice and truth so that we can see the fulfillment of Your Word.

Matthew 6:33

But seek first His kingdom and His righteousness, and all these things will be given to you as well.

Lord, give our leaders a heart to seek You above all else. May they govern according to the truths of Your kingdom, knowing this will bring the greatest blessing and the greatest reward. Remind them when they give in to the fear of man. Lead them to trust You as they make decisions based on Your laws and not on men's opinions.

Romans 13:1

Let everyone be subject to the governing authorities, for there is no authority except that which God has established. The authorities that exist have been established by God.

Father, You are the origin of all authority and the only one who can grant it. Your authority is based on good and not evil; righteousness and not wickedness. Help us to distinguish the difference between godly authority and fleshly control. Set apart those who carry the mark of Your favor and the fruit of Your blessing.

Romans 13:4

For the one in authority is God's servant for your good. But if you do wrong, be afraid, for rulers do not bear the sword for no reason. They are God's servants, agents of wrath to bring punishment on the wrongdoer.

God, You provide us with governing authorities so there can be peace in the land. Show us clearly those who have been called by You with a heart to serve the people and not themselves. Show favor and honor to those who are prepared to deal with wrongdoers and bless those who do good. May we see and recognize those leaders who govern in the way You designed so that all people will have the freedom to choose You.

Romans 13:6

This is also why you pay taxes, for the authorities are God's servants, who give their full time to governing.

Lord, I pray that those who have been elected as public servants would remember that they are Your servants, first. Impress upon them the favor and blessing that comes when they serve the people out of reverence for You. May our government leaders walk in the fear of the Lord and bring righteous judgments on our behalf.

1 Peter 2:13-14

Submit yourselves for the Lord's sake to every human authority: whether to the emperor, as the supreme authority, or to governors, who are sent by Him to punish those who do wrong and to commend those who do right.

You have asked us, Lord, to submit to those authorities who lead in the way You designed. You desire for our leaders to punish those who do wrong and commend those who do right so there can be peace in the land. Distinguish those leaders who use their authority justly and honor You in their positions. Show us how to support and encourage those who govern according to Your principles and pray for those who don't.

NOTES

NOTES

WORDS FOR RIGHTEOUS LAWS

2 Chronicles 19:7

Now let the fear of the Lord be on you. Judge carefully, for with the Lord our God there is no injustice or partiality, or bribery.

Release the fear of the Lord upon those who make laws in our nation, Lord. Start in our community and then our state. May the seriousness of their position be evident as the weight of Your presence is felt. Remove any who have gained their position through bribery or false pretense. Give us officials who will rule justly without partiality. May each one know they must eventually answer to You for their decisions.

Psalms 1:1-3

Blessed is the one who does not walk in step with the wicked or stand in the way that sinners take or sit in the company of mockers, but whose delight is in the law of the Lord, and who meditates on His law day and night. That person is like a tree planted by streams of water, which yields its fruit in season and whose leaf does not wither - whatever they do prospers.

May our nation be blessed through our laws, Lord. May we not look to the wicked for counsel or expect the sinner to bring us truth. May our delight be in Your Word that brings life and liberty. Bring us elected officials who revere Your Word and seek to uphold it through the laws they make. May we see the fruit of obedience and faithfulness to Your plumbline of truth and Your heart for justice.

Psalms 19:7-9

The law of the Lord is perfect, refreshing the soul. The statutes of the Lord are trustworthy, making wise the simple. The precepts of the Lord are right, giving joy to the heart. The commands of the Lord are radiant, giving light to the eyes. The fear of the Lord is pure, enduring forever. The decrees of the Lord are firm, and all of them are righteous.

Father, I ask that the laws in this land reflect Your heart and character towards Your creation. May our laws refresh us by being trustworthy and easy to understand. May our laws bring a sense of freedom and safety. May the laws give greater understanding to what is true and good in order for peace to reign. May our laws be pure in their intent and long-lasting in their impact. May we become a righteous people that shine forth Your glory for others to see.

Psalms 89:14

Righteousness and justice are the foundation of Your throne; love and faithfulness go before You.

I pray that the laws of this land will reflect Your righteousness and Your justice, Lord. May those who lead this nation understand the blessing of governing according to Your laws and precepts. Turn the hearts of our leaders to seek You for direction when making decisions so that our nation will be firmly established for generations to come.

Proverbs 21:3

To do what is right and just is more acceptable to the Lord than sacrifice.

Holy Spirit, remind our elected officials that doing the right thing carries great weight in the spirit. Show them the results of doing things Your way instead of their own. Teach them to uphold the laws of the land and not sacrifice truth and justice for personal gain.

Proverbs 24:24-25

Whoever says to the guilty, "You are innocent," will be cursed by peoples and denounced by nations. But it will go well with those who convict the guilty, and rich blessing will come on them.

Lord, cleanse this nation of any leader that rewards the guilty and punishes the innocent. Remove from office those who use their authority for personal gain or ill will. But for those who are not afraid to convict the guilty, even with threats and intimidation, may they reap the blessings from above that become self-evident to those who mock. Increase those who rule in righteousness and remove those who do not.

Proverbs 28:5 (ESV)

Evil men do not understand justice, but those who seek the Lord understand it completely.

Lord, show us which government leaders truly walk in the fear of the Lord. By their wisdom may they be known. By their depth of understanding and insight separate out those who look to You for counsel, versus those who look to themselves. Give our leaders a desire to gain understanding from Your Word so they can exercise justice without restraint.

Proverbs 29:7

The righteous care about justice for the poor, but the wicked have no such concern.

Lord, expose those politicians and public officials who care little for the poor or weak. Expose their hidden agendas and reveal the true state of their hearts. Bless the righteous who walk in compassion for those who are vulnerable and grant them increased favor.

Ecclesiastes 8:11

When the sentence for a crime is not quickly carried out, people's hearts are filled with schemes to do wrong.

Bring justice quickly to our legal system, Lord! May those presiding in our courts follow through with sentences and punishments against wrongdoers. May the consequences of evil be dealt with speedily to give the people hope. May it be clear what happens when laws are broken so as to deter the rebels and criminals. Turn the hearts of the people to love justice and obey our laws.

Jeremiah 22:3

This is what the Lord says: Do what is just and right. Rescue from the hand of the oppressor the one who has been robbed. Do no wrong or violence to the foreigner, the fatherless or the widow, and do not shed innocent blood in this place.

Lord, speak to our legal representatives to execute severe consequences on those who hurt the weak and the vulnerable. Give them a deep conviction that would protect our young and all who are oppressed by trafficking and abuse. Give our lawmakers wisdom and understanding in carrying out justice to send a message to those who have shed innocent blood. May the fear of the Lord fall through the laws that are established in this land to protect and secure our children.

Micah 6:8

He has shown you, O mortal, what is good. And what does the Lord require of you? To act justly and to love mercy and to walk humbly with your God.

May we keep our laws simple and based on Your truth, Lord. May we be just towards one another and treat one another fairly. May we have mercy towards those who struggle with sin and long to be set free. May we walk in humility before You and others. May we be a people that please You by reflecting Your heart of both mercy and truth.

Matthew 23:23-24

Woe to you, teachers of the law and Pharisees, you hypocrites! You give a tenth of your spices - mint, dill and cumin. But you have neglected the more important matters of the law - justice, mercy and faithfulness. You should have practiced the latter, without neglecting the former. You blind guides! You strain out a gnat but swallow a camel.

Establish integrity in our court system, God. Establish a love for Your laws in every part of our culture, starting in the Church. May we as a people love justice, mercy, and faithfulness. May we esteem those who obey the law and seek to maintain a high standard of conduct and business in this nation. Remove those in positions of authority who are blind to what is most important and give us representatives who are passionate about the truth and compassionate towards their fellow man.

John 14:15

If you love Me, keep My commandments.

May the fear of the Lord rest upon those who follow You, Lord, to be the first to obey the laws. Give us a greater conviction in pursuing the kinds of laws that reflect Your heart and character in how we live. May we see the charge You have given us to steward this land and be an example to those around us. May we follow Your laws with joy and freedom so that others will see the blessings that come from doing things Your way.

Romans 7:7

What shall we say, then? Is the law sinful? Certainly not! Nevertheless, I would not have known what sin was had it not been for the law. For I would not have known what coveting really was if the law had not said, "You shall not covet."

Father, I ask for laws to be established that would remind people of what is good and right. For those who create our laws, may they see the Word of God as a template for justice. May they recognize Your wisdom in the laws You already established which have been proven to bring peace and stability to peoples and nations. May there be a fresh revelation of how secure and free a people can be when there are good laws in place.

Romans 13:9-10

The commandments, "You shall not commit adultery," "You shall not murder," "You shall not steal," "You shall not covet," and whatever other command there may be, are summed up in this one command: "Love your neighbor as yourself." Love does no harm to a neighbor. Therefore, love is the fulfillment of the law.

Stir in our hearts a greater love for our fellow man, God. May those who follow You be the first to model and demonstrate love and mercy towards others. May our laws be governed by this purity of love that seeks the best for one another and calls each other to account when the law of love is broken. Give us Your heart with which to execute our laws so that all are treated fairly and given the opportunity to experience the power of Love.

1 Timothy 1:8-11

We know that the law is good if one uses it properly. We also know that the law is made not for the righteous but for lawbreakers and rebels, the ungodly and sinful, the unholy and irreligious, for those who kill their fathers or mothers, for murderers, for the sexually immoral, for those practicing homosexuality, for slave traders and liars and perjurers - and for whatever else is contrary to the sound doctrine that conforms to the gospel concerning the glory of the blessed God, which he entrusted to me.

Thank You, Lord, for laws that keep the rebels and sinners from having free rein in our cities, states, and nation. Make the boundaries clear to those who execute justice so that the innocent will be protected and the guilty will be punished. May our justice system be founded on the principles of truth, justice, and liberty. Remind us that laws are for our good and necessary to maintain peace and freedom for all.

James 3:17-18

But the wisdom that comes from heaven is first of all pure; then peace-loving, considerate, submissive, full of mercy and good fruit, impartial and sincere. Peacemakers who sow in peace reap a harvest of righteousness.

May those who create our laws do so with the wisdom from heaven. May our laws be peace-loving, considerate, submissive to Your Word, full of mercy and good fruit. May they be impartial and free of bias. May they be true and right and bring peace to all. May our laws reap a harvest of righteousness in our cities and spread to other cities, states, and nations. Let the wisdom of heaven rule and reign in our land.

1 John 3:4

Everyone who sins breaks the law; in fact, sin is lawlessness.

Lord, free us from the spirit of lawlessness that has permeated the earth. Where sin has established a stronghold, convict Your people and draw them to repentance. In our own community, may the citizens see the negative effects of allowing sin to rein free. Move upon the hearts of the people to desire righteousness and see the blessing of obeying Your laws and doing what is right.

NOTES

NOTES

Words to Secure Our Cities

Exodus 33:14

The Lord replied, "My Presence will go with you, and I will give you rest."

Surround this city with Your presence, Lord! Give us rest on every side as we lift up Your Name above every other name. May Your peace overshadow Your people to give them confidence and boldness in continuing to declare the truth. Go before us and establish our steps as we enlarge the boundaries of Your Kingdom in this city.

2 Chronicles 20:15b

Do not be afraid or discouraged because of this vast army. For the battle is not yours, but God's.

Thank You, Lord, for fighting the battles that are Yours alone. Thank You for Your angelic host that are warring the principalities over this city and responding to our prayers. Help us to do our part in displacing the lies and ungodly beliefs that have attracted dark forces to our city. May we demonstrate Your Kingdom so powerfully that the vast armies aligned against us will be powerless against us!

Esther 6:9

Then let the robe and horse be entrusted to one of the king's most noble princes. Let them robe the man the king delights to honor and lead him on the horse through the city streets, proclaiming before him, "This is what is done for the man the king delights to honor!"

I declare that righteous leaders in this city will have a platform from which to speak. I declare that the favor of the Lord will be upon those who bring hope and light to the city. May city officials recognize those who truly love the city and recognize them for their truth and integrity. Grant increased favor to Your servants, Lord, so the entire city can see and hear the good things You have done.

Psalms 31:19-20

How abundant are the good things that You have stored up for those who fear You, that You bestow in the sight of all, on those who take refuge in You. In the shelter of Your presence, You hide them from all human intrigues; You keep them safe in Your dwelling from accusing tongues.

Father, I pray for any in our city who are being persecuted for their faith or being threatened because of their testimony. Hide them in the shadow of Your wings and protect them from the enemy's crosshairs. May they be kept safe and secure and able to continue in their service unto You. May they know the joy of sharing in the fellowship of Your sufferings, realizing the power of the truth to which they testify.

Psalms 34:7

The angel of the Lord encamps around those who fear Him, and He delivers them.

Thank You for the fear of the Lord that keeps and protects us, Lord! May Your presence surround those who have been faithfully serving You and obeying Your Word. Deliver us from evil eyes and those who would seek to take us down and destroy our testimony. May all the doubters and accusers be amazed at the sovereign protection and power of the Lord!

Psalms 55:9

Lord, confuse the wicked, confound their words, for I see violence and strife in the city.

I declare that all the plans and schemes of the enemy will become twisted like a knot and unable to gain any traction in this community. I declare that their communications would be confused and their words be like static. Lord, shut down the violence and strife in this city by releasing a fog over the enemy. May they not see, hear, or understand what to do because of the power of Your presence over this city.

Psalms 89:15-17

Blessed are those who have learned to acclaim You, who walk in the light of Your presence, Lord. They rejoice in Your name all day long; they celebrate Your righteousness. For You are their glory and strength, and by Your favor You exalt our horn.

Lord, may all those in this city who trust in You shine forth like gold! May their witness and testimony be so powerful as to bring light and life to all that is dead. May those who follow You be filled with joy and celebrate Your goodness. May You lift up those who give glory to Your Name so that Jesus would be known in our town.

Psalms 101:7
No one who practices deceit will dwell in My house; no one who speaks falsely will stand in My presence.

Lord God, I ask that You remove any and all who are practicing deceit in places of authority in this city. Especially in the Church, I ask that the fear of the Lord would fall on any leader who has been compromised or has fallen into sin. Cleanse and sanctify the leadership of this city so that we can stand in righteousness and truth for the sake of Your Name.

Psalms 107:6-9
Then they cried out to the Lord in their trouble, and He delivered them from their distress. He led them by a straight way to a city where they could settle. Let them give thanks to the Lord for His unfailing love and His wonderful deeds for mankind, for He satisfies the thirsty and fills the hungry with good things.

Lord, may this city become a refuge and haven for those who are hungry and thirsty. May this city be a place of salvation and restoration. May we establish godly foundations on which to build a lasting legacy and abundant inheritance for all who settle here. Empower Your Ecclesia in this city to be agents of transformation and givers of hope.

Psalms 121:7-8
The Lord will keep you from all harm - He will watch over your life; the Lord will watch over your coming and going both now and forevermore.

Lord, keep watch over the gates of this city and protect us from intruders and thieves. Release Your angelic host to guard the doorways, both natural and spiritual, so that we will not give access to the enemy. Help us establish altars of Your presence that will supersede and nullify the demonic altars of sin and compromise. May our worship, praise, and prayers be so powerful, no evil spirit will have influence or impact in this city.

Psalms 127:1

Unless the Lord builds the house, the builders labor in vain. Unless the Lord watches over the city, the guards stand watch in vain.

Bless the watchmen in this city, Lord! Bless those who stand by night and stay alert to spiritual activities. Raise up this next generation to continue the call and stand guard over this city. Reveal Your heart and Your ways to Your servants, the prophets and intercessors, so that we can partner with You in establishing Your Kingdom here.

Proverbs 8:1-3

Does not wisdom call out? Does not understanding raise her voice? At the highest point along the way, where the paths meet, she takes her stand; beside the gate leading into the city, at the entrance, she cries aloud.

We invite and welcome the spirit of wisdom to this city! May our leaders heed wisdom's call and learn that which will bring the greatest blessing to our city. Separate out man's intellect from heaven's wisdom and empower our city leaders to turn their ear to those who speak with truth and revelation from above.

Isaiah 1:26

I will restore your leaders as in days of old, your rulers as at the beginning. Afterward you will be called the City of Righteousness, the Faithful City.

Restore righteous leaders to this city, Lord! Raise up officials and law enforcements agents with a heart after You! Speak to those with gifts of leadership to have a heart for the city. Pour out favor upon those You have called so all can see the hand of God and the gift they will bring to this region. Bring us shepherds after Your own heart who will lead with compassion and truth, mercy and justice.

Isaiah 8:13-14

The Lord Almighty is the One you are to regard as holy, He is the One you are to fear, He is the One you are to dread. He will be a holy place; for both Israel and Judah He will be a stone that causes people to stumble and a rock that makes them fall. And for the people of Jerusalem He will be a trap and a snare.

Spirit of the Living God, fall upon this city with the fear of the Lord! May there be a divine separation between those who are true and faithful to the Lord and those who are compromised and counterfeit. Purify the Church of the city so that no unclean or religious spirit would tarnish or spoil the true gospel of the Kingdom. Offend our minds to get to our hearts! May we stand in awe and reverence at the holiness of Your name.

Isaiah 35:8-10

And a highway will be there; it will be called the Way of Holiness; it will be for those who walk on that Way. The unclean will not journey on it; wicked fools will not go about on it. No lion will be there, nor any ravenous beast; they will not be found there. But only the redeemed will walk there, and those the Lord has rescued will return. They will enter Zion with singing; everlasting joy will crown their heads. Gladness and joy will overtake them, and sorrow and sighing will flee away.

I speak over our roads and highways, Lord! I declare that every road that leads in and out of this city will be marked by holiness and righteousness. I declare that no unclean thing will have access and no illegal activity will be allowed. Shut down all traffic into this city with immoral or illegal agendas. Release Your angels to cover this city with songs of joy and gladness. May all who travel through here experience the presence of Your Spirit and the joy of the Lord!

Isaiah 63:8-9

He said, "Surely they are My people, children who will be true to Me;" and so He became their Savior. In all their distress He too was distressed, and the angel of His presence saved them. In His love and mercy He redeemed them; He lifted them up and carried them all the days of old.

Your love and mercy towards Your children is great, Lord! You are not apathetic towards our plight, but feel our pain and are ready to respond to any calamity or distress. I call upon the angel of Your presence to come and save those who are despondent and unaware of Your love. Rescue us from those who oppress us. May salvation come to those who see the power of Your love as You come and redeem this city.

Zechariah 2:5

"And I Myself will be a wall of fire around it," declares the Lord, "and I will be its glory within."

Lord, I ask that You place a firewall of Your Spirit around this city. Release Your angelic warriors to stand guard and protect this city from intruders and marauders. May the reality of Your Spirit burn in people's hearts and make them hunger for even more of Your presence and power. May that fire be a light and shining example of the supremacy of Your Kingdom and the glory of the King.

Luke 4:28-30

All the people in the synagogue were furious when they heard this. They got up, drove Him out of the town, and took Him to the brow of the hill on which the town was built, in order to throw Him off the cliff. But He walked right through the crowd and went on His way.

Thank You for supernatural protection, Lord! Even when our enemies seek to destroy us, You cover us and empower us to escape their traps. Watch over those who are bold and courageous to take a stand in this city and speak the truth. Protect them and deliver them from trouble. May the power of Your Spirit be evident to all who watch so that they will have a revelation of Your power for those who believe.

John 1:4-5

In Him was life, and that life was the light of all mankind. The light shines in the darkness, and the darkness has not overcome it.

Shine Your light on this city, Lord! I speak life to all that is dead here and resurrection power to those who are living in a grave of sin. Thank You, Lord, for the power of Your Name to dispel the darkness and bring hope and promise. I declare that the light over this city will overwhelm the darkness and that all who are searching for truth will find it.

John 17:11b

Holy Father, protect them by the power of Your Name, the Name You gave Me, so that they may be one as We are one.

Make us one, Lord! May all who follow You be of one mind and heart so that this city will have authority before the throne. Bring us together, even in our diversity and unique gifts. May we see the blessing and benefit we are to each other and hear Your heart together. May we be one unified voice in this city so that our prayers will be effective and our witness bring impact to our region. For the glory of Your Name alone.

Acts 6:9-10

Opposition arose, however, from members of the Synagogue of the Freedmen (as it was called) - Jews of Cyrene and Alexandria as well as the provinces of Cilicia and Asia - who began to argue with Stephen. But they could not stand up against the wisdom the Spirit gave him as he spoke.

Release the spirit of wisdom and revelation upon us, Lord, so that those who oppose us will be silenced. Give us words from heaven and testimonies that cannot be denied. Raise up those who boldly testify about You and speak to city officials in unmistakable ways. Guard and protect them with angelic assistance and keep them safe as they speak with the clarity of heaven.

Acts 8:6-8

When the crowds heard Philip and saw the signs he performed, they all paid close attention to what he said. For with shrieks, impure spirits came out of many, and many who were paralyzed or lame were healed. So there was great joy in that city.

Raise up Your ministers, Lord, who are unafraid to demonstrate the power of Your Kingdom in this city. May deliverance come to many who are bound by evil spirits at the preaching of Your Word. May joy erupt in this city as testimonies of healing and deliverance spread far and wide! Draw people to the realities of Your Kingdom through supernatural manifestations that bring many to salvation.

Acts 8:12-13

But when they believed Philip as he proclaimed the good news of the kingdom of God and the name of Jesus Christ, they were baptized, both men and women. Simon himself believed and was baptized. And he followed Philip everywhere, astonished by the great signs and miracles he saw.

Lord, bring forth the evangelists and those with a passion for the lost! May the gospel of the Kingdom be preached and demonstrated throughout our city with great power to break the spell of witchcraft and sorcery. May any who practice the dark arts in this city be miraculously saved by seeing the true demonstration of the Kingdom through Your servants.

Acts 18:9-10

One night the Lord spoke to Paul in a vision: "Do not be afraid; keep on speaking, do not be silent. For I am with you, and no one is going to attack and harm you, because I have many people in this city."

Lord, may this city be so full of believers in Christ that the enemy has no access or authority. May our boldness increase as we join together in faith and proclaim the truth of Your Kingdom. Thank You for the protection that comes when Your people unite for one cause. Draw us together that we might grow deeper in fellowship and stronger in our resolve to see Your Kingdom come in this place.

Acts 19:15-17

One day the evil spirit answered them, "Jesus I know, and Paul I know about, but who are you?" Then the man who had the evil spirit jumped on them and overpowered them all. He gave them such a beating that they ran out of the house naked and bleeding. When this became known to the Jews and Greeks living in Ephesus, they were all seized with fear, and the name of the Lord Jesus was held in high honor.

Lord, I ask that those who are using Your Name for their own glory and benefit would have a wake up call! May the fear of the Lord fall upon this city and the reality of demonic influence be exposed. May there be a clear separation between those leaders who walk in true authority and those who only seek fame and recognition. May the Name of Jesus not be a byword, but a powerful sword in our hands to cut the lies and demonstrate that which is true.

NOTES

WORDS FOR CULTURAL TRANSFORMATION

Esther 2:21-23

During the time Mordecai was sitting at the king's gate, Bigthana and Teresh, two of the king's officers who guarded the doorway, became angry and conspired to assassinate King Xerxes. But Mordecai found out about the plot and told Queen Esther, who in turn reported it to the king, giving credit to Mordecai. And when the report was investigated and found to be true, the two officials were impaled on poles. All this was recorded in the book of the annals in the presence of the king.

Lord, may we take our place at the city gates where people of influence meet. Show us where to go so we can be in the right place at the right time for Kingdom impact. Give us favor with city officials. Give us eyes and ears to see what You are doing and take action on what You tell us. May we be conduits of truth and those who speak a good word to those in positions of power.

Psalms 107:33-38

He turned rivers into a desert, flowing springs into thirsty ground, and fruitful land into a salt waste, because of the wickedness of those who lived there. He turned the desert into pools of water and the parched ground into flowing springs; there He brought the hungry to live, and they founded a city where they could settle. They sowed fields and planted vineyards that yielded a fruitful harvest; He blessed them, and their numbers greatly increased, and He did not let their herds diminish.

Lord, may Your presence transform this city and make it a place of provision and blessing. Redeem our ground and make it productive. Restore this land to Your creation design that it would be fruitful with plenty of bounty for all. May our labors yield a great harvest that would show the abundance of Your house. Transform every part of our city so that it brings glory and honor to You.

Daniel 1:17-18

To these four young men God gave knowledge and understanding of all kinds of literature and learning. And Daniel could understand visions and dreams of all kinds. At the end of the time set by the king to bring them into his service, the chief official presented them to Nebuchadnezzar.

Give us an increase of knowledge and understanding that would set us apart from nonbelievers. May we be so filled with wisdom that secular leaders would seek out our counsel and insight. Grant favor to those You have anointed in this and open doors so they can influence our leaders behind the scenes. May a spirit of wisdom and revelation increase upon this next generation to be major change agents in the city square and in our nation.

Matthew 5:13

You are the salt of the earth. But if the salt loses its saltiness, how can it be made salty again? It is no longer good for anything, except to be thrown out and trampled underfoot.

Holy Spirit, keep us hungry for Your Word and passionate about the truth. May we share our faith out of conviction and not under compulsion. May our testimonies stir people to faith and bring the lost to You. Teach us how to impact our city and be set apart, not as irrelevant, but influential. Make us salty so we can bring out the best in others through the power of Your Name.

Matthew 5:16

In the same way, let your light shine before others, that they may see your good deeds and glorify your Father in heaven.

Let my light shine, Lord! Lead me as I look for ways to demonstrate the power of Your Name to those in my community. May I not be a person who just talks about my faith but acts on it. May my heart reflect Your love and compassion for others in my actions so that hearts will be drawn to You. Teach Your Church how to engage with our community so that our faith will be evident in how we do things and how we care for others.

Matthew 28:19-20

Therefore, go and make disciples of all nations, baptizing them in the name of the Father and of the Son and of the Holy Spirit, and teaching them to obey everything I have commanded you. And surely I am with you always, to the very end of the age.

You have called us to disciple entire nations, Lord. Open doors for us to share our faith in every sphere of our culture. May we declare Christ in every business, government office, theater, sports arena, public school, and hospital. Stir believers in this city to be change agents in their sphere of influence. May we not only bring people to salvation, but show people how to live in a way that brings blessing, honor, and life that counts for eternity.

Mark 16:15
He said to them, "Go into all the world and preach the gospel to all creation."

Lord, You've instructed us to preach the gospel to all creation. That means to get outside the Church walls and declare Christ everywhere we go! May we fulfill our commission and impact our community so powerfully it will redeem and restore all who are lost.

Acts 1:8
But you will receive power when the Holy Spirit comes on you; and you will be My witnesses in Jerusalem, and in all Judea and Samaria, and to the ends of the earth.

Fill us with Your Spirit, Lord, so our witness will be more than just words, but a demonstration of Your power to save, heal, and deliver. May the followers of Christ in this community know the gifts of the Spirit that enable us to express Your heart more fully. May our testimonies ignite hearts to love and draw others to salvation. Increase our influence as we faithfully share the truth and proclaim Jesus to all who will listen.

Acts 8:26-27
Now an angel of the Lord said to Philip, "Go south to the road - the desert road - that goes down from Jerusalem to Gaza." So, he started out, and on his way he met an Ethiopian eunuch, an important official in charge of all the treasury of the Kandake (which means "queen of the Ethiopians"). This man had gone to Jerusalem to worship.

Holy Spirit, lead us to city officials and people of influence who are secretly searching for truth. Give us favor with city leaders who are ready to follow You and be filled with authority from heaven. Empower us to teach Your Word clearly and to empower others to follow You. Bring divine appointments that will determine destinies and enlarge Your Kingdom.

Acts 16:14-15

One of those listening was a woman from the city of Thyatira named Lydia, a dealer in purple cloth. She was a worshiper of God. The Lord opened her heart to respond to Paul's message. When she and the members of her household were baptized, she invited us to her home. "If you consider me a believer in the Lord," she said, "come and stay at my house." And she persuaded us.

Holy Spirit, open doors to reach and influence business owners in our city and impact them with the gospel. Reveal whose hearts are ready to receive truth and to influence those around them. Soften hearts of those who carry weight in this city so they will look to believers for instruction and counsel.

Acts 17:22-23

Paul then stood up in the meeting of the Areopagus and said: "People of Athens! I see that in every way you are very religious. For as I walked around and looked carefully at your objects of worship, I even found an altar with this inscription: to an unknown god. So you are ignorant of the very thing you worship - and this is what I am going to proclaim to you."

Lord, give us eyes to see our city by the Spirit and distinguish the godly from the ungodly. Give us the needed wisdom to call attention to those idols that are having influence in our community and call people to a higher path. Give us discernment to judge rightly and to speak in a way that challenges people's thinking and breaks the spell of the enemy's lies. May Your name be exalted in this city and may our shrines and memorials reflect only that which is good and true in Your eyes.

Acts 23:11

The following night the Lord stood near Paul and said, "Take courage! As you have testified about Me in Jerusalem, so you must also testify in Rome."

Lord, grant courage to those You have called to speak to rulers and governors. Enlarge their influence and empower them by Your Spirit to influence those who lead in positions of power. May we be ready to go wherever You send us and know that You go before us and prepare the way for Kingdom impact.

2 Timothy 2:2

And the things you have heard me say in the presence of many witnesses entrust to reliable people who will also be qualified to teach others.

Lord, show us those You have called to leadership in this city. Show us who You have equipped to teach and train others in the ways of righteousness. Give us spiritual fathers and mothers with a desire to disciple the next generation to bring long-lasting transformation.

1 Peter 3:15-16

But in your hearts revere Christ as Lord. Always be prepared to give an answer to everyone who asks you to give the reason for the hope that you have. But do this with gentleness and respect, keeping a clear conscience, so that those who speak maliciously against your good behavior in Christ may be ashamed of their slander.

Holy Spirit, teach us how to share our faith in the workplace and in our city streets. May we be so contagious that people will ask why we are so hopeful and filled with joy. May we bring change to those we meet because of what we carry. May our words and actions cause people to desire truth and a personal relationship with You.

NOTES

ABOUT THE AUTHOR

Wanda has been in ministry for over 35 years as a worship leader, teacher, author, deliverance counselor, and speaker. She is an ordained minister, commissioned fivefold leader, and passionate about interpreting life from heaven's perspective. Since an unexpected angelic encounter in 2002, Wanda ministers through a spirit of wisdom and revelation that empowers believers to know their authority, embrace their calling, and demonstrate heavenly realities on the earth (Ephesians 1:17).

She has produced six books as well as numerous video and audio teaching series which are available through her website (wandaalger.me) and Amazon. She hosts a blog as well as several social media platforms including YouTube, Rumble, Telegram, Truth Social, and Facebook.

She is married to Bobby Alger, Lead Pastor of Crossroads Community Church in Winchester, Virginia which they founded together in 1998. They have three grown children and a growing number of grandchildren.

VISIT WANDA'S WEBSITE at wandaalger.me where you can find her latest articles, prophetic words, and videos, in addition to all her teaching resources, prayer guides, and an online library of topical studies for further research and prayer.

Made in USA - Kendallville, IN
42138_9780999675236
10.25.2022 1736